MIDLAND LOCOMOTIVES

This picture of Johnson compound No. 2635 (later No. 1004) at Kentish Town was clearly taken on almost the same day and from almost the same position as *Plate 210* in Volume 1 but is, if anything, even more clear. It reveals that at least this example and No. 2634 (see Volume 1, *Plate 211*) were given the fully 'decorated' crimson livery with many embellishments compared with, say, No. 2632 (*Plate 287*, Chapter 9).

Authors' Collection

AN ILLUSTRATED REVIEW OF

MIDLAND LOCOMOTIVES

FROM 1883

BY

R. J. ESSERY & D. JENKINSON

VOLUME TWO
PASSENGER TENDER CLASSES

WILD SWAN PUBLICATIONS LTD.

© Wild Swan Publications Ltd. and R. J. Essery & D. Jenkinson 1988
ISBN 0 906867 59 2

ERRATA TO VOLUME ONE

A number of errors, many of them typographic and obvious, occurred in Volume One. Those known to the authors are listed below.

Contents page. Appendix 1 should be page 187.

Page 4. Plate 7. Despite the information given on the reverse of the original photograph, the location is Bradford Forster Square.

Page 9. Plate 14. No. 990 was the second engine built, No. 999 was the first and 998 the last.

Page 12. Plate 22. No. 535 was originally MR No. 69 not No. 6.

Page 17. Plate 31. No. 3371 was originally MR No. 2094 not MR No. 1892.

Page 27. Plate 47. No. 44 became MR No. 118 in 1907 not MR No. 119.

Page 34. Plate 58. The location is Walsall.

Page 35. Plate 60. We can now confirm that the square white board with a diagonal black cross is a route indicator for trains working over the Metropolitan widened lines, and in this picture is hung out of use on the front of the side tank. The extension pieces behind the lamp brackets for carrying these boards in service are also clearly seen.

Page 37. Plate 64. No. 1142A became MR 1526 not MR No. 1527.

Page 39. Plate 70. An awful error. We incorrectly referred to another ex Severn & Wye engine. The correct caption should read 'No. 1607, built in 1862 as No. 223. It became No. 223A in 1890 and No. 1604 in 1907. It became LMS No. 1607 in 1923 and was withdrawn in 1928.' We will illustrate the locomotive described in Plate 70 Volume 1 in Volume 3.

Page 42. Plate 77. No. 2458 was built with condensing gear but it was removed shortly after the locomotive entered service. Note the plate on the smokebox side. No. 2458 was refitted with condensing gear again in July 1903.

Page 43. We failed to record that in 1907 Nos. 2317/18 and 2341 were curved framed locomotives (but not to the later standard designs) although numbered within the straight frame number series.

Page 46. Plate 83. Provides a good example of the problem of recording the history of Kirtley goods engines. We stated that No. 386 was withdrawn in 1904. This is correct, a Kirtley 0-6-0 No. 386 was withdrawn that year but we now believe that the locomotive illustrated with that number was 'old No. 269' built by Robert Stephenson in 1853 and renumbered No. 386 in 1904 (after the original No. 386 was withdrawn). It then became No. 2306 in 1907 and lasted until withdrawal in 1917.

Page 55. Fig. 4. No. 19 is the locomotive handbrake. A more correct description of the driven wheels would be: 'driving wheels' are those on the crank axle while 'coupled wheels' are the remainder. The position of the balance weights, which were altered slightly c.1880 is different. On the coupled wheels they are opposite the crank and on driving wheels they are adjacent to the crank.

Page 58. Plate 92. No. 71 was built in 1876.

Page 60. Plate 97. We incorrectly described this locomotive as a Belpaire. It is, of course, an 'H' boilered 4-4-0.

Page 63. Figs. 10 and 11. Captions transposed. The drawing is incorrect. The radius of the dome is shown as 11½. It should be 1' 1½" and struck from the centre line of the dome.

Page 67. Under the heading 'Lubricators' we gave Plate 104. It should have been Plate 114 — a picture of a '483' class rebuild which shows the mechanical lubricator used by the LMS on their standard locomotives.

Page 82. Fig. 16. This otherwise excellent drawing shows the brake pull rods 'outside' the wheels whereas they should be 'inside'.

Page 103. Plate 163. 'Plate 105' should read 'Plate 165'.

Pages 132/3. Plates 208/9. We should perhaps have made it clear that lining around the base of the chimney was confined to locomotives with drumhead smokeboxes, and, of course, No. 1757 did not have one.

Page 143. Plate 223. No. 2458 became 1917 not 1937, and '7237' should read '7217'.

Page 146. Plate 230. 'Toolbox' should read 'sandbox'.

Page 177. Plate 268. Should read 'In 1907 it became No. 507 and was fitted with an 'H' boiler and in 1912 it was renewed to '483' class.

Designed by Paul Karau
Typesetting by Berkshire Publishing Services
Printed and bound by Butler & Tanner Ltd., Frome

Published by
WILD SWAN PUBLICATIONS LTD.,
1-3 Hagbourne Road, Didcot, Oxon, OX11 8DP

CONTENTS

An unidentified single at St. Pancras loco yard c.1895. This close-up view reveals a number of interesting points, pit holes in the buffer heads, paint blistering on the smokebox door, the practice of putting a single coupling link around the top lamp iron and finally the method of arranging the front coupling. Note the pre-1903 lamp iron position and that the bogie bearings are outside the frames.

National Railway Museum

INTRODUCTION

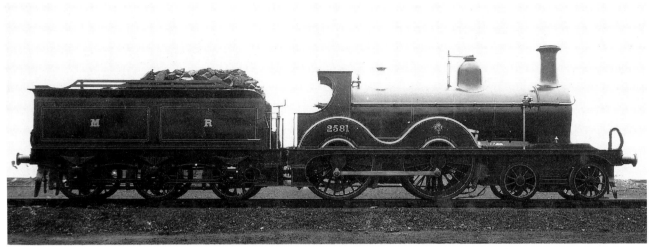

No. 2581 was one of ten locomotives built by Beyer Peacock in 1900, the final series of 6 ft 6 in driving wheel engines (see Chapter 5).
National Railway Museum

The generally favourable reaction given to Volume 1 of this survey was a source of great pleasure to us and in this book we commence our more detailed look at the Midland's engines in the hope that it will continue to give pleasure to our readers. It is, however, very different in form from that which was first envisaged and indeed promised at the end of Volume 1 (page 205) and for this change we owe readers an explanation and perhaps an apology.

Soon after compiling Volume 1 of this series — and not the least reason why the interval between then and now has been rather longer than we had hoped — we began to realise that if we were to offer the same sort of detailed coverage of MR locomotives as our publisher had already pioneered with his definitive LSWR locomotive series, then the subject would simply not allow itself to be compressed into two additional volumes and still maintain the sort of size/price ratio which would be acceptable to readers. Not for the first time in our joint researches, we had underestimated the size of the task, a fact which became increasingly obvious as we came to grips with the realities and complexities of Midland Railway locomotives. It has, in the event, turned out to be one of the hardest tasks we have ever undertaken jointly and we soon began to realise why no-one else had ever tackled the problem before! Therefore, from the outset, we would like to thank our publisher for agreeing to this major re-casting of the detailed story and enduring our constant changes of plans.

We shall continue, as already stated, to confine attention mostly to the pre-group story of those engines which survived to the amalgamations of 1923, but have now elected to divide our survey into the *three* categories which the Midland recognised, viz., Passenger Tender;

Tank (all types); Freight Tender. Even so, there was still no room for the Joint Lines (S & DJR/M & GNR) to be covered properly. This subject will, therefore, be offered as a further (smaller?) volume in the fullness of time. Also, for reasons outlined below, some of our friends will deal in detail with the early Kirtley period, with which will also be incorporated, purely for convenience, a study of those post-1883 engines, like the American 2−6−0s, which did not reach the LMS.

This part of our survey, therefore, considers the Midland's passenger tender engines from the start of the 'red' period to the railway grouping of 1923. Some references will be made to the LMS continuation but, for the most part, the latter period has already been covered in Volume 4 of our companion series, *An Illustrated History of LMS Locomotives*. As far as is possible we have tried to offer a fairly standard method of presentation, explained in detail in the notes on page xi. However, since a few reviewers of Volume 1 have somewhat misunderstood our criteria, it may be helpful to re-state the principal areas with which we shall concern ourselves.

The starting point is generally c.1883, for reasons explained in some detail in Volume 1. We are therefore covering the Midland during the 'red engine' period, including all Johnson/Deeley/Fowler designs, but leaving the detailed study of many earlier Kirtley engines to a companion volume in preparation by some of our friends and which will in due course be published uniform with this series. In essence, our choice of Kirtley classes to cover in detail has been determined by the simple expedient of whether or not the particular type survived to the end of the Midland period. Thus, for example, we do include some of the 2−4−0s and 0−6−0s, but not the 2−2−2s. Neither have we gone too much into the

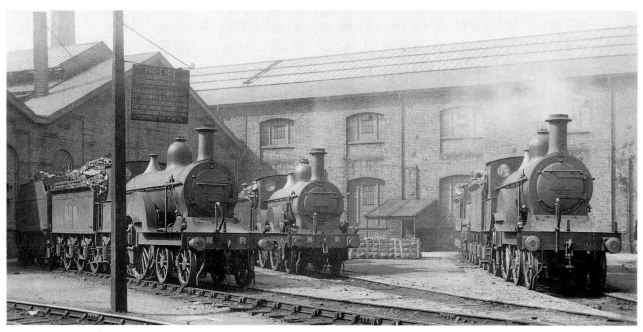

Midland engines at Kentish Town on 31st May 1944.   *H. C. Casserley*

pre-1883 state of any of the Kirtley engines, choosing to start our detailed coverage of these classes in which might be called their 'Johnsonised' form, and going on from there. In the case of the Johnson engines built before 1883, the only serious omission will be a discussion of their green liveries.

As always we shall continue to concentrate on the principal outward and visible changes to be seen and will not dwell too much on the technical story which, along with detailed specifications, can be found elsewhere for most classes, although we do touch upon the story in places and in some of the tables. We came to the subject via the modeller's bench and discovered that the biggest single problem to resolve was what the engines actually looked like during the various periods of their, often very long, lives. Consequently, although we have not written specifically for the modeller, we cannot deny that the modeller's needs have been a very vital factor in the treatment we have adopted. Thus we make no apology for concentrating heavily on liveries and fundamental anatomical changes, since these are the very details we have found lacking elsewhere. Judging by the reaction to many of our previous books, this area is of interest to a considerable number of non-modellers too, so we continue unashamedly on the same line of investigation.

That these are all arbitrary decisions cannot be denied, but we hope they may help to bring order out of chaos in what was undoubtedly a most confusing series of engines. As ever, we are conscious that we may well be working in an area 'where fools rush in and angels fear to tread' but this is in part borne out of our frustration that none of the so-called experts have, thus far, even dared to tackle the subject in a general way! We have even tried, to the best of our ability, to offer some sort of explanation for

some of the more interesting and at times inexplicable events which took place, for in our view, the 'why' is often as interesting as the 'what' even if it is dangerous ground to cross. We hope that our opinions are readily identifiable from the pure facts and if our endeavours do no more than stimulate more 'hard' information, then we shall be well pleased. We have also sought to offer a few generalisations, hopefully not unreasonably based, in order to help readers get to grips with the subject, even though we realise that this approach may not suit the rivet counters!

As usual we owe considerable thanks to a large number of friends and acquaintances, especially in the search for photographs, and would like to thank them all. In this volume we are particularly indebted to: Roger Carpenter, the late A. G. Ellis, David Hunt, Bernard Mathews, Bill Stubbs, Peter Truman, David Tee, David White, Laurie Ward, Ken Woodward, and the library staff at the National Railway Museum, all of whom assisted in Volume 1. Newcomers to Volume 2 include: Eric Lancaster, the late R. E. Lacy, Vic Forster, Barry Lane, Adrian Tester, Ken Stores, Roy Anderson, Gordon Coltas, Les Hanson, H. C. Casserley, and the Historical Model Railway Society. We would also like to record our special thanks to Stephen Summerson who devoted many hours to checking the manuscript and offered much helpful advice.

Finally, should readers be able to add to or correct our data, we would hope they will write via the publisher. We have tried to eliminate errors but have no doubt that a few might not have been identified. These are entirely our fault and we apologise for them.

RJE   *DJ*
Solihull   *Knaresborough*
1988   *1988*

INTRODUCTION

NOTES ON THE USE OF THIS BOOK

OTHER PUBLISHED REFERENCES

To save space and cost, we have not thought it necessary to fill the pages with great lists of numbers and neither have we included over-long technical specifications. In these two areas we have given the minimum information consistent with positive identification of type. However, we do think that readers who wish for more in this area will find the following books quite useful: *Derby Works and Midland Locomotives*, J. B. Radford, Ian Allan 1971; *British Locomotive Catalogue 1825-1923 Vol. 3A*, B. and D. Baxter, Moorland Publishing 1982 (Note: this volume does contain errors so treat with caution); *Midland Railway Locomotive Album*, Robin Higgins, Vintage Carriage Trust; *S. W. Johnson, Midland Railway Locomotive Engineer Artist*, Jack Braithwaite, Wyvern Publishing; *Locomotive and Train Working in the Nineteenth Century*, E. L. Ahrons, reprinted from various issues of *The Railway Magazine*; *The Midland Railway*, Hamilton Ellis, Ian Allan.

DIAGRAMS/DRAWINGS

We have included a number of diagrams and drawings in the text. Some of the drawings have been specially prepared and may be considered accurate, others have been used before. The diagrams are less helpful in this respect, often being deficient in detail and at times incorrect, sometimes embracing more than one visible variant within a wheel arrangement. However, they do assist in providing a convenient 'shorthand' identification (below). Indeed a skilled draughtsman armed with a General Arrangement drawing before rebuilding may, with the aid of the diagram, photographic and other information, be able to produce a drawing for a class which was never the subject of an 'official general arrangement detailed drawing'!

IDENTIFICATION OF TYPE

This subject is more thoroughly covered in Chapter One, but our normal method of identification of class, other than by wheel arrangement, is to quote the first running number allocated, e.g. '1400' class for the celebrated 6 ft 9 in Johnson 2—4—0s. This method is used throughout, where relevant, supplemented by references to engine diagram number(s) and/or subsequent 'popular' designations, if thought helpful in context, e.g. 'Compound', 'Belpaire', etc.

LOCOMOTIVE NUMBERING

Where engines were involved in the great 1907 renumbering (by wheel arrangement and power class see Volume 1, page 22) both numbers are quoted where necessary. In general, the *final* pre-1907 number is regarded as definitive in the case of engines which had carried several numbers prior to the big 1907 re-organisation. A full 1907 renumbering list is in Volume 1, page 187. In point of fact, virtually all the engines covered in this book carried 1907 numbers, and for many of them, of course, this was the only number anyway.

POWER CLASS

Although numerical assessment of power was not adopted in its final form until the 20th century, it is difficult to write about MR engines at any period without reference to their subsequent power designation(s). This has been done wherever it seems helpful to understanding. Power class references can always be distinguished from numerical class designations by the fact that the power class figure (1 to 4) always *follows* the word 'class'. Thus, for example, while '483' class is a designation of a specific type, class 2 is a definition of power, which could and did embrace several types.

LIVERY

The description of liveries is covered in detail in Volume 1, including a list of abbreviated definitions of the styles on page 114. This method of livery summary will be adopted throughout this volume and, for convenience, the definitions relevant to this part of the work are repeated below:

MR Green — Pre-November 1883 livery. Could be either Kirtley Dark or Johnson Light Green.

Early Crimson Lake — Implies the pre c.1890 period when certain 'below the footplate' lining was not present.

Full and 'Decorated' Crimson Lake — Implies the period c.1890-1905 when additional lining was used below the footplate and elsewhere. While extra lining was universally used, the term 'decorated' is particularly appropriate when describing the ornate additional lining used by certain paintshops during the mid/late 1890s until after the turn of the century. This additional lining was most frequently applied to the more important passenger locomotives but was also placed on certain tank engines.

Simplified Crimson Lake or Deeley livery — Describes the simplified lining practices introduced by Deeley c.1905 which saw the level of lining gradually reduced over a 2-3 year period to less than that used during the Early Crimson Lake livery period. During this period black was introduced to replace the red used hitherto for wheels and the outside of the frames. This term also covers the LMS 1923-28.

Post 1928 Crimson Lake — This was almost identical to the pre-1928 style except that the locomotive running number was moved from the tender or tank side to the cab or bunker side. During this period there were variations in the shape and style of transfers used and the lining changed from pale cream to chrome yellow c.1936.

Intermediate Passenger Livery — This describes the black livery with red lining introduced in 1928 by the LMS for many locomotives which hitherto had been painted Crimson Lake.

Full BR Livery — Describes the lined black LNWR style livery adopted by British Railways and applied to certain ex-MR passenger locomotives (tender and tank).

WHEEL DIAMETERS

For a given wheel arrangement, the driving wheel diameter is often a useful differentiation of type (e.g. the 4—4—0s). Although driving wheel diameters are normally quoted to the nearest half-inch, there is, in fact, no significant difference (beyond tyre thickness) between, for example, nominal 7 ft 0 in and 7 ft 0½ in wheels, both of which sizes could have been worn down to about 6 ft 10 in or less after a typical lifespan before new tyres were fitted. Indeed, because of the effect of tyre wear, there is a strong case for disregarding wheel diameter differences which were less than 3 inches and there is certainly no cause for the pedant to get too neurotic about this matter. However, since changes in nominal driving wheel diameter frequently caused changes in *visual* characteristics (e.g. splasher dimensions on the 4—4—0s), there is a case for considering them with reasonable accuracy. This we have tried to do.

It should be noted that some other records give differing wheel dimensions (usually varying by ½ in). For reasons explained in Chapter One, most of our dimensions (where applicable) are taken from the company's 1903 reference.

It is not often that one can feature a human interest story but this view of 2—4—0 No. 1402 outside Lancaster shed coaling stage was submitted by a reader of Volume 1. Taken in the early years of this century, it shows his grandfather, driver Lancaster, with both his engine and fireman, plus the shed foreman.

E. Lancaster

INTRODUCTION

This photograph of Midland engines grouped around the turntable inside Kentish Town shed was taken on the same day as that on page viii.

H. C. Casserley

TENDERS

Although Midland engines exchanged tenders quite frequently, there was a fair degree of association of particular tenders (or groups of tenders) with specific locomotive types. Tender variations are, therefore, usually covered within the class sections rather than being dealt with separately, although if space permits, we may go into the subject more thoroughly in a later volume. Unlike the LNWR, for example, the Midland did not generally return an engine to traffic after repair with the first convenient tender to hand.

LOCOMOTIVE DETAILS

Small variations in detail as they affected MR engines 'across the board' are covered in Volume 1, Chapter Three, and their substance will not be repeated in this volume. However, where relevant, changes from the 'norm' will be discussed in the class chapters.

SEQUENCE OF TREATMENT

Most chapters give a general review followed by a more detailed class-by-class survey. In the analysis of each class, a consistent order of treatment will, in general, be followed, namely:

1. Date and number built, including original running numbers and a summary of the class as handed over to the LMS in 1923.
2. Analysis of visual characteristics 'as built' (or, in the case of pre-1883 designs, 'as at 1883').
3. Subsequent visual changes as a result of rebuilding (if any) after 1883.
4. Tender types – and variations if any.
5. Liveries carried during MR period (with examples).

Preserved MR No. 1000 — the overlarge shed plate has now been replaced.

National Railway Museum

CHAPTER ONE

LOCOMOTIVE CLASSIFICATION

WE begin this volume with a look at the Midland Railway's overall method of locomotive classification. We think it is particularly important to deal with this subject for two reasons: firstly, because to the best of our knowledge, it has never before been examined in print; secondly, and perhaps more important, a more complete understanding of the subject will enable readers to follow the story which we will try to unravel in these volumes.

The principal period of Midland locomotive history under review is what we have chosen to call the 'red engine era', namely from the end of 1883 until the Midland Railway became part of the LMS in 1923. Inevitably, we continue the story through the period of LMS ownership and to some extent until the final days in BR traffic, but the emphasis after the Midland Railway ceased to exist is considerably reduced. Equally the period before 1883 is less fully documented by us, but, in order to ensure a smooth hand-over to our two friends who are writing the story of the Kirtley engines together with the 'Green Livery period', we must, in some cases, commence our story before our chosen date of 1883. None the less, in terms of locomotive classification, we shall follow the principles laid down by Johnson and generally refer to all Kirtley engines as 'Kirtley' with the added qualification of 'Passenger' or 'Goods' and to add the word 'Tank' if they were not of a tender configuration. We are thus able to leave the explanation of the full Kirtley MR locomotive classification to the writers of the later volume. To aid exact identification still further, we will use accepted class descriptions in the chapters, e.g. Kirtley Passenger — '800' class, etc.

The arrival of Johnson heralded a period of great change on the Midland and it would be surprising if locomotive classification had not been one of the areas where Johnson changed existing Midland Railway practice. We touched upon the subject briefly in Volume 1 page 22, and the subject of power classification was dealt with on page 163. We now propose to go into these subjects in much greater detail.

The basic principle adopted by the Midland Railway was for Derby-built engines to be known by an order number and for contractor-built locomotives to have a class letter allocated to them, but there were exceptions to the rule. Whilst these are generally covered in the tables with this and subsequent volumes, it is worth drawing readers' attention to some of them here. For example the 0—4—4Ts built at Derby in 1876 (1907 Nos. 1226-1235) were referred to as Class C or Order No. 1. This suggests that the order number system was not introduced until Johnson had been at Derby for a few years after taking charge on 1st July 1873.

Incidentally, the sequence of 'new orders for locomotives' began in 1874 with a batch of 0—6—0Ts known as 'class A',

followed by the 'class B' 0—6—0s, both types being contractor-built. Then came 'class C Order No. 1' which preceded the 'class D' 0—4—4Ts about to be built by Neilsons. Therefore it suggests to us that for a short time there may have been an intention to classify all MR locomotives by a class letter. If so, this policy was soon changed. The next batch of Derby-built locomotives was a series of ten Johnson 2—4—0s in 1876 which were similar to Kirtley's '1070' class and are referred to by Derby as Order 97. However, the system can still not have been fully operative because even as late as 1881 the Neilson-built 2—4—0s Nos. 1502-1531 did not receive a class letter — they were simply known as 'like O 232' which were the 1879 build at Derby which we have chosen to call the '1400' class. However, after this things more or less settled down until 1900. Of course one should not overlook the fact that there wasn't a class I; after all it could be mistaken for class 1 (one). Instead, following the class H 0—6—0s, came the six-coupled goods engines which would have been class I but instead they were simply known as 'Neilson Goods'.

The final anomaly came in 1900 when a batch of ten 4—4—0s was ordered from Beyer Peacock. Because they were almost identical to a class of M & GN locomotives currently being built by Beyer Peacock, they were known officially as 'Like C — M & GN', but they probably should have had a class letter. These engines were virtually the same as the Derby-built engines dating from 1888-1891, i.e. the '1808' class, to order 678 (see Table 1). Nevertheless, apart from these few exceptions, the system worked well and the principle of Derby Works order numbers (a series which encompassed not only new locomotives, but rebuilds, tenders, new frames, etc.) was carried through not only Johnson's time and the remainder of the Midland Railway's independent existence, but right through the LMS era into the British Railways period, where we end our story. Not only were Johnson's engines long-lived but so were some of his organisational methods!

In compiling this and subsequent volumes of this series, we have used a document whose full title is 'Photographs and leading particulars of MR Locomotives'*. It is dated 1st July 1903 but the copy we have was in use for a year or so after that date and kept up to date at least until 1904. It has been our principal source of official information and forms the basis of the tables used in the class chapters. Naturally, information for the post-1903 period has come from elsewhere and we have tried to identify these sources wherever possible. Our reason for adopting this approach is simply to ensure that we do not add further to the existing confusion surrounding the classification of Midland Railway

---

* A copy is now at the National Railway Museum. The authors were advised of the original at the Science Museum by Adrian Tester.

TABLE 1

INDEX OF ORDERS

ORDER	TYPE	PAGE	Nº OF GENERAL DRG	ENGINE NUMBERS.	ORDER	TYPE	PAGE	Nº OF GENERAL DRG	ENGINE NUMBERS.
Kirtley Pass.?	P	26		2.3.5.7.12.40-49.72.76. 90-92.95.134-136.148.490-909	496	G.T	53	78-1055	1090-1092.1094.1095. 1677-1686
Kirtley Goods	G	44		224-229.240-360.371-663 696-779.830-879.910-1069	499	G.T	53	78-1055	1687-1696.1096-1100 1698-1707
1	B.T	35	75-341	6.15.18.137.140-144.147	530	G	41	85-2215	1718-1727
96 R	P	25		810-812.815.817	538	B.T	32	81-1591	1708-1717
97	P	24	75-462	1.9.10.13.70.71.73.74.96.146	544	G	41	85-2218	1738-1747
like 97	P	24	---	1070-1069 (Sharps)	554	P.B	17	85-2311	1728-1737
107	P	21	76-566-75-391	50-59	589	B.T	32	81-1591	1748-1757
155 R? 779	P P	23 25	76-721	8ll.8.3.814.816.818.819 101-110	615	P.B	17	85-2311	1758-1767
204	G.T	53	78-1055	1377-1386	617	G	41	85-2218	1768-1777
218	G.T	53	do	1347-1356.1387-1396	633	G	41	-do-	1778-1797
232	P	22		1400-1409	655	S.B	5	87-2547	25-29
like 232	P	22		1502-1531 Milton	663	G	41	85-2218	1808-1817
239	G.T	51	75-1055	220-221.1410-1417	678	P.B	16	88-3074	1798-1807
240	G	42	80-1379	1452-1461	713	G	40	69-3187	1818-1822
262	G.T	53	78-1055	1410-1419	734	P.B	16	88-3074	30-32.34.1853
273	P	22		1462-1491	745	S.B	5	89-3225	1823-1832
275	P	22	80-1376	1452-1501	763	B.T	32	81-1591	37.1854-1857
279	P	22	do	1472-1481	796	S.B	5		1858-1867
263	P	21		111-114.89.	809	S.B	5		202 1428 1430 1697 See duplicates
289	B.T	32	81-1591.51-1596	1532-1551	816	S.T	81	83-1890	200.201.213.214.217.222
340	G.T	52	78-1055	1552-1561	824	G.T	53	78-1055	223.1093.1101.1431
341	S.T	81	83-1890	1322 -1326 see duplicates	654	G.T	51	78-1055	1102-1106.1843-1847
370	P.B	18	82-1757	1552-1571	669	G.T	53	-do-	203.1848-1852.1973-1976
400	P.B	18	do	1572-1581	883	G.T	53	-do-	880-889
414	G.T	51	76-1055	210-212.215.216.218.219. 1397-1399	920	P.B	16	88-3074	11.14.80-87
					924	G.T	53	78-1055	1977-1981
415	B.T	32	81-1591	1632-1636	935	S.B	4		1868-1872
430	P.B	18	82-1757	1657-1666	968	G.T	52	76-1055	1982-1991
460	B.T	32	81-1591	1637-1650	981	B.T	31	91-3479	202.1322-1326 1428-1430.1697
					991	G.T	51	78-1055	1992.1107-1115

INDEX OF ORDERS

ORDER	TYPE	PAGE	Nº OF GENERAL DRG	ENGINE NUMBERS.	ORDER	TYPE	PAGE	Nº OF GENERAL DRG	ENGINE NUMBERS.
998	S.B	4		8.24.33.35.36.38.39. 122.132.145.	2328	G	35¾		240-244.2736-2740
1080	S.B	4		4.16.17.94.97-100 129.133.	2458	P.B	7	02-5255	820-829
1094	S.B	4		149.170-178	2517	S.T	79		1159-1153
1124	S.B	3	94-4043	179-183	2530	G	35¾		245-254
1162	S.T	80	83-1890	1116 -1120 see Duplicates	2601	P.B	7	Cancelled	830-839
1235	P.B	13	92-3761	184-193	2651	B.T	Cancelled		
1276	P.B	13	-do-	161-164.194-199	2652	G	35¾		255-264
1353	G	37	89-3230	361-370	2675	G Rebuilt	83		1808-1822; 11; 14; 80-87.
1395	G.T	49	94-4010	1121-1130	2675¹	"	84		2581-2590
1410	P.B	13	92-3761	230-239	2676	"	85		161-164; 184-199; 230- 239; 2203-2217.
1454	P.B	3		75-77.79.86.	2676¹	"			
1458	P.B	14		156-160	2676²	"			
1460	P.B	15		1667.1668.1672.1675.1676	2677	Goods Rebuilds	35¾		361-370;1798-1807;1873-1972;2011-2182 2217-2552; 2591-2740;2661-2700; 2141-2770 &
1474	S.B	2	97-4397	115-119	2677¹	"	35X		1698-1717; 1758-1797 264-2634
1534	S.T	80	83-1890	2359.2360.1131-1133 See Duplicates	2692	G	35¾		265-274
1552	S.T	79		1134 -1138 see Duplicates	2694	C	Cancelled		
1597	P.B	15		150.153-155.204-209	2726	P.B.	82		840-849
1602	B.T	29	94-4003	690-695.780-783	2741	Motors	0		1 & 2
1635	P.B	12		60-66.93.138.139					
1659	S.B	2	97-4397	120.121.123-128.130.131					
1707	P.B	15		1669.1671					
1834	P.B	12		67-69.151.152.165-169					
1869	Belp.	6		800-804.2606-2610					
1926	S.B	1	00-4753	19-23.2601-2605					
2041	P.B	9	00-4732	805-809.2636-2690					
2072	P.B	15		1670.1673.1674					
2109	Comp	6		2631-2635					
2135	Belp.	7	02-5255	2781-2790					
2196	B.T	26	94-4003						
2250	Belp	7	02-5255	810-819					

TABLE 2   *INDEX OF CLASSES*

CLASS	TYPE	PAGE	N° OF GENERAL DRG	ENGINE NUMBERS	CLASS	TYPE	PAGE	N° OF GENERAL DRG	ENGINE NUMBERS
Dubs (Cond)	B.T	33		784 – 799	N Vulcan	G.T	50	91-3628	1993 - 2012
A Neilsons	G.T	54		1116 - 1120, 2253 - 2256	O Sharps	P.B	13	92-3761	2203 - 2217
A Vulcan	G.T'	54		1131 - 1141	P Vulcans	B.T	30	92-3806	2218 - 2227
B Kilsons	G	43	74 - 151	1142 - 1161	P2 Dubs	B.T	27	94-4003	2228 - 2232
B Dubs	G	43	do	1162 - 1181	Q Sharps	G.T	49	94.4010	2248 - 2252
B Beyers	G	43	do	1182 - 1201	Q Stephensons	G.T	49	do	2361 - 2380, 2571 - 2580
B Neilsons	G	43	do	1202 - 1251	R Sharps	P.B	10	93-4443	2421 - 2440
C Beyers	P.B	11	93-3926	2581 - 2590	S Vulcan	G.T	48	98-4450+31	2441-2460, 2741-2750
D Neilsons	B.T	34	75 - 265	1252 - 1281	T Neilsons	P.B	9	00-4732	2591 - 2600
E Dubs	P	21	76.566-75.391	1282 - 1311	U Vulcan	G.T	47	00-4870	2751 - 2760
F Vulcans	P.B	20	75.471	1312 - 1321	U 2 Vulcan	G.T			2761 - 2780
G Dubs	P.B	19	76.656	1327 - 1346	Baldwin	Mogul	45	In folio	2501-2510, 2521-2540
H Dubs	G	42	77.754	1357 - 1376	Schenectady	Mogul	46	do	2511 - 2520
H Stephenson	G	42	80.1379	1432-1451, 1462-1471					
H Beyers	G	42	82.1695	1582 - 1631					
Neil. Goods	G	39	89.3230	1873 - 1972					
J Kilsons	G	38	90.3447	2023 - 2062					
J Dubs	G	38	do	2063 - 2092					
J. 2 Dubs	G	38	do	2133 - 2162					
K Dubs	B.T	31	91-3479	1833-1842, 2013-2022					
K.2 Dubs,94	B.T	29	94.4003	2233 - 2247					
K.2 Dubs,93	B.T	28	do	2611 - 2630					
L Sharps	P.B	14	92-3721	2183 - 2202					
M Sharps	G	37	89.3230+97.4402	2093-2132, 2259-2283					
M Neilsons	G	37	97.4402	2284 - 2358					
M Kilson	G	37	do	2391 - 2420					
M Neilson	G	37	do	2461 - 2490					
M Vulcan	G	37	do	2491-2500, 2541-2550					
M Dubs	G	37	do	2551 - 2570					
M Kilsons	G	36	do	2641 - 2660					
M Sharps	G	36	do	2661 - 2680					
M Neilsons	G	36	do	2681 - 2735					

locomotives and their leading dimensions. Let us give some examples.

It could be argued that others writing and recording details years ago have established precedents which should be followed, and in general we accept this point in so far as it is compatible with the official record. However, for example, unlike some other railway companies, the Midland considered that an extra half-inch *cylinder* diameter merited a new class identification, whereas some writers have divided into separate classes locomotives which were, within up to a 3-inch difference in the *driving wheel diameter*, identical machines and classified as such by the Midland. The company was less obsessed about driving wheel diameter as far as locomotive classification was concerned, than it was about cylinders. e.g. Diagram 21 Johnson 2—4—0s (see Table 8 Chapter 4). This policy may be seen as rather surprising when set against the minor changes the company actually made with its driving wheel sizes during the construction of the 2—4—0 and 4—4—0 designs (see Chapters 4 and 5). For our part, we take the view that anything less than 3 inches difference in driving wheel size is not very important, but it does mean that various writers have divided up the company's locomotive fleet according to their own ideas and one writer's view may not coincide with another's! This is not to say that either is right or

wrong, it's merely a question of individual interpretation in the absence of published official information. But even with the information which *was* published, one cannot always be on safe ground. Much depends upon the date of the official information; this, too, varied as we will see. For example, the tyre thickness changed at about the turn of the century and, as will be seen from the tables, nominal wheel diameters increased as a result of these thicker tyres. This, in turn, led to altered 'official' wheel sizes for older locomotives. Compare the values in Table 3, for example, with those in the class chapters.

Another source of apparently conflicting information concerns heating surfaces. More than one formula can be used to establish this figure and it was not until 1914 that a single formula was agreed by all the Locomotive Engineers in the Kingdom. Examination of the tables will, in consequence, reveal apparent contradictions, but remember these are the actual figures recorded at the time by the Midland, they are not typographical errors! Similarly the method of calculating engine weights varied, so readers should not be too concerned if they find that the figures quoted in this volume vary from those found elsewhere. It's probably just a question of different 'official' figures being quoted. We have already mentioned cylinder enlargement and reboilering together with rebuilding, all of which further confused the subject, but when one considers that the Midland was in the business of maintaining over 2,500 locomotives to work its traffic and not concerned with making life easy for latter day enthusiasts, then perhaps these different sets of official figures begin to make sense!

We have mentioned the 1903 record which from now on we will refer to as the '1903 Engine Diagram Book'. This fascinating document uses descriptions which have, by and large, fallen out of use. There is a delightful period 'ring' to them; the descriptions are set out below and are used in some of the tables.

SB Single Bogie Passenger
PB Passenger Bogie
P Passenger without Bogie
BT Bogie Tank
G Goods
GT Goods Tank
ST Saddle Tank

We come now to the two lists of engine classifications, commencing with Table No. 1. This is an index of orders for Derby Works and contains some valuable information. Whilst we repeat the order numbers in later tables, together with the 1903 diagram page numbers, we have not repeated the GA drawing number. This useful piece of information enables locomotive drawings to be accurately identified by readers. The note on the table, 'see duplicates', refers to a separate list of locomotives which in 1903 had been replaced by new engines and which were now carrying a duplicate number, i.e. with an 'A' suffix (see Volume 1, page ix). We deal with any such locomotives in the detailed class chapters.

Table No. 2 provides the index of classes which came from the outside contractors and which were given specific letters or other identity.

Table No. 3 updates matters somewhat and is a 1916 list which relates the pre- and post-1907 engine numbers, indicates the maker, date when new and original order number or class description, together with the rebuild/s order numbers and confirms the 1916 driving wheel diameters. By this date we have thicker tyres in universal use.

Returning to 1903, we have in Table No. 4 a list of the 'engines running on July 1st 1903' (this list, of course, includes locos at works), and this shows another important fact which must be considered when classifying Midland locomotives. If one looks at the heading '6 wheels coupled goods', item number 8, we have the goods engines with outside frames and cranks. Now, as every student of the Kirtley goods engines knows, there were three distinct groups called the '240', '480' and '700' classes, which generally referred to the straight frame (earlier) and two curved frame (later) series. The fact is that by 1903 the Midland had decided to lump them all together and recognised but one variety, all 723 of them! Straight frame, curved frame, it mattered not a jot, they were allocated one page, No. 44, in the diagram book regardless of the fact

PASSENGER ENGINES

Type	Engine Nos	Old Engine Nos	Makers	Date New	Order No or Class	Order Nos (Rebuild)		Dia. of Drivingwheels
2-4-0	1 — 19	Various 76a-164a	M.R.Co	1866-8				6'-3"
	20 — 22	153a-155a	"	1874				
	23 — 34	165a-169a. 60a-66a	"	1870				
	35 — 62	600a. 602a-606a. 608a-629a	NEILSON	"				
	63 — 67	136a. 139a. 93a. 22a. 23a	M.R.Co	1871				6'-9"
	68 — 87	890-909	NEILSON	"				
	88 — 126	Various 2-148. 19a-152a	M.R.Co	1872-5				
	127 — 146	1070-1089	SHARP STEWART	1874-5				6'-3"
	147 — 156	19.10.13.70.71.73.74.96.146	M.R.Co	1876	0-97			
	157 — 186	1282-1311	DUBS	"	CLASS E			6'-6½"
	187 — 191	50-54	M.R.Co	"	0-107			
	192 — 196	55-59	"	"	"			6'-9"
	197 — 206	101-110	"	1877	0-179			7'-0½"
	207 — 216	1400-1409	"	1879	0-232			6'-9"
	217 — 221	111-114. 89	"	1880	0-283			6'-6½"
	222 — 231	1472-1481	"	"	0-279			
	232 — 241	1482-1491	"	"	0-273			6'-9"
	242 — 271	1502-1531	NEILSON	1881	LIKE 0-232			
	272 — 281	1492-1501	M.R.Co	"	0-275			7'-0½"
4-4-0	300 — 308	1312-1320	KITSON	1876-7	CLASS F			6'-6½"
	310 — 327	1327-1331. 1333-1345	DUBS	1877	" G	0-3492		7'-0½"
	328 — 337	1562-1571	M.R.Co	1882	0-370	0-2676a	0-3544a	
	338 — 347	1572-1581	"	1882-3	0-400		G7 BOILER	6'-9"
	348 — 357	1657-1666	"	1883	0-430	H CLASS BOILER	(SATURATED)	
	358 — 367	1738-1747	"	1885-6	0-554	0-2676b	0-3544b G7 BOILER	7'-0½"
	368 — 377	1748-1757	"	1886	0-615	H CLASS BOILER	(SATURATED)	
	378 — 387	1808-1817	"	1888	0-678	0-2675	0-3462	
	388 — 392	1818-1822	"	"	0-734		G7 BOILER	6'-6½"
	393 — 402	80-87. 11. 14	"	1891	0-920	H CLASS BOILER	(SATURATED)	
	403 — 422	2183-2202	SHARP STEWART	1892	CLASS L	0-3021	0-4311 G7 BOILER	7'-0½"
	423 — 427	156-160	M.R.Co	1896	0-1458	H CLASS BOILER	(SUPERHEATED)	
	428 — 442	2203-2217	SHARP STEWART	1893	CLASS O			
	443 — 452	184-193	M.R.Co	1894	0-1235	0-2676 H CLASS BOILER	0-4476	6'-6½" (SATURATED)
	453 — 462	194-199. 161-164	"	"	0-1276	0-3602	G7 BOILER	7'-0½"
	463 — 472	230-239	"	1895	0-1410	G7 BLR. SATURATED (460 & 465 ONLY)	(SUPERHEATED)	(SUPERHEATED)
	473 — 482	2581-2590	BEYER PEACOCK	1900	LIKE C (M & G N)	0-2675a H CLASS BOILER		
	483 — 492	1667-1676	M.R.Co	1896-1901	0-1460. 1707. 2072	0-3021a	0-3942	
	493 — 502	150. 153-155. 204-209	"	1897	0-1597	H CLASS BOILER	G7 BOILER (SUPERHEATED)	
	503 — 522	2421-2440	SHARP STEWART	1899	CLASS R			
	523 — 532	60-66. 93. 138-139	M.R.Co	1898	0-1635	0-3021b	0-4116	7'-0½"
	533 — 542	67-69. 151-152. 165-169	"	1899	0-1834		G7 BOILER	
	543 — 552	805-809. 2636-2640	"	1901	0-2041	H CLASS BOILER	(SUPERHEATED)	
	553 — 562	2591-2600	NEILSON	"	CLASS T			
4-2-2	600 — 604	25-29	M.R.Co	1887	0-655			7'-4½"
	605 — 607	30-32	"	1888	0-745			
	608 — 609	1853. 34	"	1889				7'-6½"
	610 — 614	1854-1857. 37	"	"	0-796			7'-4½"
	615 — 619	1858-1862	"	1889-90	0-809			
	620 — 624	1863-1867	"	"				
	625 — 629	1868-1872	"	1891	0-935			
	630 — 639	8. 122. 132. 145. 24. 33. 35. 36. 38. 39	"	1892	0-998			
	640 — 649	4. 16. 17. 94. 97-100. 129. 133	"	"	0-1080			7'-6½"
	650 — 659	149. 170-178	"	1893	0-1094			
	660 — 664	179-183	"	"	0-1124			
	665 — 669	75-77. 79. 88	"	1896	0-1454			
	670 — 674	115-119	"	1896-7	0-1474			
	675 — 684	120. 121. 123-128. 130. 131	"	1899	0-1659			7'-9½"
	685 — 694	2601-2605. 19-23	"	1899-1900	0-1926			
4-4-0	700 — 709	2606-2610. 800-804	M.R.Co	1900-1	0-1869		0-4132 G8a BOILER (SUPERHEATED)	
	710 — 719	2781-2790	"	1902	0-2135			
	720 — 729	810-819	"	"	0-2250			
	730 — 739	820-829	"	1903	0-2468		G8a BOILER	6'-9"
	740 — 749	830-839	"	1903-4	0-2601		(SUPERHEATED)	
	750 — 759	840-849	"	1904-5	0-2726			
	760 — 769	850-859	"	1905	0-2798			
	770 — 779	860-869	"	"	0-2918			
4-4-0	990 — 998		M.R.Co	1909	0-3371		0-3943 G9a BOILER (SUPERHEATED)	6'-6½"
	999		"	1907	0-3139			
	1000 — 1004	2631-2635	"	1902-3	0-2109		0-3945 G9a BOILER (SUPERHEATED)	
	1005 — 1014	1000-1009	"	1905	0-2889		0-4211	7'-0"
	1015 — 1034	1010-1029	"	1906	0-2998		(G9a BOILER. SUPERHEATED)	
	1035 — 1044		"	1908-9	0-3410		1040 ONLY.	

TABLE 3

TANK ENGINES

TYPE	ENGINE Nos	OLD ENGINE Nos	MAKERS	DATE NEW	ORDER No OR CLASS	DIA. OF DRIVINGWHEELS
	1200 – 1205	690a – 695a	BEYER PEACOCK	1869		5'-3"
	1206 – 1225	780a – 783a, 784-799	DUBS	1870		
4	1226 – 1235	85,86,87,140-144,147	M.R.Co	1875	O-1 OR CLASS C	5'-4"
–	1236 – 1265	1262-1281, 1292-1261	NEILSON	1875-6	CLASS D	5'-7"
1	1266 – 1285	1522-1551	M.R.Co	1881-2	O-288	
–	1286 – 1290	1632-1636	"	1883	O-415	
4	1291 – 1310	1637-1656	"	1883-4	O-460	
	1311 – 1320	1718-1727	"	1885	O-538	
1	1321 – 1330	1728-1737	"	1886	O-589	
–	1331 – 1340	1823-1832	"	1889	O-763	
0	1341 – 1350	822-826,207,1424-1430,1687	"	1892	O-941	5'-4"
	1351 – 1370	1833-1842, 2008-2022	DUBS		CLASS K	
	1371 – 1380	2216-2227	NEILSON	1893	• P	
	1381 – 1385	2228-2232	DUBS	1895	• P2	
	1386 – 1400	2233-2247	"		• K2	
	1401 – 1410	690-695, 780-783	M.R.Co	1898	O-1602	
	1411 – 1430	2611-2630	DUBS	1900	CLASS K2	
0	1500 – 1504	1372a -1376a	M.R.Co	1883	O-341	
–	1505 – 1507	1424a, 1430a, 1687a	"	1889-90	O-816	
4	1508 – 1512	1116a -1120a	"	1893	O-1162	
–	1513 – 1517	2259, 2260,1133a -1133a	"	1897	O-1534	3'-10"
4	1518 – 1522	1134a -1138a	"		O-1552	
–	1523 – 1527	1139a -1143a	"	1903	O-2517	
0	1528 – 1532		"	1907	O-3081	
	1600 – 1604	203a,201a,222a,1096a,1096a	KITSON, WILSON, M.R.Co	1847-8, 1855-60	MISCELLANEOUS	4'-3"
	1606 – 1608	1124a -1126a	VULCAN	1880-82-86		
	1610 – 1619	580a - 589a	BEYER PEACOCK	1871	KIRTLEY	
	1620 – 1659	1102a -1115a,1116-1120,2753-2756,1112a-1180a,1131-1141	NEILSON & VULCAN	1874-6	CLASS A	
	1660 – 1669	1377-1386	M.R.Co	1878	O-204	
	1670 – 1689	1347-1356, 1347-1356	"	1878-9	O-218	
	1690 – 1699	220,1729,1920-1927	"	1879	O-239	
	1700 – 1709	1410-1419	"	1880	O-262	
0	1710 – 1719	1552-1561	"	1882	O-340	
–	1720 – 1729	210-212, 215, 216, 218, 219, 1397-1399	"	1883	O-414	
6	1730 – 1744	1677-1686,1090-1092,1094,1095	"	1884	O-496	
–	1745 – 1759	1687-1696, 1096-1100	"	1884-5	O-499	
0	1760 – 1769	200, 201, 213, 214, 217,222,1346,1093,1101,1431	"	1889-90	O-804	
	1770 – 1779	1843-1847,1102-1106	"	1890	O-854	
	1780 – 1789	203,1848-1852,1973-1976	"	"	O-869	4'-7"
	1790 – 1794	1977-1981	"	"	O-924	
	1795 – 1804	880-889	"	"	O-883	
	1805 – 1814	1982-1991	"	1891	O-968	
	1815 – 1824	1992, 1127-1135	"	"	O-991	
	1825 – 1844	1893-2010	VULCAN	1892	CLASS N	
	1845 – 1854	1121-1130	M.R.Co	1895	O-1395	
	1855 – 1859	2294-2298	SHARP STEWART		CLASS Q	
	1860 – 1889	2361-2390	STEPHENSON	1899	"	
	1890 – 1899	2571-2580		1899-1900	"	
	1900 – 1919	2441-2460	VULCAN		CLASS S	
	1920 – 1929	2741-2760	"	1901	"	
	1930 – 1939	2751-2760	"	1902	CLASS U	
	1940 – 1959	2761-2780	"	"	CLASS U2	
0-6-4	2000 – 2019		M.R.Co	1907	O-3187	5'-7"
	2020 – 2039				O-3258	

GOODS ENGINES

TYPE	ENGINE Nos	OLD ENGINE Nos	MAKERS	DATE NEW	ORDER No OR CLASS	ORDER Nos (REBUILD)	DIA. OF DRWHEELS
	2300 & 2301	376, 345	HAWTHORN	1850, 1853			
	2302 – 2307	266,412,670,460,366,922	STEPHENSON	1852-3			
D	2309 – 2316	654,281,1052,459,490,406,588,542	KITSON	1852-4			
O	2318	373	SHARP STEWART	1855			
U	2319 & 2320	420, 421	KITSON	1856			
B	2323 – 2340	VARIOUS 368 -485	STEPHENSON	1856-9			
L	2342 – 2365	" 300-557	M.R.Co	1858-60			
E	2366 – 2386	" 460-1067	FAIRBAIRN	1860-62			
	2388 – 2397	448,449,572,525,526,572,330,558,571	M.R.Co	1861-2			
F	2398 – 2458	VARIOUS 302 -564	STEPHENSON	1863-6		H CLASS BOILER No 2431 & 2434, H CLASS BOILER No 2472 }O-3007	
R	2459 – 2497	" 290-650,604,631	M.R.Co	1863-7			
A	2498 – 2531	" 558 -649	KITSON	1866-8			
M	2532 – 2549	610-619, 621-625, 677-620	SHARP STEWART	1867-8			
E	2550 – 2567	631-636, 626-640	DUBS	1868		H CLASS BOILER No 2567, H CLASS BOILER No 2559 }O-3007	
D	2568 – 2582	671 -681,665,292,301,304	"	1868			
	2583 – 2591	650-665, 657-659	YORKS. ENG. Co	1868-9		H CLASS BOILER No 2583	
O	2592 – 2631	700-719,760-779	DUBS	1869-70			
–	2632 – 2651	720 -739	NEILSON	"			
6	2652 – 2661	740-749	KITSON	"			
–	2662 – 2671	750-759	FOWLER	1870			
0	2672 – 2695	VARIOUS 229 -699	M.R.Co	1869-71			
	2695 – 2715	" 223-667	VULCAN	1870-71			
	2712	456	FAIRBAIRN	1860			
D	2716 – 2769	VARIOUS 438 -1053	DUBS	1871-3			
O	2770 – 2789	910-929	NEILSON	1871-2			
U	2790 – 2804	VARIOUS 225-667	M.R.Co	1872-3			
B	2805 – 2829	" 309-926	VULCAN	1872-4		(E CLASS BOILER) O-3336	
L	2830 – 2843	267,258,257,375,274,361,383	"	1874			
E	2844 – 2863	1042-1051, 1054-1063	DUBS	1873-4		(D CLASS BOILER) O-3336	
	2864 – 2867	1064,1065,1067,1069	"	1874			
	2900 – 2929	1142-1161,361-385,400-406	KITSON	1875-6	CLASS B		4'-11"
	2930 – 2959	1162-1191	DUBS	1875	"		
	2960 – 2989	1192-1221	BEYER PEACOCK	1876	"		
S	2990 – 3019	1222-1251	NEILSON	"	"		
	3020 – 3039	1357-1376	DUBS	1878	CLASS H		5'-3"
F	3040 – 3049	1452-1461	M.R.Co	1880	O-240		
R	3050 – 3079	1432-1451,1462-1471	STEPHENSON	1880-1	CLASS H		
A	3080 – 3129	1582-1631	BEYER PEACOCK	1882-4	"		
M	3130 – 3139	1698-1707	M.R.Co	1885	O-530		
E	3140 – 3149	1708-1717	"	"	O-544		
D	3150 – 3159	1758-1767	"	1886	O-617	O-2677a (H CLASS BOILER)	4'-11"
	3160 – 3169	1768-1777	"	1887	O-633		
O	3170 – 3189	1778-1797	"	1887-8	O-663		
–	3190 – 3199	1798-1807	"	1888	O-713		
6	3200 – 3299	1873-1972	NEILSON	1890-1	"		
–	3300 – 3339	2073-2096	KITSON	1891-2	CLASS J		
0	3340 – 3369	2062-2096	DUBS	1891	"		
	3370 – 3409	2093-2132	SHARP STEWART	1892	CLASS M		
	3410 – 3459	2133-2182	DUBS	1892-4	CLASS J2		
	3460 – 3469	361 - 370	M.R.Co	1894-5	O-1353		
	3470 – 3544	2084-2258	NEILSON	1896-7	CLASS M	O-2677 (H CLASS BOILER)	
	3545 – 3569	2259-2283	SHARP STEWART	1897	"		
	3570 – 3599	2391-2420	KITSON	1899-1900	"	NOTE – Nos 3006,3336,3367 TO O-2677b	
S	3600 – 3629	2461-2490	NEILSON	"	"		
I	3630 – 3649	2491-2510	DUBS	1900	"		
N	3650 – 3669	2491-2500, 2541-2550	VULCAN	"	"		O-4745 H BOILER (SATURATED)	5'-3"
G	3670 – 3689	2641-2660	KITSON	1901	"		
L	3690 – 3709	2661-2680	SHARP STEWART	"	"		
E	3710 – 3764	2681-2735	NEILSON	1901-2	"		
	3765 – 3774	2736-2740, 240-244	M.R.Co	1903	O-2326		
	3775 – 3784	245 -254	"	"	O-2530		
	3785 – 3794	255 -264	"	1904	O-2655		
	3795 – 3804	265 -274	"	"	O-2695		
	3805 – 3814	275 -284	"	1906-7	O-2851		
	3815 – 3834		"	1908	O-3344		
	3835		"	1911	O-4000		
	3836		"		O-4201		

that this same page records cylinder diameters of 16½", 17" and 18" x 24" stroke! There was also included an extra page which summarised where they were originally built, and this information concerning origin of the post-1903 survivors is given in Table 3. On the other hand, the single frame Johnson goods engines, a series numbering 865 by the date of this return, was divided into no less than nine varieties, and of these nine most folk would now regard eight of them simply as 'Class 2', using the power class nomenclature. In a recently published book by Jack Braithwaite entitled *S. W. Johnson, Locomotive Engineer Artist*, there are lists of MR locomotives as classified by the author. When dealing with the nine varieties of goods engines, he identifies only *four* varieties. A well known historian of Midland locomotives, who apparently influenced Braithwaite's compilation, when questioned about this apparent anomaly, said, 'There was little difference dimensionally or

mechanically between them.' He was referring to a variety which Braithwaite considered to be but one class but which the Midland, in 1903, had broken into several different ones, as indeed we shall do in Volume 4.

All views are, in fact, right. There is little difference; yet with other classes similar minor differences led to an official sub-division, so it really all depends upon one's personal viewpoint and the background against which these assessments are made. For our part, we have recorded the Midland's official viewpoint wherever possible and where this is not practical, we have occasionally suggested our own method of classification.

To round off the chapter, there is the question of power classification which has to be considered. As discussed in Volume 1, it was decided in 1905 to display the power classification for goods tender engines on the engine cab by means of a brass numeral, the Kirtley 0—6—0s being

4—4—0 No. 2183 in original condition is seen here at an unknown location. As the first member of the '2183' class, it marked the beginning of the enlargement of the slim-boilered 4—4—0. Its story is told on page 109.
C. M. Doncaster

TABLE 4

| | TYPES | | | | | No. OF ENGINES | | |
	GENERAL	DISTINCTIVE		VARIETIES	REGULAR STOCK	DUPLICATE STOCK	TOTAL
1	NON COUPLED PASSR	1	WITH BOGIE	5	95	-	95
		2	NO BOGIE	2		2	2
2	4 WHEELS COUPLED PASSENGER	3	INSIDE FRAMES AND BOGIE	14	302	-	302
		4	INSIDE FRAMES NO BOGIE	6	199	18	217
		5	OUTSIDE FRAMES & CRANKS NO BOGIE	4	4	72	76
		6	COMPOUND WITH BOGIE	1	2	-	2
3	G WHEELS COUPLED GOODS	7	INSIDE FRAMES	9	865	-	865
		8	OUTSIDE FRAMES AND CRANKS	1	723	-	723
		9	MOGUL OUTSIDE CYLINDERS	2	40	-	40
4	4 WHEELS COUPLED PASSR TANK	10	TRAILING BOGIE	8	205		205
		11	TRAILING BOGIE OUTSIDE FRAMES & CRANKS	3	16	10	26
		12	LEADING BOGIE OUTSIDE CYLINDERS	1	-	5	5
5	G WHEELS COUPLED TANKS	13	SIDE TANKS	12	322	31	353
		14	SADDLE TANKS	3	-	1	1
		15	BACK TANKS	5	-	9	9
		16	SIDE TANKS OUTSIDE CYLINDERS	2	-	2	2
6	4 WHEELS COUPLED	17	SADDLE TANKS	3	2	23	25
					2775	173	2948

ENGINES RUNNING ON JULY 1ST 1903

generally in class 1, the unrebuilt and small Johnson 0—6—0s in class 2 and the H-boilered 0—6—0s in class 3. During 1906 the principle was extended to the various passenger tender classes, again in three divisions. These were later expanded to four classifications and, because only 4—4—0s and 0—6—0s were involved, the accepted method of description through common usage became, for example, class 1 0—6—0 or class 1 freight, and similarly for the passenger engines. To identify them more closely, other descriptions were sometimes used, such as class 2 superheater or class 1 Kirtley 2—4—0, etc.

It should not, therefore, surprise readers to learn that in these volumes we choose to use a variety of descriptions, adopting the version which we feel to be the most appropriate in context. We use order numbers or letters to indicate certain batches and we regularly encompass these batches under an overall 'accepted usage' class heading, e.g. '1562' class. We also relate them to the 1903 diagrams in the tables and to the 1910 and 1919 engine diagrams (some of which we illustrate) in the class chapters. The difference between these later diagrams was explained on page ix in Volume 1. Finally, in several instances, we also use the power classifications and popular names, e.g. 'Compounds' and 'Belpaires', to assist a fuller understanding; we hope that readers will agree that this method best suits the modern approach to the subject.

To round off the classification story, before commencing the detailed examination of the various passenger tender classes in this volume, we conclude this chapter with Table 5, a list of engines built by the Midland after the 1903 Engines Diagram Book was produced.

TABLE 5

Order No.	Date	Qty.	1907 Engine Nos.	
2726	1904/5	10	750-759	
2798	1905	10	760-769	
2821	1906	10	3805-3814	
2889	1905	10	1005-1014	
2918	1905	10	770-779	
2998	1906	20	1015-1034	
3031	1907	5	1528-1532	
3139	1907	1	999	
3187	1907	20	2000-2019	
3258	1907	20	2020-2039	
3306	1908	1	2299	
3344	1908	20	3815-3834	
3371	1909	9	990-998	
3410	1908/9	10	1035-1044	
4000	1911	1	3835	
4001	1911	1	3836	
4482	1919	1	2290	
4991	1917	15	3837-3851	
5064	1918	10	3852-3861	
5127	1918	10	3862-3871	
5168	1918/9	15	3872-3886	
5233	1919	15	3887-3901	
5308	1920	15	3902-3916	
5335	1920/1	20	3917-3936	
5432	1921/2	50	3937-3986	Built by Armstrong Whitworth and Co.
5469	1921	20	3987-4006	
5528	1921/2	5	1533-1537	
5530	1921/2	20	4007-4026	

Apart from 0/5432 all were built at Derby.

Plate 1. 2—4—0 No. 77A perfectly exemplifies the '156' class during the late 1890s and early 1900s. Its numbering was complex. Starting as No. 111 in 1867, it went onto the duplicate list in 1880. It was restored to the capital list as No. 80 in 1888, in 1891 it became 80A, in 1895 it was renumbered 77, and in 1896 77A. There matters remained until 1907 when it became No. 11, and it retained this number until withdrawal in 1928. It is seen here in full crimson lake livery, a form typical of the 1896-1901 period when it carried this number. In earlier 'red' days there would be less lining below the footplate.

Collection Bernard Mathews

CHAPTER TWO

KIRTLEY 2-4-0 CLASSES

Plate 2. '800' class 2—4—0 No. 64 in its immediate pre-Johnson condition. It was given the Johnson treatment in 1882 at which point it probably changed tender and the locomotive itself took up the same configuration as shown at *Plate 4*. Note the different pattern of Kirtley tender, probably of 2,000 gallon capacity, compared with *Plate 3* which is of 1,600 gallon. This view also shows a dark green engine.

Authors' Collection

DURING the middle part of the 19th century, the six-wheel locomotive was virtually the norm for all types of railway working and in the long distance passenger business, the 2—2—2 wheel arrangement was the most commonplace. However, as train weight increased, more adhesion was called for and the 2—4—0 type, already widely used as an alternative to the 0—6—0 for goods working, tended to be developed (with larger wheels) until it eventually became possibly the most characteristic form of express power on the majority of British lines.

Not all engineers liked the 2—4—0 for passenger working — feeling that the 'single driver' type was more free running, not having coupling rods. We shall have cause to return to this particular theme in Chapter 7, but at the moment, suffice it to say that Matthew Kirtley seemed to have no fear of using a 2—4—0 for the heavier Midland expresses — even though he had also built numerous 2—2—2 engines. Of the several 2—4—0 designs he initiated, the earliest to concern us in this particular work are the two double-framed series introduced in 1866 and 1870 respectively. These were the '156' and '800' classes. One pre-1883 view is given at *Plate 2* to show the 'seed corn' from which they were developed during subsequent regimes.

They were truly astonishing engines, like many another Kirtley design and, thanks mainly to a series of re-boilering activities, their lives were prolonged well into the LMS period without them ever really losing their mid-19th century character. In fact, they proved literally indestructable in one instance — '156 Class' No. 158A, now preserved in the National collection.

At the start of the period of our survey both types had mostly received new, larger Johnson boilers with Johnson cabs and, for the most part were to exchange their original Kirtley 'horseshoe' tenders for the larger capacity Johnson pattern although this took some time to complete. Whether the increased capacity was mainly to give greater operational flexibility or perhaps carry more water for the large new boilers, we are not sure. Perhaps there was even something fundamentally wrong with their original tenders — a tendency to axlebox overheating? However, the Kirtley type tender continued in use well into LMS days on goods engines.

Thus, the starting point in our story is represented more or less by the condition illustrated at *Plates 2 & 3*. From this point we shall deal with two classes separately.

Plate 3. '156' class 2—4—0 No. 104A, taken sometime after 1882 when it received its first Johnson boiler, and before rebuilding with a larger Johnson boiler in 1898. It should be noted that these first Johnson boilers appear to have been pitched lower, a feature covered more completely in a later volume. The engine may be green or red in this view and, in its later, re-boilered form, became No. 6 in 1907 and was withdrawn in 1932. *Authors' Collection*

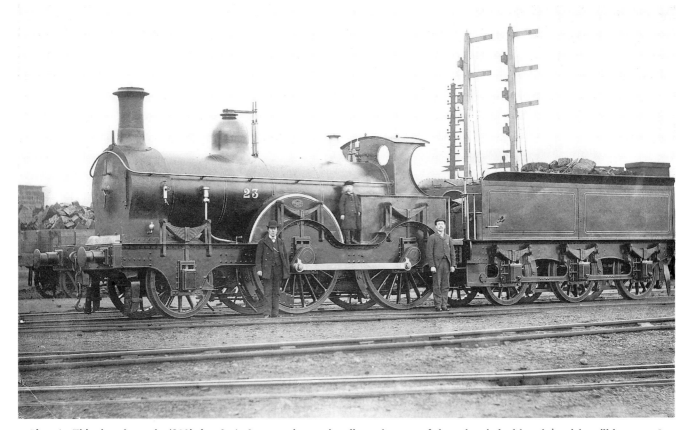

Plate 4. This view shows the '800' class 2—4—0 type as it was virtually at the start of the red period, although it might still be green. It received its Johnson boiler as early as 1882 when engines were still green and it was certainly photographed prior to 1890. The locomotive was built in 1871, became No. 23A in 1900, No. 67 in 1907 and was withdrawn from service in 1925. Note the large tool box on the rear of the tender. Whether green or red, the lining is typical of the 1880s. Note the absence of lining on the lifeguards (guard irons) or brake block hangers, springs or end spring brackets. However, unlike later period pictures, the front corner of the cab is lined on both the front and side. Note also the lack of a front vacuum hose. *Collection Bernard Mathews*

156 CLASS

Summary:

Twenty-nine engines built at Derby 1866-1874. The MR numbers of the 22 surviving locomotives immediately prior to renumbering in 1907: 156A, 158A, 159A, 89A, 118A, 104A, 105A, 106A, 107A, 76A, 77A, 157A, 119A, 79A, 116A, 160A, 161A, 163A, 164A, 153A, 154A, 155A. 1907 numbers (respectively) 1-22, all to LMS except No. 20. All rebuilt by Johnson. Class extinct 1947. No. 158A, by then No. 20002, was withdrawn for preservation and is now part of the National Collection.

Tenders

In 1903 the tender allocation included:

1600 gallon	No. 104A
2000 gallon	Nos. 89A, 159A
2200 gallon	Nos. 158A, 153A
2750 gallon	Nos. 76A, 79A, 105A, 154A, 160A, 161A, 164A, 157A, 116A, 163A
2950 gallon	Nos. 77A, 106A, 107A, 119A, 156A, 118A

Later c.1910

The allocation was as below:

2750 gallon	3, 4, 6, 7, 10-19
2950 gallon	1, 2, 5, 8, 9, 20, 21, 22

These engines were an enlargement of an earlier Kirtley design and E. L. Ahrons said of them ' . . . *for their size, there are no better engines in the country today.*' There were never many of them, only 29 in total and of these the last five were actually erected after Johnson had taken over (although for the Midland at this time 29 was a large number for a single class of passenger engines). No fewer than 22 remained in service to be given 'pole' position (Nos. 1-22) in the new 1907 lists and all but one of these (No. 20) reached the LMS. Three survived until the 1940s and the last withdrawal, No. 2 (latterly LMS No. 20002), was preserved in 1947. It now carries No. 158A again but this is not historically accurate (see below).

Apart from the last five (reboiled during 1886-91) the bulk of the '156' class had received their first new boilers during 1880-2 before the change to red livery. There were, however, a few examples (believed to be old Nos. 103, 109, 114, 116, 117, 161, 163 and 164) which were reboilered in the mid-1880s and were, presumably, always red thereafter. It seems probable that Johnson tenders began to be fitted at this reboiling, or shortly thereafter. During the 'red' period, all would certainly have received the early crimson lake style followed in the 1890s by the 'full' treatment (e.g. *Plate 1*) but it seems unlikely that they were ever given much in the way of decorated styles towards the turn of the century.

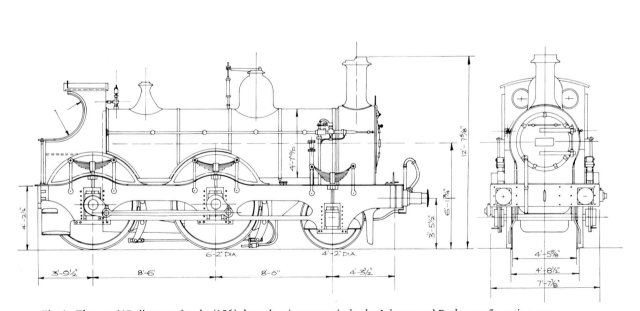

Fig. 1. *The two MR diagrams for the '156' class, showing respectively the Johnson and Deeley configuration, are inaccurate and have not been reproduced. However, they also show different tender sizes as well and this information has been incorporated in the summary. Instead we have included a detailed drawing of the '156' class in Deeley condition, which is based on measurements of the preserved No. 158A. For reasons explained in the text, no tender drawing is offered.*
Original drawing by K. C. Woodhead, traced by Carl Legg

Plate 5. Very few pictures exist to show locomotives with smokebox door numberplates which have an A suffix. This '156' class locomotive was built in 1874 as No. 153 and went onto the duplicate list in 1897. Ten years later it became No. 20 and was withdrawn in 1921. This picture illustrates a locomotive with a flat Deeley smokebox door, Johnson style handrail and a flowerpot chimney which doesn't suit this class at all. Note the 2,200 gallon tender.

Collection Bernard Mathews

Plate 6. 2—4—0 No. 159A as running c.1905, also with a flowerpot chimney. This is another example displaying a smokebox door numberplate with an A suffix. Built in 1866 as No. 159, the locomotive went onto the duplicate list in 1896, became No. 3 in 1907 and was withdrawn in 1928. Only the boiler bands adjacent to the smokebox and cabfront are lined and there is no lining on the front end of the cabside panel. Clearly this is Deeley's new livery before the introduction of tender numerals. *National Railway Museum*

Deeley 'front ends' began to be fitted slightly before 1907, sometimes with flowerpot chimneys (*Plate 5*), but the characteristic condition after the renumbering was with normal Deeley chimney/smokebox − a configuration they retained until scrapping. The longer term survivors eventually became black during LMS days (*Plates 11 & 12*) and more details of the LMS period are given in our companion work *An Illustrated History of LMS Locomotives, Vol. 4*.

According to some official diagrams dated c.1910, tenders were either of the 2750 gallon or 2950 gallon variety, and the division of the types was a bit arbitrary. However, a 1903 official record exhibits a wide variety of types and we have recorded the relevant numbers in the

class summary. This is probably as near a correct division as is likely to be possible at this range in time. Talking of tenders, it is, of course, the tender of the preserved 158A which gives rise to the inaccuracy of presentation.

No. 158A had been preserved long before the creation of the National Railway Museum, at a time when, for some reason, there was an absolute fetish for preservation 'as built'. Never mind that the engine had spent most of its time in Johnson/Deeley condition, it was a Kirtley engine so it must be given a Kirtley tender! No-one seemed to appreciate that the old tenders vanished from this class, mostly before 1900, that the larger boiler was a Johnson-inspired change or that the 'front end' was Deeley. If it

Plate 7. Cab interior of '156' class 2−4−0 No. 10 showing the interior cab treatment during the Deeley period. Between waist and roof, the colour was buff, usually grain finished. The roof was white and below the waist, surfaces were black at this time. Compare this view with that of No. 104A (*Plate 194*, Volume One). Note the lower boiler pitch in the earlier view.   *National Railway Museum*

Plate 8. Although there is no visible sign of MR on the bufferplank, we think that on this picture at Barnt Green it is just obscured. The view is recorded as having been taken in July 1921 and shows an interesting front end: Johnson handrails and dished smokebox door with the vertical handle – more usually associated with the flat smokebox door but not uncommon on the dished door if the continuous handrail was retained. Built in 1868 as No. 163, it went onto the duplicate list in 1894 as No. 163A. Becoming No. 18 in 1907, it was withdrawn in 1934.

W. L. Good

Plate 9. '156' class No. 5 in LMS crimson lake at Derby in June 1925. The locomotive appears to be newly repainted and so, presumably, has just gone from MR to LMS livery. Dating from 1867 as No. 102, it became No. 102A in 1879 and then in 1890 it was restored to the capital list as No. 118. Seven years later, in 1897, it was back onto the duplicate list as No. 118A. 1907 saw it become No. 5, and as such it lasted until withdrawal in 1928.
W. L. Good

had simply been left as withdrawn it would have been truly representative of the 1938-47 period, and with a Deeley chimney c.1910-47. Now it is representative of no specific period, more's the pity.

It is, of course, nice to be able to examine a venerable Kirtley tender and maybe we are being a little over-sensitive about the fine detail, but one of us has to live with the problem on a semi-permanent basis at the NRM. On this score, old 158A is a most curious hybrid indeed for it is impossible to give it a correct colour scheme. The irony is that a much more suitable 2950 gallon tender is hitched onto 4−2−2 No. 673 which could well have been preserved with the 3500 gallon version it was built with. But then, MR 1000 has an ex-S & DJR tender; so, all told, these three famous preserved MR types do have their problems. It is, of course, better than if they had been scrapped, and it probably does not matter too much to most people, but we feel it should be on record as it were. Now, if anyone could find another tender for No. 673 — say a 3500 gallon one!

Clearly, the '156' class engines were more generally versatile than the '800' class (overleaf) and lasted rather better than their more numerous and, nominally, younger sisters. They were certainly a good investment and we doubt if the HSTs will last in service for 80 years!

Plate 10. A close-up of the driving wheel splasher and spring of the preserved No. 158A. *Authors' Collection*

Plate 11. No. 2 in LMS plain black livery at Kings Norton on 10th March 1932 heading a local passenger train. This locomotive, the last to survive, was built in 1866 as No. 158. It went onto the duplicate list as No. 158A in 1896. Becoming No. 2 in 1907, it became No. 2002 in 1934, was withdrawn in 1947 and became part of the National Collection (see main text). *W. L. Good*

Plate 12. 2—4—0 No. 20012 at Bedford in March 1937. This was the final style for this class — usually plain black finished with approx. 8 inch handpainted numerals on the cabside and smokebox door. No number plate was used. Built in 1867 as No. 110, it became No. 110A in 1879 and ten years later it was back on the capital list as No. 20. By 1892 it was on the duplicate list again as No. 20A, then in 1894 it changed to 157 and in 1896 to 157A. In 1907 it became No. 12 and remained so until 1934 when it was renumbered 20012. Finally, in 1945, the locomotive was withdrawn from service.

A. G. Ellis

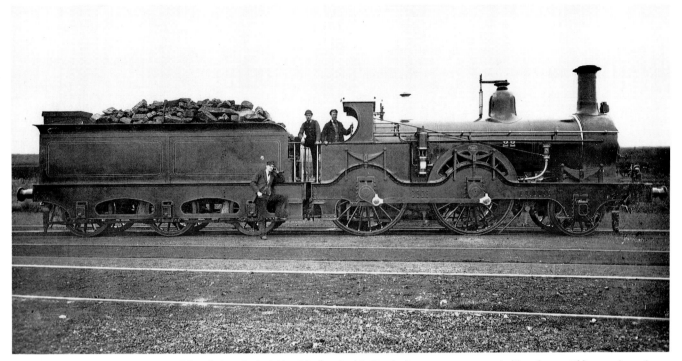

Plate 13. This interesting view of '800' class 2−4−0 No. 22, fitted with Westinghouse pump was probably taken at Skipton where the engine was based. It was one of the first Johnson rebuilds (in 1876) and still retains its 'open' front splasher in spite of the other obvious Johnson changes. Note, too, the early Johnson style tender with 'inside' springs. These were later altered. The engine is unquestionably green but we cannot say precisely how long it remained like this before adopting the more normal configuration. No. 22 became 22A in 1900 and No. 66 in 1907.   *National Railway Museum*

800 CLASS

Summary

Built at Derby and by Neilson & Co.
The 18 Derby-built locomotives were equipped with lever and quadrant type reversing gear.
The 30 Neilson-built engines had a screw reversing gear which was vertical, with a wheel on the top on the first ten locomotives to be built and horizontal on the remainder. The final six locomotives built at Derby had 3 ins shorter wheelbase between the driving wheels and a shorter firebox. While these were not considered to be the same class by the Midland Railway Company when built, they are all included within this series as far as this volume is concerned. The five survivors of this batch in 1907 became 63-67.
Three locomotives, Nos. 801A, 807A and 3, were withdrawn in 1905.
The MR numbers of the 45 surviving locomotives immediately prior to renumbering in 1907: Derby-built — 165A-169A, 60-66A, 138A, 139A, 93A, 22A, 23A. Became 23-34, 63-67. Neilson-built — 800A, 802A, 806A, 808A-829A. Became 35-62. 1907 numbers 23-67 with only 24 survivors to the LMS in 1923. Allocated to Engine Diagram 7 in 1910. Generally equipped with 2,950 gallon tenders (No. 165A ran with 3,250 gallon tender c.1903). Class extinct 1936.

It is interesting that the two long-lived Kirtley 2−4−0 designs were both highly regarded from the outset. We have already quoted Ahrons' comment on the '156' class and he was later, in the same book, to refer to the '800' class as ' . . . one of the most celebrated classes of express engines that ever ran in this country'.

As part of his general policy of increasing engine power, partly in response to the comments of the locomen, Kirtley built the first of the '800' class engines in 1870 in a very similar style to the '156' series but with 6 inch bigger driving wheels and enhanced cylinder/boiler output. They were thus altogether bigger machines and 48 were built. Johnson was so impressed with their performance and, presumably, by their rugged construction, that by 1882 he had reboilered the lot and given them even bigger cylinders, now 18 inch diameter. Some of them had the stroke lengthened as well, but this was deemed too expensive a modification (it would involve *inter alia*, completely new crank axles and valve eccentrics) so the majority retained their 24 inch stroke.

This rebuilding was just completed at the start of our detailed period of study and their early history will be more fully considered in a later volume. *Plate 4* shows the Johnson version. It was probably in this form that they first gained wide attention and for some 20 years they remained little further changed. In the early 1880s, they were much used on the still fairly new Settle-Carlisle line, and, for working the Scottish expresses, some of them were Westinghouse fitted (*Plates 13 & 14*). They were not, however, confined to the north and found employment throughout the system.

Plate 14. '800' class 2—4—0 No. 802. This photograph, at an unknown location, was taken before March 1901, when the locomotive went onto the duplicate list. However, the reader's attention is drawn to the Westinghouse pumps and brake gear fitted to several members of the class (see also *Plate 13*). The lining on the locomotive is very clear and the Johnson built-up chimney should be noted. No. 802 became 802A and in 1907 was renumbered No. 36. Withdrawal was in 1924.

Collection David White

Plate 15. '800' class No. 826A was photographed between 1903 and 1907 when it became No. 59 (see *Plate 19*). This beautifully crisp view shows a version of the final 'full' livery before the Deeley simplifications. The guard irons are lined but the spring brackets and brake hangers are not and there is no lining on the cab front and weatherboard. This may have been a first stage simplification since late 19th century views show lined brake hangers, for example, and lining on the corner of the cab and weatherboard. *Authors' Collection*

This upgrading by Johnson − as with his work on the later 2−4−0 series − is interesting when set alongside the story of his 4−4−0s (Chapter 5). The latter wheel arrangement was introduced in 1876 but it was not until 1881 that the last of the 2−4−0s (Johnson's 7 ft series) came out, and, for much of the 1880s and 1890s, the 2−4−0s remained in the front line, thus justifying continued attention, which policy, of course, embraced the '800' class. It is recorded that these engines remained in main line service for almost 30 years after rebuilding, and the reason is not difficult to seek.

After Johnson's ministrations, which also went with the fitting of new 2950 gallon tenders, the '800' class were, for all practical purposes, virtually brand new machines during the first decades of the 'red' period and few visible changes took place. We cannot say when the last one became red, but c.1886 would, possibly, be a fair assumption. They were, of course, all rebuilt before the end of the 'green'

period, so would obviously keep this colour scheme for a few years after 1883. However, being in the forefront of activities, they would be early candidates for the new colour scheme.

With this scheme, the general arrangement is as shown at, for example, *Plate 14*, one of the more interesting points being the position of the numbers on the boilerside. In all conscience, there was little enough room for them on the cabside, as the LMS was to find later. As the Midland moved into what we have called the 'full' and 'decorated' period of the 1890s, most available evidence suggests that apart from getting 'MR' on the tender and a little more elaboration below the footplate, the '800' class, like the '156' class engines, were not normally given any highly embellished liveries.

Deeley's front end duly appeared, along with the new livery and numbers (*Plate 18*), and the engines mostly remained in mainline service throughout the Edwardian

Continued on page 24

Plate 16. '800' class 2—4—0 No. 805A at Leeds fitted with a cast iron Johnson chimney — compare with No. 802 in *Plate 14*. This picture is broadly contemporary with *Plate 15* but shows lining on the cab corner. However, the tender has the new style Deeley treatment, so again there has been some simplification. No. 805 went onto the duplicate list in 1901, became No. 39 in 1907 and was withdrawn in 1926. Note the unidentified 4—4—0 with flat Deeley smokebox door and smokebox door numberplate which can just be seen behind the tender coping of the 2—4—0.

J. H. Wright

Plate 17. No. 820A, photographed between 1903 and 1907, is superficially as *Plates 15/16* but note the single line only round the *whole* tender side. Simplification of tender lining was quite common for a few years before the new large tender numerals came into use, but until 'MR' was abandoned, the normal solution was to line *both* tenderside panels round the edge of the beading. No. 820A received its 'A' suffix in 1903 and became No. 53 in 1907. It was withdrawn in 1927. *Authors' Collection*

Plate 18. No. 27 was originally No. 169 and is shown at Birmingham New Street on 21st August 1912. Note the flat smokebox door and the retention of the original Johnson continuous handrail. The No. 3 district plate Birmingham, and locomotive number painted onto the headlamp can clearly be seen. Many of the '800' class retained the continuous front handrail for a period, even after fitting with dished doors. *W. L. Good*

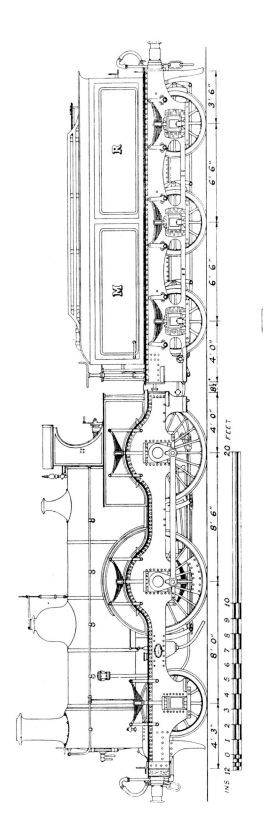

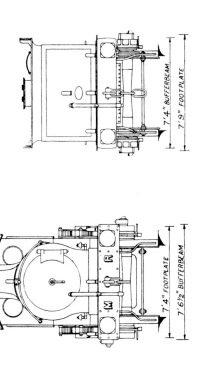

Fig. 2. This drawing of an '800' class locomotive is based upon a drawing produced by the late J. N. Maskelyne, A.I. Loco. E., for Model Railway News which was published in the May 1940 issue of that magazine. The drawing depicts the locomotive in its Johnson condition with the Johnson 'front end' but features incorrect tender spring hangers and brackets.

Plate 19. '800' class No. 59 at St. Pancras in the standard Deeley configuration. Even though the smokebox door is not visible, the handrails clearly terminate at the front edge of the smokebox. We include this rear view, as with *Plates 21 & 23*, more than partly to help modellers.
National Railway Museum

Plate 20. This three-quarter rear view of No. 63 (later 63A, then No. 31) taken c.1895 should also be of help to modellers.

C. M. Doncaster

period. Three only failed to be renumbered in 1907, but thereafter withdrawal was much more rapid than for the numerically smaller '156' class. Only 24 reached the LMS and this company continued to withdraw them quite quickly.

This more rapid withdrawal compared with the '156' class, was, we think, very much bound up with the great 4—4—0 passenger engine renewal programme (see Chapter 5). With their bigger wheels, it would, perhaps, be harder to find suitable alternative work for the '800s' than the '156s', which were often used for pilot purposes. The '800' class was essentially an express passenger type, and, historically speaking, this type of locomotive was never quite as long-lived (on any company) as the smaller wheeled engines, which could usually be found some sort of alternative occupation over a rather longer time-span. The MR never,

as far as we know, deliberately classified any engine as 'mixed traffic' in the modern sense; but it undoubtedly used smaller wheeled passenger engines for goods trains and also employed vacuum-fitted goods engines on some local passenger services. The '156' class could, therefore, continue for a bit longer than the '800' class. Moreover, the somewhat more numerous and newer Johnson '1400' class had the same size wheels as the Kirtley '800s' and seems to have been the preferred choice for retention in the 6 ft 8 in to 6 ft 9 in category, especially when rebuilt with a new Belpaired boiler (Chapter 4).

Nevertheless, the last of the '800' class, LMS No. 20060, was not withdrawn until 1936, some 65 years old at the time and probably with its original frames — not a bad achievement.

TABLE 6: KIRTLEY PASSENGER 2—4—0 CLASSES

1903 Diagram Page No.	Order No. or Class	Built by	Qty. built	Date of building	Pre 1907 numbers	1907 renumbering	Cylinders	BOILER Centre Line	Diameter	Length	Tubes	Diameter	Working Pressure	FIREBOX Length	Grate Area in sq. ft.	Total Heating Surface in sq. ft.	WHEELS Leading	Driving	Tyres	ENGINE WEIGHT Empty	Loaded	REMARKS
58	MR	Derby	29	1866-68 1873-74	Various 76A-164A	1-22	18″ × 24″	not quoted	4' 2″	10' 6″	244	1¾″	140 PSI	5' 11″	17.5	1246	4' 2½″	6' 2½″	not quoted	37.7.1	40.10.2	Known as 156 class. Originally 16½″ × 22″ cycls.
25	Kirtley Pass.	Neilsons	30	1870	800-829	35-62	see remarks	not quoted	4' 2″	10' 6″	246	1¾″	see remarks	5' 11″	17.5	1260	4' 2½″	6' 8½″	2¾″	36.3.1	39.12.2	Known as 800 class. diagram page 25 is annotated Eng. 811 18″ × 26″ 160 PSI Engs. 814, 816, 813, 818, 819 18″ × 26″ 140 PSI Eng. 817 18″ × 24″ 160 PSI
60		Derby	18	1870-71	60, 61, 62, 63, 166-169, 64-66, 165, 3, 22, 23, 93, 138, 139	23-34 63-67	18″ × 24″	not quoted	4' 2″	10' 6″	244 246	1¾″	140 PSI	5' 11″	17.5	1252 1260	4' 2½″	6' 8½″	not quoted	36.3.1	39.12.2	but a very reliable source suggests that at 1st July 1903 the 160 PSI engines were 811, 814, 815 and 817. Eventually nine carried 160 PSI boilers. The 18″ × 26″ cyl engines were 169, 800, 804, 805, 807, 811, 813, 814, 816, 818, 819, and the remainder were 18″ × 24″. All were originally 17″ 24″. *Source 1903 Engine Diagram Book.*

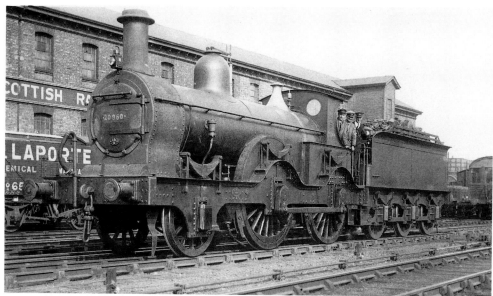

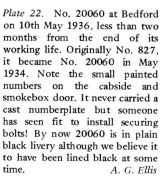

Plate 22. No. 20060 at Bedford on 10th May 1936, less than two months from the end of its working life. Originally No. 827, it became No. 20060 in May 1934. Note the small painted numbers on the cabside and smokebox door. It never carried a cast numberplate but someone has seen fit to install securing bolts! By now 20060 is in plain black livery although we believe it to have been lined black at some time.   *A. G. Ellis*

Plates 21 (opposite) & 23. It was our original intention to give only one cab interior view of the '800' class but the late acquisition of a second view made us feel that the subtle differences visible on the two pictures should be featured.   *National Railway Museum*

Plate 24. '890' class 2—4—0 No. 901 more or less as built in 1871. It is recorded as not having been rebuilt until 1886, but it clearly already has a Johnson chimney and may have had a new smokebox door pretty soon. This represents the condition of many of this class at the start of our survey and No. 901 is not likely to have lost its green livery until rebuilt. It became No. 79 in 1907 and was scrapped in 1919.

Authors' Collection

CHAPTER THREE

TRANSITIONAL 2-4-0 CLASSES

Plate 25. '1070' class 2—4—0 No. 1075 very soon after building in 1874. Although a posthumous design, the Kirtley influence is still strong — tender splashers, dome, etc. This picture shows very clearly the design relationship between this 6 ft 2½ in type and the Derby batch of the almost contemporary '890' class as shown at *Plate 26*. No. 1075 was fully 'Johnsonised' in 1889, became No. 132 in 1907 and was scrapped in 1933.   *Authors' Collection*

WE have chosen to use the word 'transitional' to cover the next group of 2—4—0s (1907 Nos. 68-156) because, although instigated by Kirtley, they were built across the period when, following his death, he was replaced by Johnson. Moreover, many of them were actually built in the Johnson period and their physical character strongly anticipated what might be called the true Johnson 2—4—0s (Chapter 4) and unquestionably influenced Johnson's own later designs.

The principal and obvious difference distinguishing the final Kirtley 2—4—0s from their predecessors was the abandonment of full double frames. However, although the coupled wheels had conventional inside frames, the leading wheels were still carried in outside bearings but now mounted in a substantial plate, in effect an outer frame which extended rearwards to form a much deeper than usual footplate angle and which became characteristic of all Johnson's 2—4—0 types as well. A similar construction was adopted for the trailing wheels and footplate angle of the bogie 4—2—2s (Chapter 7).

As with the double-framed '156' and '800' series covered in Chapter 2, the new designs came in the same two driving wheel sizes, nominally 6 ft 8½ in and 6 ft 2½ in, but this time the large-wheeled version, the '890' class, came first and was indeed designed by Kirtley himself in 1871, the early examples featuring his characteristic double folding smokebox door (*Plate 24*). The smaller wheeled variety,

the '1070' class, introduced in 1874, was in effect a posthumous Kirtley design built at the start of the Johnson period (*Plate 25*). Twenty were built in 1874-5 and another ten, slightly modified, in 1876, later being sometimes referred to as the '1' class.

890 CLASS

Summary

Built by Neilson & Co. and Derby 1871-1875.
MR numbers of locomotives which were renumbered in 1907, 50 of which reached the LMS in 1923:
Neilson-built — 890-909. 1907 numbers 68-87.
Derby-built — 2, 95, 90, 148, 92, 125, 5, 12, 123, 127, 19, 40, 41, 43, 46, 49, 91, 67, 121, 69, 131, 132, 151, 152, 47, 7, 72, 78, 42, 45, 44, 48, 124, 126, 128, 130, 120, 135, 136. 1907 numbers 88-126.
It is believed that they were ultimately fitted with Johnson 3250 gallon tenders, but a number ran with 2950 gallon tenders at some time.
Class extinct 1938.

The '890' class was dimensionally on a par with the preceding '800' class, but was essentially a more modern concept altogether. However, at the start of our period of survey, the engines had not as yet wholly been reboilered by Johnson, although they did carry much Johnson detail.

Plate 26. The Derby batch of '890' class 2—4—0s is fairly well typified by No. 151, still with Kirtley type boiler, splashers and dome, but fitted with Johnson chimney. No. 151 was built in 1874 but was not one of those which received a Johnson boiler between 1875-8 (see text). It therefore remained in the condition illustrated until fully 'Johnsonised' in 1888. The date of the picture is not known but the engine could well be a red one. Note the family resemblance to No. 1075 (*Plate 25*). No. 151 became No. 110 in 1907 and was scrapped in 1931. *Authors' Collection*

Plate 24 shows the appearance of the Neilson build after which the rectangular lower cabside treatment was changed to the form shown at *Plate 26*. The Derby-built locomotives were in this form, mostly with the more modern smokebox door style as well. However, the first six of this later series retained the old 'folding' doors with the new cabside 'splasher', but they all had cabs not weatherboards.

Many were built after Kirtley had gone and six of the last seven (built 1874-5) were given Johnson design boilers and domes *from new*. This boiler was then subsequently applied, retrospectively to many of the earlier examples during the 1875-8 period but by no means to all of them. Thus, at the time of the change to red livery in and after 1883, the '890' class probably presented quite a mixed bag of visual styles. At the same time, since the old fashioned Kirtley folding smokebox doors could be replaced without renewing the boiler itself, this may have happened quite quickly — probably before any became red.

Just after the livery change and from 1885-95, Johnson enlarged the cylinders (as for the '800' class), rebuilt the splasher sides to his own conventional pattern on the whole class of 62 engines, and fitted those *not so far carrying them* with his own design of boiler. The engines then took up the more familiar configuration of *Plate 27*. This 1885-95 rebuilding was accompanied by the fitting of new 3250 gallon tenders and, of couse, all engines were given crimson lake livery after this more fundamental rebuilding. Thus at last, and for the first time, there was 'visual stability' within the class.

At the same time, it should be made clear that many '890' class engines ran on well into the red period before losing their many Kirtley-inspired features (tenders, pierced splashers, domes etc.) and it is a near certainty that those of

them not rebuilt until the later 1880s and early 1890s would probably have been repainted red, at least once, before their major reconstruction. Regrettably, we have no knowledge of paint dates. However, most of the relevant rebuilding dates and so forth are recorded in such sources as *British Locomotive Catalogue, SLS Journal*, etc., and interested readers (especially modelmakers) ought to be able to make some fairly accurate assessments from these sources and the above review, assuming say 4-5 years between re-paints. In fact, the actual painting interval was probably somewhat less than this.

When the second style rebuilding was completed in 1895, the '890' class were visually part of the pure 'Johnson' family and at first glimpse indistinguishable from the genuine article. They remained thus until the start of the 'front end' modification by Deeley from 1904 onwards and this became their final anatomical state, e.g. *Plate 31*. Unlike later 2—4—0 designs, none of them were given Belpaire boilers in LMS days.

They were highly regarded engines and only three had gone by the 1907 renumbering and of the remaining 59, there were still 50 left when the LMS was formed. Withdrawal then speeded up and the last to go was No. 92 (now No. 20092) in 1938.

As far as MR decoration was concerned, we have mentioned the situation down to 1895, by which time the full crimson livery was normal (e.g. *Plates 27/8*). As with their predecessors, we do not think they were serious candidates for the special decorative embellishments, but there could have been exceptions. Thereafter came some simplification followed by the new Deeley livery (*Plates 31 & 32*) which, with LMS markings, lasted until 1928 after which black was the normal colour of any survivors.

Plate 27. This lovely view of No. 905 (rebuilt to this configuration in 1888) typifies the undiluted Johnson version of the '890' class towards the end of the 1890s, in full crimson livery. It became No. 83 in 1907 and was scrapped in 1928, guard irons, brake hangers and even the 'rebuilt' plate above the leading wheel all carry lining typical of the late 19th century. *National Railway Museum*

Fig. 3. This drawing shows ED8 produced in 1910 for the '890' class and illustrating the Deeley configuration.
National Railway Museum

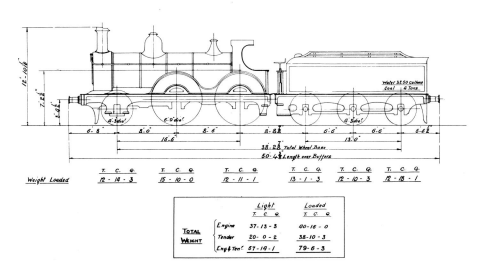

2—4—0 PASSENGER ENGINE

Plate 28. The livery of No. 151A is superficially as *Plates 27/30*, but there is some reduction of lining below the footplate and the tender side panels are in the later quasi-Deeley style. The Johnson chimney appears a bit 'top heavy' (probably a 'trick of the light') and is associated with a new Deeley smokebox door and what looks like the original Johnson boiler. The engine looks quite different from its condition when built (*Plate 26*). Note the brass numeral '1' on the cabside confirming a c.1906/7 date.
Authors' Collection

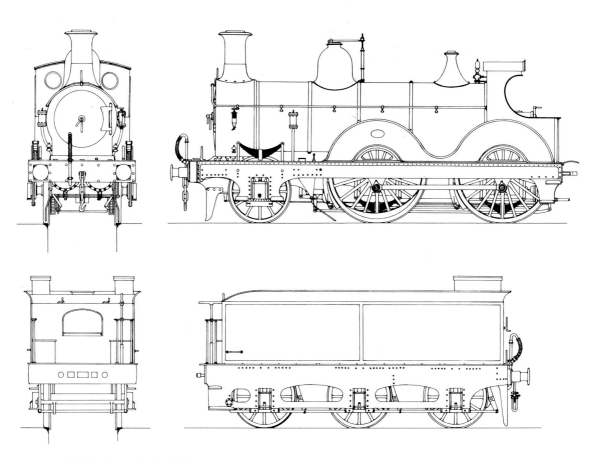

Fig. 4. This drawing of the '890' class 2—4—0 was prepared by David Hunt and represents the second Johnson rebuilt condition of the locomotive with a built-up chimney. The tender is of 2,750 gallon capacity with brake rods outside the wheels and the old wooden brake block hangers moved forward and iron brake blocks fitted. This class of tender was, of course, fitted to other locomotives, but by c.1903 the 2,950 gallon was the smallest size of tender then coupled to this class of locomotive. *David Hunt*

SCALE - FEET

0 1 2 3 4 5 6 7 8 9 10

Plate 29. This view of No. 902 (later No. 80) must have been taken in about 1905 as it carries the earlier emblem and no power class number. The engine is in virtually full livery (there is lining on the guard irons), the tender is in the simpler Deeley style and the cabside emblem is of the old type. This combination, while not unique, was somewhat rare. The tender itself seems quite high-sided compared with the engine and looks almost like a 3,500 gallon replacement. In the left background a much smaller tender can be seen carrying the full Johnson lining with 'MR' on the tender rear. No. 902 was one of quite a number of this class to get a new Deeley smokebox door *before* receiving the full Deeley 'front end'. *Authors' Collection*

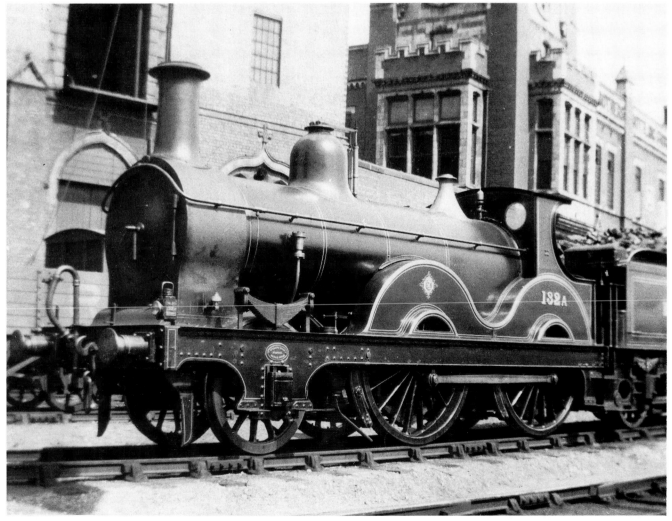

Plate 30. No. 132A prior to becoming No. 109 in 1907. Built in 1874 as No. 132, the locomotive is seen here in pure Johnson condition. As No. 109 it lasted until 1927 when it was withdrawn from service by the LMS. Note the lining on the spring brackets but not the springs or the buckle. This view complements *Plate 27* by giving more detail of the 'front end'. Both engines are in identical livery.

National Railway Museum

Plate 31. This right-hand view of No. 77 in Deeley livery shows the large ejector (which is only on this side of the locomotive) attached to what appears to be a thick handrail which is in fact part of the ejector. By now No. 77 displays the full Deeley 'front end' treatment. No. 77 started life as No. 899, becoming No. 77 in the 1907 renumbering scheme and being withdrawn in October 1934. The picture was taken at Crewe and the carriages are from the North Staffordshire Railway.
Authors' Collection

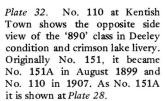

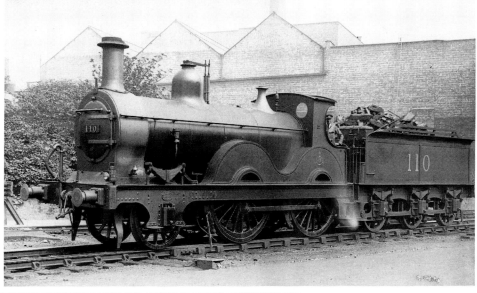

Plate 32. No. 110 at Kentish Town shows the opposite side view of the '890' class in Deeley condition and crimson lake livery. Originally No. 151, it became No. 151A in August 1899 and No. 110 in 1907. As No. 151A it is shown at *Plate 28.*
Authors' Collection

Plate 33. 2-4-0 No. 96 at Stratford-upon-Avon on 8th April 1924. Note the dished smokebox door with the small vertical handle, the latter feature being more normally found on the flat smokebox door. It was, however, usually retained on dished doors if the engine also kept its continuous front handrail. Note the absence of any sign of MR or LMS identity on either the cabside or front buffer plank. Originally No. 123, this locomotive became No. 123A in 1899 and No. 96 in 1907. *W. L. Good*

TRANSITIONAL 2−4−0 CLASSES

Plates 34 & 35. These last two views of '890' class 2−4−0s show the typical LMS liveries of the type − red (pre-1928) and lined black (post-1927). No. 97 was built as No. 127 in 1873 (scrapped in 1928) and No. 70 was one of the pioneer engines, No. 892, built in 1871. It lasted until 1932.

A. G. Ellis

Plate 36. This immaculate ex-works view of '1070' class 2—4—0 No. 1072 (1907 No. 129) gives an excellent impression of the 'as built' condition of these engines. Note the very early use of the 'built-up' Johnson chimney — a shape soon to become very familiar. It seems certain that some of these engines became red while still in this external form.
National Railway Museum

1070 CLASS (INCLUDING '1' CLASS)

Summary

Built by Sharp Stewart 1874-1875 ('1070' class)
Original MR numbers immediately prior to the 1907 renumbering — 1070-1089.
1907 numbers — 127-146, all except No. 141 reaching the LMS in 1923.

Built at Derby 1876 ('1' class)
Similar to '1070' class when built but with different motion. Only the intermediate valve spindles were different. In addition the '1' class had a higher pitched boiler than the '1070' class when built.
Original MR numbers immediately prior to the 1907 renumbering — 1, 9, 10, 13, 70, 71, 73, 74, 96, 146.
1907 numbers — 147-156, of which all reached the LMS except Nos. 148/51.

Both classes allocated to ED 10 in 1910.
Types extinct 1933 ('1070' class), 1950 ('1' class). It is believed that ultimately they were all fitted to 3250 gallon tenders, although c.1903 Nos. 1, 9, 10, 70, 71, 73, 74, 96 were coupled to 2950 gallon tenders.

The '1070' class, although designed by Kirtley, arrived during the first part of Johnson's term of office and, although the engines were delivered much as Kirtley had intended them to be, Sharp Stewart fitted them with Kirtley boilers, but Johnson pattern chimney (*Plate 36*). Their relationship to the '890' class was quite obvious but there were some differences in motion detail as well as the self-evident reduction in wheel size to 6 ft 2½ in.

Some of the '1070' class seem to have been delivered new with modified 'closed in' splashers (*Plate 37*), or had

them altered soon after building, but we have been unable to establish the exact situation.

The inevitable rebuilding with Johnson boilers and larger cylinders did not begin until 1887 and was completed in 1890. Consequently it is once again a reasonable certainty that some of them were repainted red after 1883, still in the external style of *Plates 36 & 37*. After rebuilding, they assumed the familiar Johnson style (*Plate 38*) and in this form were always red.

Before this happened, however, in 1876 Derby had built another batch of ten 6 ft 2½ in 2—4—0s, basically similar to the '1070' class in size but with different motion and Johnson P boilers, and external treatment much more typically 'Johnson'. They had characteristic Johnson chimneys and domes and an early version of the famous safety valve casing which was fitted to a number of the early Johnson classes, but the splasher treatment showed some Kirtley influence and they all had inside spring Johnson tenders (*Plate 39*). Fitted with Westinghouse pumps, they were intended for the Carlisle workings on the opening of the Settle-Carlisle and were generally known as the '1' class.

There would be some logic in regarding these engines as the first of the true Johnson breed, but their derivation from the Kirtley design was so obvious that we prefer to consider them as representing the end of the 'transitional' phase. When rebuilt (1887-90), they were indistinguishable from the rebuilt '1070s' and once again it is a fair bet that some of them became red *before* rebuilding. From here onwards, the two series will be considered together.

Plate 37. This undated view of the last of the '1070' class 2−4−0s No. 1089 (1907 No. 146) shows the same Kirtley boiler plus Johnson chimney characteristics of *Plate 36* but the closed in splasher treatment gives it a more modern appearance even than the '1' class engines when built (*Plate 39*), yet the works plate is the official Sharp Stewart type. The engine is not recorded as having been rebuilt until 1888, when it received a Johnson boiler anyway. It therefore seems likely either that many were delivered with closed splashers from new or that this feature was a fairly speedy modification before rebuilding. The lining layout on this engine could relate to either the Johnson green livery or the early crimson lake style but we think green to be marginally the more probable. Undoubtedly, however, one or two of the '1070s' would have been painted red in this external form. *National Railway Museum*

Plate 38. '1070' class No. 1080 (later No. 137) was rebuilt to this form in 1888 but by the time of this undated picture, was carrying more lining below the footplate than was probably the case when first rebuilt. We therefore deduce the picture to be from the later 1890s. *Authors' Collection*

Plate 39. '1' class 2—4—0 No. 9 'as built'. Although of poor quality, this picture does show just sufficient detail to give the general character of this first Johnson style (see text). No. 9, of course, green at this time (c.1876), was rebuilt with 18 in. cylinders in 1887, became No. 148 in 1907, and was withdrawn in 1912.   *Authors' Collection*

Plate 40. This picture of No. 1070 displays a locomotive with heat-damaged paintwork — not an unusual state of affairs as readers will note from a variety of photographs used in this volume. It shows good 'below footplate' detail of the full crimson livery of the later 1890s. The headlamp gives the depot as Peterborough and the driver as C. Smith. Built in 1874 as No. 1070, it became No. 127 in 1907 and was withdrawn in 1933.   *National Railway Museum*

Plate 41. '1070' class 2−4−0 No. 142 was photographed at Bolton Trinity Street when working a Blackburn−Chinley service. Originally No. 1085, it was withdrawn in December 1931. Note the Johnson front end with the smokebox door numberplate and Deeley-style 'dog' type rim fastenings, neither of which, in our view, suited this style of door.
Collection V. Forster

TABLE 7: SUMMARY OF THE TRANSITIONAL 2−4−0 CLASSES

1903 Diagram Page No.	Order No. or Class	Built by	Qty. built	Date of building	Pre 1907 numbers	1907 renumbering	Cylinders	BOILER					Working Pressure	FIREBOX		Total Heating Surface in sq. ft.	WHEELS			ENGINE WEIGHT		REMARKS
								Centre Line	Diameter	Length	Tubes	Diameter		Length	Grate Area in sq. ft.		Leading	Driving	Tyres	Empty	Loaded	
26	Kirtley Pass.	Neilsons	20 42	1871-75	890-909 Various 2-152	68-87 88-126	18″ × 24″	not quoted	4′ 2″	10′ 4″	246	1⅝″	140 PSI	5′ 11″	17.5	1244	4′ 2½	6′ 8½″	2¾	36.0.2	39.10.2	Known as the 890 class. Originally 17″ × 24″ cyls.
24	Sharps like 97	Sharp Stewart	20	1874-75	1070-1089	127-146	18″ × 24″	7′ 1″	4′ 2″	10′ 4″	244	1⅝″	140 PSI	5′ 11″	17.5	1235	4′ 2½	6′ 8½″	2¾″	36.1.1	39.0.0	Known as the 1070 class.
	97	Derby	10	1876	Various 1-146	147-156																As 1070 class but with different motion referred to as the 1 class. Originally 17″ × 24″ cyls.
																					Source 1903 Engine Diagram Book.

As with the '890' class, the 6 ft 2½ in 2−4−0s ran in their 'pure' Johnson condition only for some 15-20 years (on average) before being modified to the full Deeley front end configuration. As usual, there were some intermediate stages on the way (e.g. *Plates 41-3*) but, eventually, all settled down in the form of *Plate 45*.

In terms of livery, some of the engines are likely to have carried the early crimson style if rebuilt before c.1892/3. Thereafter, the more fully lined treatment would be typical, well exemplified by *Plate 40*. We have no record of any 'decorated' styles for this group. Judging from pictures, fewer than usual carried what might be called transitional livery styles from c.1904-6 and most engines seem to have gone direct to the pure Deeley style with large tender numerals.

All thirty engines were renumbered in 1907 and 27 lasted to the 1923 grouping. Scrapping thereafter took place quite quickly, mostly during the pre-1928 livery period of the LMS. A handful of survivors lasted long enough to be repainted black (*Plate 46*) and four of the '1' class engines (Nos. 150/3/5/6) lasted long enough to become the oldest Johnson 2−4−0 engines to receive G6 Belpaire boilers in LMS days. One of these, by then LMS No. 20155, actually lasted until BR days (allocated BR No. 58020 but never carried) and became the very last survivor of all the ex-MR Johnson 2−4−0s.

There was no real significance in the fact that the last survivor was one of the oldest built. Virtually all the longer lived Johnson 2−4−0s, i.e. those which received LMS 2XXXX series numbers — had received Belpaire boilers in LMS days and since it was, in effect, the age of the boiler fitted to an engine which, as much as anything, determined its withdrawal date, given sound frames and motion, it is natural that any which had been given Belpaires would last longer.

Plates 42 & 43. These two views of Nos. 139 and 141 (originally Nos. 1082/4) both show the flat Deeley door with continuous handrail and both seem to bear the identical Deeley livery of the 1906 and later period. However, and even discounting the less than perfect picture quality, the lining on No. 141 seems much bolder. It was stated in Volume One that the Deeley livery eventually had its line thickness specified at a wider dimension than we believe was the case in earlier days. These pictures hint (but do not prove) that this change may have taken place some time early in the life of the Deeley style. More evidence would be welcome. *Authors' Collection and Collection Bernard Mathews*

Plate 44. This somewhat indifferent picture of the original '1' class 2—4—0 (new No. 147) at Derby in 1921 is of principal interest not so much in showing the final front end configuration but because it reveals an extraordinary double row of rivets round the smokebox door rim. We have seen only one other similar example, No. 737, and can offer no explanation. *Authors' Collection*

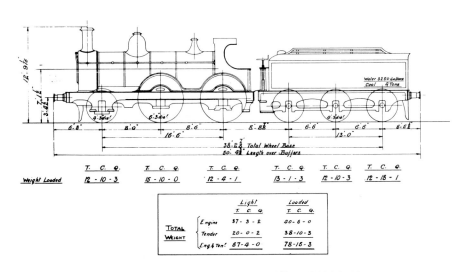

2—4—0 PASSENGER ENGINE

Fig. 5. ED10 was issued in 1910 and at this time referred to the whole series of 6 ft 3 in 2—4—0s from Nos. 127-156. The diagram illustrates the early Deeley condition with flat smokebox door.

Plate 45. This April 1923 view at St. Albans shows No. 127, the pioneer '1070' class 2–4–0, in the external configuration most typical of this series during the '1907 to withdrawal' period. The livery is perfectly standard Deeley style. An interesting, if peripheral, point is the different 'riding height' of the two tenders featured in the view. They are both standard 3,250 gallon types but that of No. 171 appears to have a new set of tyres (and probably newer springs) than that of No. 127 whose tyres (and springs?) are virtually life expired. If nothing else, the picture demonstrates the utter stupidity of quoting a railway wheel diameter to an accuracy of half an inch!

Plate 46. Relatively few of the '1070' or '1' class engines achieved the post-1927 LMS livery, lined black with gold characters, shaded red, borne by No. 132 (originally No. 1075) in this view taken at Northampton St. Johns in 1931.   *L. Hanson*

Plate 47. '1' class 2–4–0 No. 150 was one of four of this group to be fitted with a type G6 Belpaire boiler – in this case in 1926. Note also the 'pop' safety valves. The livery is pre-1928 LMS red – basically the Deeley livery with LMS emblem. No. 150 was built as No. 13 in 1876 and withdrawn (somewhat surprisingly for a Belpaired 2–4–0) as early as 1928, only two years after conversion.

National Railway Museum

Plate 48. '1282 class' 6 ft 6 in 2—4—0 No. 1309 (later No. 184) as built with Westinghouse brake equipment in 1876. Note the early pattern tender and the curved arrangement of the cabside numerals. The engine is certainly green. This was one of six examples to have the coupling rods removed in 1886 for experiments with steam sanding gear. This picture may be considered as typifying the first batch of Johnson 2—4—0s prior to the start of the 'red' period. *Authors' Collection*

CHAPTER FOUR

JOHNSON 2-4-0 CLASSES

THE Johnson 2—4—0 classes which came after the '1' class were amongst the most well-loved and characteristic products of this celebrated artist-engineer. They were built during a six year period from 1876-1881 and, all told, 125 examples were put in service. Although, nominally, these engines were divided into a whole series of separate classes, they were essentially all built to the same basic configuration and mechanical layout (see Table 8). Moreover, they all looked very much alike save for wheel diameter, so we propose to depart from our standard chapter layout and start with an extended analysis of the whole series. Indeed, it could be said that Johnson did not truly design a 2—4—0. Instead it could be argued that he developed the design of the inside frame Kirtley 2—4—0.

The essential 'Johnson' 2—4—0 was clearly derived from its Kirtley predecessors (Chapters 2 & 3) and its ultra-clean visual lines clearly developed out of the '890', '1070' and '1' class engines. One simple visible distinguishing point which always differentiated the 'true' Johnson from the '890', '1070' and '1' series was the shape of the outer frame, which took the form of a deep footplate angle below the cab. On the genuine Johnsons it swept down in a continuous curve to form the rear footstep support, whereas on the earlier engines the footstep support was riveted behind this feature.

The various sub-groups of the whole series of 125 engines as identified by the Midland Railway in 1903, are given at Table 8. Most of these sub-divisions were identified as separate classes by contemporary observers and as such have been described in these terms by many subsequent writers, including ourselves. However, we have inserted one or two additional comments in the 'remarks' column to aid understanding.

The building of the 2—4—0s was divided, essentially, into two phases, not unconnected with Johnson's work on 4—4—0 engines at the same time (Chapter 5). Fifty 2—4—0 engines were built during 1876-7 with 17½ in x 26 in cylinders and towards the end of this phase Johnson simultaneously introduced two 4—4—0 equivalents, sharing the same mechanical specification, but with marginally larger boilers — and we do mean marginally. The 'P' class boiler fitted to

Plate 49. Photographed at Elstree c.1904, '1492' class 7 ft 0 in 2—4—0 No. 1495 (later No. 275) appears to be carrying full crimson livery. The newer splasher shape is clearly obvious.

Authors' Collection

MIDLAND LOCOMOTIVES

TABLE 8: SUMMARY OF THE JOHNSON 2—4—0 CLASSES

1903 Diagram Page No.	Order No. or Class	Built by	Qty. built	Date of building	Pre 1907 numbers	1907 renumbering	Cylinders	BOILER Centre Line	Diameter	Length	Tubes	Diameter	Working Pressure	FIREBOX Length	Grate Area in sq. ft.	Total Heating Surface in sq. ft.	WHEELS Leading	Driving	Tyres	ENGINE WEIGHT Empty	Loaded	REMARKS
21	E	Dübs	30	1876	1282-1311	157-186	18″ × 26″	7′ 1½″	4′ 2″	10′ 4″	246	1¾″	140 PSI	5′ 11″	17.5	1244	4′ 2½″	6′ 6″	2¾″	36.9.3	39.12.1	Known as 1282 class. Built with 17½″ × 26″ cyls.
	107	Derby	5 5	1876	50-54 55-59	187-191 192-196												6′ 6″ 6′ 8½″				Referred to as modified 1282 class.
	283	Derby	5	1880	111-115	217-221												6′ 6″				Known as 1282 class.
22	232	Derby	10	1879	1400-1409	207-216	18″ × 26″	7′ 2″	4′ 2″	10′ 4″	246	1¾″	140 PSI	5′ 11″	17.5	1244	4′ 2½″	6′ 8½″	2¾″	36.18.0	40.0.2	Known as 1400 class (except for 1492-1501).
	Like 232	Neilsons	30	1881	1502-1531	242-271												6′ 8½″				No class letter given to Neilson build.
	273	Derby	10	1880	1482-1491	232-241												6′ 8½″				
	275	Derby	10	1881	1492-1501	272-281												7′ 0″				Ahrons regarded these as 101 class. It is not clear why the Midland did not allocate them to Diagram 23 when 101 class received 18″ cyls.
	279	Derby	10	1880	1472-1481	222-231												6′ 8½″				Engines built to GA 80/1376 shown as built with 6′ 9″ driving wheels and 2950 gallon tenders (quoted as 3000 gallon).
23	139	Derby	10	1877	101-111	197-206	18″ × 26″	7′ 3½″	4′ 2″	10′ 4″	246	1¾″	140 PSI	5′ 11″	17.5	1244	4′ 2½″	7′ 0″	2¾″			Originally 1347 class (1347-56) renumbered in 1879 (101-111) and then referred to as 101 class. Built with 17½″ × 26″ cyls.

Source 1903 Engine Diagram Book

the 2—4—0s was 2 inches shorter than the 'B' class of the 4—4—0s, had identical diameter and firebox length and was only 16 sq. ft* less in heating surface (see Tables 8 and 9). In later years the 'B' class boiler was put on the 2—4—0s as well. There was a minor difference with the eccentric rods, these being shorter on the 4—4—0s.

After the initial thirty 4—4—0s, Johnson reverted to the 2—4—0 arrangement and built 75 more examples during 1879-81, retaining the 'P' boiler, but this time with the slightly enlarged (18 in x 26 in) cylinders first used on the *second* series of 4—4—0s, except that 111-115 (217-221) of 1880 had 17½ in cylinders when built. These 2—4—0s looked no different from their predecessors but, for convenience, we shall refer where necessary to these two basic groups of 2—4—0s (as differentiated originally by cylinder size) as the 'first' and 'second' batches respectively.

At this range in time, it is impossible to know why Johnson experimented with both wheel arrangements. The 4—4—0 was still a somewhat new concept (in British terms) so perhaps he felt it prudent to continue with the well-proven and traditional six-wheel engine. The latter would be less costly to build if nothing else, although the 4—4—0 might show some advantages at higher speeds because of the better guiding properties of the leading bogie and it may have been the latter point which eventually won the day. At all events, after 1881 all subsequent Midland Railway passenger tender engines had a leading bogie and the 2—4—0 had reached the limit of its development.

Be that as it may, there was no profound difference in power output between the 2—4—0s and their equivalent 4—4—0 types during the latter part of the 19th century and the early part of the 20th. Thus it was that the Johnson 2—4—0s remained in the front line (along with the rebuilt Kirtley 2—4—0s and the slim-boilered 4—4—0s and 4—2—2s) until the wholesale physical enlargement of the express passenger fleet in the Edwardian (and subsequent) periods.

So much by way of background, which is continued in the next chapter as it affected the 4—4—0 series. It is now time to turn to the 2—4—0s in more detail and they will be considered in *1907 number* order, which generally reflected their order of building.

The first batch of 50 engines with 17½ in cylinders built during 1876-7 exhibited no fewer than three wheel dimensions. By far the most numerous were the 30 engines of the 1282 class built by Dübs & Co. with 6 ft 6 in wheels (*Plate 48*); in 1907 they became Nos. 157-86. They are of some additional interest in that the first twenty were fitted with Smith's simple vacuum brake, whereas the last ten had Westinghouse brakes. At a later date, six of these last ten (pre-1907 Nos. 1306-11) while based at Hellifield, had their coupling rods removed in 1886 and ran as experimental 'singles' for a time to test the new steam sanding gear. This served as a prelude for the large scale re-introduction of the single driving wheel locomotive which Johnson began in 1887 (see Chapter 7).

While Dübs & Co. were building the '1282' class, Derby simultaneously started the construction of another 20 engines wherein some variety of wheel diameters was present. The first to appear were five engines of the '50' class (1907 Nos. 187-91) which were identical in all significant respects to the Dübs '1282' class. Why the whole group of thirty-five 6 ft 6in engines was not given the same class designation is something of a mystery.

Even more odd, in terms of designation, were the next five 2—4—0s from Derby (1907 Nos. 192-6). These had 6 ft 8½ in wheels but were still referred to as the '50' class. By all logic they should have been called the '55' class, given the then current thinking; presumably they were '50' class because they were part of the same order as the five Derby-built 6 ft 6 in engines and in 1903 were still grouped together on the same diagram. They undoubtedly set the style for the numerous 6 ft 8½ in engines (with 18 in cylinders) of the second 2—4—0 batch of 1879-81.

The final engines of the 'first' 2—4—0 batch appeared from Derby in 1877 when Johnson introduced the 7 ft wheel onto the Midland with the ten 2—4—0s of the '1347'

* One source gives it as 8 sq ft.

Plate 50. '101' class 7 ft 0 in 2−4−0 No. 102 (originally '1347' class No. 1348, later No. 198) posed for the official photographer in the Derbyshire Peak District in the late 1890s. The engine has full livery but retains the original splasher shape with 'flattened' section between the wheels. It trails a Johnson tender with 'outside' springs. Compare with *Plate 48.*   *National Railway Museum*

class. They were fairly swiftly renumbered 101-10 in 1879 and were afterwards referred to as the '101' class, becoming Nos. 197-206 in 1907 (*Plate 50*).

This proliferation of wheel diameters within what was, in essence, the same type of locomotive, seems somewhat unnecessary to modern eyes and no less an authority than the late Roland Bond (the last 'steam' CME of British Railways and an ex-Derby man, to boot), has stated that anything less than a six inch difference in wheel diameter was, in his view, something of an unnecessary luxury! Perhaps Kirtley had it right all along when eventually he settled for 6 ft 2½ in and 6 ft 8½ in as his two diameters in the 2−4−0 field. However, late 19th century thinking placed great store by subtle differences of this nature and it was not until the 20th century that it became quite clear

that a 'general utility' engine with wheels about 6 ft diameter could do just about everything except at the extremities (high-speed passenger and heavy freight) of the operating spectrum − hence the Stanier class 5, amongst others.

Johnson, however, was a profoundly sophisticated engineer by late 19th century standards and it can therefore be safely assumed that he had sound reasons for the various experiments, which included the fact that the valve events dictated dimensional changes, together with the belief that certain routes should have particular wheel dimensions.

According to Ahrons, the 6 ft 8½ in wheel was later to be enlarged to 6 ft 9 in in the second 18 in cylindered batch of Johnson 2−4−0s, but the other two sizes remained unchanged. However, this extra half inch is not recorded on

Plates 51 & 52. Opposite side views of possibly the most well-known of the Johnson 2—4—0s — the 6 ft 9 in '1400' class. These pictures show more or less 'as built' locomotives, both in red livery but retaining the original splasher shape (see page 51). No. 1474 (later No. 224) is carrying the early crimson livery (albeit with 'MR' on the tender) with considerably less lining below the footplate than No. 1401 (later No. 208) which has the full livery. It must be admitted that superficially they look very much alike and it needs a magnifying glass on the original pictures to be absolutely certain.   *Authors' Collection*

Plate 53. '50' class 6 ft 6 in 2−4−0 No. 54 (later No. 191) showing the original 'inside spring' Johnson tender carried initially by the earlier Johnson 2−4−0s. The engine is in 'as built' condition and is shown in green livery.   *Authors' Collection*

the 1903 Midland diagrams, so we will refer to them as 6 ft 8½ in locomotives even though the G.A. (80/13376) gives 6 ft 9 in as the driving wheel diameter.

In 1907 number order these were as follows:

Nos. 207-16 – '1400' class	6 ft 8½ in wheels	(10)
Nos. 217-21 – '1282' class	6 ft 6 in wheels	(5)
Nos. 222-71 – '1400' class	as 207-16	(50)
Nos. 272-81 – '1492' class or '101' class	7 ft 0 in wheels	(10)

Examples of two of these three sub-categories are given at *Plates 49 & 51* visually identical to the earlier batches of 2−4−0s. This identity was made even closer when virtually all the first 50 had their cylinders enlarged to 18 in generally some ten to fifteen years after first building.

Thus, in summary, the 125 Johnson 2−4−0s could be categorised as follows, all being essentially the same but for wheel size:

6 ft 6 in engines	40
6 ft 8½ in engines	65
7 ft 0 in engines	20

Interestingly, the vast majority had wheels between 6 ft 6 in and 6 ft 8½ in and were probably indistinguishable in terms of effectiveness 'on the road'. Oddly, however, (see Chapter 5) the contemporary 4−4−0s tended (mostly)

to settle down at either 6 ft 6 in or 7 ft 0 in driving wheels with relatively fewer at the 6 ft 9 in size.

Turning now to the tenders fitted to these engines, the first batch of 50 seem to have come out with Johnson's early pattern 'inside spring' variety (*Plate 53*). These were later converted to outside springs (*Plate 54*), but they seem mostly to have been replaced by Johnson's more familiar style of tender by the early years of the 'red engine' period. Ahrons records that the '1400' class of 1879 were the 'first engines to have the more modern type of tender' and we have been able to find only one picture (*Plate 54*) of a Johnson 2−4−0, identifiably *red*, trailing anything other than the familiar Johnson style of tender with outside springs below the running plate and coal rails above the flared out top. There were, however, variations in tank capacity according to the 'class' divisions of the series. The class summaries (page 56 *et seq.*) give the officially specified type for each group. We do not think there was much changing about over the years.

Given this preliminary review, it is now possible to consider the whole of the 125 Johnson 2−4−0s as a single group in terms of their visible variations, paint schemes, etc., for the whole of the 1883 and subsequent period. For the most part, they were broadly homogenous throughout this time, and the changes which did take place were 'across the

Plate 54. '1282' class 6 ft 6 in 2—4—0 No. 1295 (later No. 170) was photographed at Gloucester in 1896, after receiving 18 in cylinders. It is coupled to a rebuilt Johnson tender now with outside springs. Besides the lack of coal rails, note the more angular 'flare' compared with the standard Johnson type. It was rare to see *red* Johnson 2—4—0 engines with this type of tender at this time.   *Authors' Collection*

Plate 55. This view shows '50' class 2—4—0 No. 52 (later No. 189) during the mid-1890s, carrying a fairly typical form of full crimson lake livery. Note particularly the brake hangers and cab interior lining at the rear of the splashers. The engine still has the original splasher shape and a 'built-up' 3-piece Johnson chimney. Other interesting features are the large toolboxes at the rear of the tender and the communication cord davit above the coal.

Authors' Collection

Plate 56. Photographed early in the 20th century in full crimson livery, '1282' class 2−4−0 No. 1298 displays almost the pure final Johnson condition of a locomotive which was fairly soon to become No. 173. Over the leading axlebox is a new boiler plate dating from 1896, the year it probably received the revised splasher shape between the wheels and a 'one-piece' Johnson chimney. To appreciate the differences, this view should be compared with *Plate 55.* Built in 1876 by Dübs & Co., the locomotive never received a Belpaire boiler before it was withdrawn in 1928. Note the '1' power classification on the cabside. *National Railway Museum*

Plate 57. This view of '1400' class 6 ft 8½ in 2−4−0 No. 1505 (later No. 245) illustrates its immediate pre-1907 condition showing some simplification in the livery, for example the tender panel lining. The works plate reads 'Rebuilt Derby 1902'. Note the absence of lining on the front splasher, brake block hangers, guard irons, springs and spring brackets. *J. H. Wright*

Plate 58. Compared with the photograph of No. 1298 (*Plate 56*) this view of sister engine No. 1301 (later No. 176) shows the pre-1907 number with livery in pure Deeley style, save for there being no power classification on the cabside. Compare also the boiler details, No. 1301 has a type where the water enters through an injector clack mounted on the side of the boiler whereas No. 1298 had the clacks mounted on the firebox back plate. As No. 176, the engine was withdrawn in 1924 still with a round-top boiler. Like No. 1298, No. 1301 was built by Dübs & Co. in 1876. *Collection Bernard Mathews*

Plate 59. '1400' class 2—4—0 No. 253 (formerly No. 1513) shows an early and typical Deeley modification, still with a continuous smokebox handrail but now with a Deeley chimney and flat Deeley smokebox door. It was photographed at Leeds c.1908-9 in the final Midland passenger livery. Converted to Belpaire form in 1927, No. 253 lasted until withdrawal in 1937.   *J. H. Wright*

Plate 60. Almost the full Deeley smokebox and chimney modifications are seen on '1400' class No. 256 (formerly No. 1576), along with the Deeley livery. However, the continuous handrail is maintained across the smokebox, thus explaining the small handle on the left of the dished door. This combination was more normally associated with the flat door (*Plate 59*). *Authors' Collection*

board' rather than 'specific to class'. However, we have divided the formal summaries (pages 56 to 67) according to official class designations.

During the late Victorian period, these engines were typically Johnson and it is unlikely that many remained green much after 1885/6, being very much 'front rank' types at the time. It seems fair to postulate that they all received the early crimson livery before the introduction of the more elaborate 'below the footplate' lining of the 1890s. This latter style, as has already been explained in detail in Volume 1, began to appear shortly after the introduction of 'MR' on the tender sides and, once again, it is fair to assume that they all in due course received a 'full' crimson livery as well. However, there is no real evidence that the 2−4−0s ever came in for quite the degree of decoration and elaboration that their contemporary 4−4−0s and 4−2−2s enjoyed. Fairly typical examples are shown at *Plates 55 & 56*, views which also demonstrate how, during the later Johnson period, an interesting change took place which considerably improved the already fine lines of these engines. As built, the splasher beading between the wheels had a noticeably flattened centre section − almost horizontal in fact − regardless of wheel diameter. In later years, well before the onset of the Deeley modifications, the splasher

shape was changed to display a continuous curve (between the wheels) of much more elegant aspect.

The differences can be seen quite clearly in many of the pictures with this chapter, but we are unable to date the change with any precision, although it could have dated from the change from 'P' to 'B' boilers. It does seem likely, however, that the change took place at or about the time of first reboilering and/or recylindering in the 1890s. This also coincided, to some extent, with the introduction of the more fully lined version of the red livery. Therefore, and bearing in mind the danger of making broad generalisations, it is likely that not all engines with the original splasher shape received a full red livery in this form. Equally, with the modified splashers, the full livery is much more probable than the earlier form.

The move to simplification of livery came, as usual, in two stages. First was the removal of tender lining to the beading and some reduction in the 'below footplate' lining (*Plate 57*). This started c.1904, more or less (but not always) coincidentally with the beginnings of the Deeley 'front end' changes. In early cases this took the form of a new smokebox door with continuous handrail, but eventually became a full new smokebox, chimney, etc. This more drastic 'front-end' change was usually associated with the

Plate 61. '1400' class No. 239 (originally No. 1489) appears to sport the normal Deeley front end with separate smokebox handrail — but the door is a flat one! Note the bright metal hinges and door seating ring. The lining on the front buffer plank appears to be broken where there are bolt heads in the way of a continuous line. No. 229 was withdrawn in June 1928 without receiving a Belpaire boiler.

Authors' Collection

use of the new Deeley livery with tender numerals, and by now most of them were also carrying their 1907 series numbers. These changes came so quickly (basically during 1904-8) that many subtle variations occurred, of which *Plates 57-61* may be regarded as characteristic examples.

There then followed a period of visual stability (represented, for example, by *Plate 62*), until early LMS days when more changes began. For a while the livery remained little changed save for the substitution of LMS emblems or markings in place of the Midland version, but then began another period of turmoil when Belpaire boilers and/or changes to black livery occurred during the later 1920s. We have gone into this in some detail in our LMS period survey* and have no wish to say everything twice, but a few comments will not be out of place to 'round out' the story.

The introduction of G6 Belpaire boilers on the Johnson 2–4–0s was the passenger equivalent of the similar conversion of the smaller 0–6–0s (see Volume 4). The engines were by then quite venerable and this form of boiler renewal might, at first, seem rather surprising. However, the G6 boiler existed and was, presumably, better in service (cheaper to maintain?) than a replacement round-top would

be. During the 1920s the LMS did not really have a suitable 'secondary' standard locomotive type (this concept did not appear until 1946) and there was a general feeling, not confined to the LMS, that lesser workings could be entrusted to older types which still had a few useful years of life left in them, given anything like a decent boiler. Engine boilers generally lasted considerably less time than the frames/motion etc. so replacing boilers was normal. Although the LMS was not as notorious as some railways at keeping its old warriors in the field, once it had decided to prolong the life of a few dozen 2–4–0s, it made sense to do so by using the final MR pattern of small boiler, the G6 Belpaire, rather than the previous round-top. The selection of engines to be so fitted probably reflected their basic frame/motion condition rather than the age of the engine as such.

Thus, although the G6 boiler was fitted entirely during the LMS period, it was a pure Midland concept and can, therefore, quite properly be considered as the final part of a long continuously evolving story. By far the majority of the long-lasting Johnson 2–4–0s had Belpaire boilers when withdrawn. The fact that it did nothing beneficial to their appearance is largely irrelevant.

*An Illustrated History of LMS Locomotives Vol. 4.

Plate 62. '1282' class No. 164, still in Midland livery, was photographed at Gloucester on 2nd June 1923. By now, as one would expect from that date, a dished smokebox door has been fitted and the original curved handrail has been replaced. Originally No. 1289, the engine was withdrawn in December 1930 after running with a Belpaire boiler during its final three years. *A. G. Ellis*

Plate 63. '1400' class 2—4—0 No. 223 (formerly No. 1473) was one of relatively few ex-MR engines to receive the 1923 LMS markings — small cabside letters. It displays all the final modifications to the round-top series and was withdrawn in this condition in 1926.

Authors' Collection

Plate 64. The combination of Belpaire boiler plus pre-1928 red LMS livery was not uncommon in the mid-1920s. This view shows '1492' class 7 ft 0 in 2–4–0 No. 280 (originally No. 1500) sometime between receiving a Belpaire boiler (1926) and scrapping (1928). The works plate reads 'LMS rebuilt Derby 1926' but it should be realised that a number of 2–4–0s ran for a short period only with Belpaire boilers before they were withdrawn, rendered surplus by downgraded 4–4–0s. The Belpaire boilers off these 2–4–0s were used with other locomotives.

Authors' Collection

Plates 65 & 66. The long-term survivors of the Johnson 2—4—0 classes became black in and after 1928, mostly with red lining — not that this was often obvious! Two characteristic examples are shown here, '1400' class No. 211 (formerly No. 1404) still round-top and one of the few 6 ft 8½ in variants of the '50' class (see page 56), and No. 20194 (formerly Nos. 57/194) with Belpaire boiler and now in the duplicate LMS 2xxxx number series dating from 1934. Both are fitted with the Stanier chimney. No. 211 was withdrawn in round-top condition in 1934 and No. 20194 lasted until 1939.

H. C. Casserley & Authors' Collection

We conclude this section with a formal class by class summary of the Johnson 2—4—0s, together with additional views which we hope will give a fully balanced survey of these very characteristic engines.

1282 CLASS

Summary

Built by Dübs & Co. 1876. Class E.
Original MR numbers 1282-1311 (6 ft 6 in wheels).
1907 numbers 157-186, all but No. 160 to the LMS in 1923.
Officially paired with 2950 gallon tenders in 1903 but later 3250 was not unusual.

50 CLASS

Summary

Built at Derby 1876.
Original MR numbers 50-54 (6 ft 6 in wheels, designated '50' class but identical, in fact, to '1282' class).
1907 numbers 187-191.
55-59 (192-196 in 1907) built with 6 ft 8½ in wheels.
Officially paired with 2950 gallon tenders in 1903 but later 3250 was not unusual.

The '50' class, consisting of ten engines built at Derby, was the curious batch with a change in driving wheel size

at No. 55 from 6 ft 6 in to 6 ft 8½ in. In all other respects the 6 ft 6 in engines were the Midland-built version of the 'E' class and put onto the same diagram — ED12 (*Fig. 6*) in 1920 having been diagram 21 in 1903. The 6 ft 8½ in engines went to ED 1/15 (*Fig. 10*) which originally in 1910 covered engines Nos. 192-196, 207-216, 222-221, but in 1919 this diagram ED1/15 now referred to all the 2—4—0s still in service!

Two of this series reached the LMS 2XXXX series, one from each wheel size and both with Belpaire boilers (Nos. 20188/94). No. 20194 was the last survivor, withdrawn in 1939 (*Plate 66*).

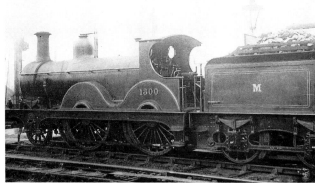

Plates 67 & 68. 'First and last condition' (well, almost) views of 6 ft 6 in '1282' class 2—4—0 No. 1300 (later No. 175). No. 1300 actually reveals the later splasher shape and rather grubby full crimson livery. It is rather interesting that the LMS, not renowned for its clean engines, ran No. 175 with Belpaire boiler and lined black livery in a rather cleaner state some 30 years later! The engine was withdrawn at the end of 1930, having received the Belpaire boiler in 1925.

Authors' Collection

Plate 69. This view of '1282' class No. 185 (formerly No. 1310) shows an LMS period Belpaire conversion of 1924 utilising Ramsbottom safety valves which it kept until at least 1936. Most of them had 'pop' valves, e.g. *Plate 68.* No. 185 had a long and interesting life. Starting out in the form of *Plate 48*, it too was used for steam sanding experiments and eventually became one of the last three ex-MR 2−4−0s, withdrawn as late as 1948 as No. 20185. *Authors' Collection*

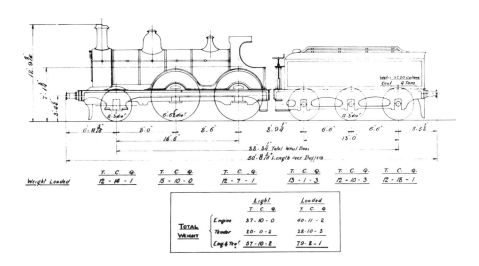

2-4-0 PASSENGER ENGINE

Fig. 6. Engine diagram 12 was issued to cover the 6 ft 6 in 2−4−0s between Nos. 157 and 191, in effect both the '1282' and '50' class (6 ft 6 in) series. The diagram shows the version with Deeley smokebox and 'flat door with continuous front handrail'. Note, however, that like all MR 2−4−0 diagrams, the drawing shows the original splasher shape (see page 51). The '1282' class designation referred to the 30 engines built by Dübs in 1876. Three of these engines reached the 1934 LMS 'duplicate' 2xxxx lists (Nos. 20157/83/5), the last two with Belpaire boilers. No. 20185 was the last survivor, withdrawn in 1948 (allocated BR No. 58021 but never carried (see Plate 69). *National Railway Museum*

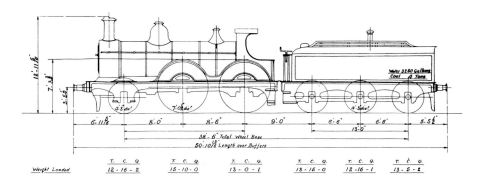

2—4—0 PASSENGER ENGINE

Fig. 7. *ED17 was one of two diagrams issued for the 7 ft 0 in Johnson 2—4—0s but was not annotated with the relevant engine numbers. However, ED18 (Fig. 12) was marked up with the numbers of the '1492' class, so we conclude that ED17 referred to the '101' class. The diagram shows the orthodox round top with full front-end modifications.* Authors' Collection

		Light T. C. Q.	Loaded T. C. Q.
TOTAL WEIGHT	Engine	38 - 5 - 1	41 - 6 - 3
	Tender	21 - 6 - 2	39 - 16 - 3
	Eng & Tenr	59 - 11 - 3	81 - 3 - 2

101 (Ex-1347) CLASS

Summary

Built at Derby 1877.
Final MR numbers prior to 1907 renumbering 101-110.
7 ft wheels.
1907 numbers 197-206, all but No. 199 to LMS in 1923.
Officially allocated 2950 gallon tenders in 1903 but later 3250 appears to be the allocated size.

The '101' class introduced the 7 ft wheel to the Midland, later adopted on a widespread scale with the 4—4—0s (see Chapter 5). It was never such a popular wheel size on the 2—4—0 engines and, in general, they did not survive for quite as long. Only No. 204 lasted beyond 1934, withdrawn as LMS No. 20204 in 1941 and by then fitted with Belpaire boiler.

Plate 70. *The pioneer 7 ft 0 in 2—4—0 No. 101, originally No. 1347, was built in 1877. Two years later it was renumbered 101 and this number was carried until 1907 when it became No. 197. This was the final number change before withdrawal in April 1924. Note the smokebox door which shows evidence of drawing air. It is seen here in full crimson lake livery and carrying the later splasher shape — compare this with* Plate 50. *Authors' Collection*

Plates 71 & 72. '101' class 2−4−0s Nos. 204/5 (formerly Nos. 108/9, originally Nos. 1354/5), both carrying Deeley livery, show the two handrail variations with the Deeley front end, both with dished doors. The lower height of the 2,950 gallon tenders fitted to this class (see diagram) is somewhat more readily discernible in these pictures than in many views of Midland engines. No. 204 (as No. 20204) was the last 7 ft 0 in 2−4−0 to be scrapped (in 1941), by which time it had a Belpaire boiler. No. 205, still round-top, went for scrap much earlier, in 1926.

Authors' Collection & Bernard Mathews' Collection

1400 CLASS

Summary

Built at Derby 1879-1881
Original MR numbers 1400-1409, 1472-1491. 6 ft 8½ in
wheels, larger cylinders than 6 ft 8½ in examples of '50'
class.
1907 numbers 207-216, 222-241, all to LMS in 1923.

Built by Neilson & Co.
Original MR numbers 1502-1531.
1907 numbers 242-271, all to LMS in 1923.

The '1400' class was clearly derived from the handful of
6 ft 8½ in so-called '50' class variants and became the most
numerous single sub-group of Johnson 2—4—0s. They were
also, in our view, the most handsome. The 6 ft 8½ in wheels
allowed a most beautiful splasher arrangement to be
achieved, especially after the initial straighter section
between the wheels had been changed to the fully curved
arrangement (see page 51).

Although the last ex-MR 2—4—0 was not a '1400', the
class itself survived, *collectively*, much better than either
the 6 ft 6 in or 7 ft engines, eight receiving LMS 1934
series 2XXXX numbers, mostly with Belpaire boilers by
this time. No. 20216 was the last to go in 1949, allocated
BR No. 58022 but never carried. It was outlived only by
No. 20155 of the official '1' class (see page 37). Thus,
the '1400' class was the longest lasting of any of the true
Johnson 2—4—0s.

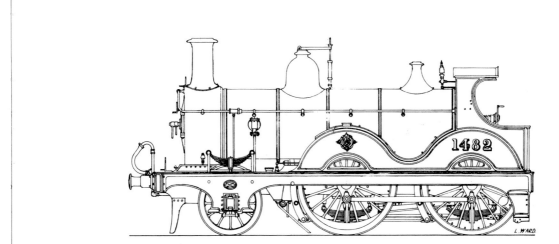

Fig. 8. *Drawing of '1400' class 2—4—0 No. 1482
in its final Johnson condition with the modified
splasher beading between the wheels.* L. Ward

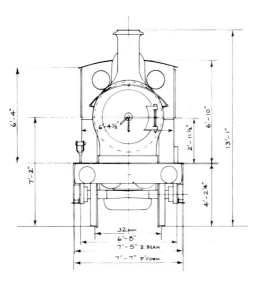

Fig. 9. *This drawing complements the side
elevation of the '1400' class 2—4—0.*
K. C. Woodhead

Plate 73. The classic '1400' class 2−4−0 in perhaps its most appealing form − full livery and modified splashers. No. 1576 was built in 1881, renumbered 266 in 1907, received a Belpaire boiler in 1927 and was scrapped, as No. 20266, in 1940. *Authors' Collection*

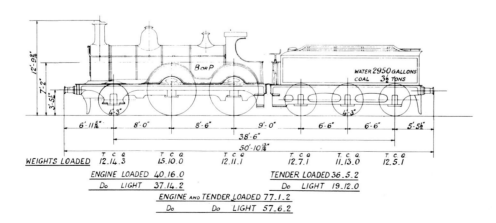

Fig. 10. ED 1/15 was issued in 1919 to cover all the 2−4−0s (!), but is in fact the diagram issued for the '1400' class now running with some Deeley modifications. It did, however, include the 6 ft 8½ in '50' class variations. The tender capacity is quoted as 2,950 gallons but it is not possible to say with certainty whether all the '1400' class carried this size of tender. Some may have had the 3,250 gallon version. Certainly the 1903 records quote both sizes of tender with these locomotives. *National Railway Museum*

Plate 74. '1400' class 2—4—0 No. 229 (originally No. 1479) in Deeley condition and livery as running from c.1910 to 1925 in which latter year it was given a Belpaire boiler. It was scrapped in 1932.

Authors' Collection

Plate 75. No. 254 (formerly No. 1514) was a late round-top '1400' class survivor, being withdrawn in late 1939 (as No. 20254) still in much the same condition as seen here. The probable livery of this early 1930 view is lined rather than plain black. *Authors' Collection*

Plate 76. Detail of Belpaired '1400' class 2−4−0 No. 261 (formerly No. 1521). The engine was withdrawn late in 1934, having run for its last eight years with Belpaire boiler. *R. E. Lacy*

Plate 77. This picture is included mainly for its curiosity value. It shows Belpaire boilered '1400' class No. 250 (formerly No. 1510) in the 1928 LMS *red* livery. It received its Belpaire boiler in 1927 and would have received a new red paint job at that time. Consequently, when the livery and insignia changes took place late in 1927, it was clearly cheaper to re-letter rather than re-paint to lined black. No. 250 was withdrawn late in 1933. *Authors' Collection*

Plate 78. This picture is a close-up of the cab and tender of '1400' class No. 213 which was withdrawn in 1934. Starting life as No. 1406, it became No. 213 in the 1907 renumbering and received a G6 Belpaire boiler in 1927. When photographed the locomotive was in black livery lined red. Note the brass '1' with the LMS addition of the transferred 'P' to achieve the post-1928 classification 1P. *Authors' Collection*

Plates 79 & 80. Front-end comparisons between '1400' class 2–4–0s in the early and late stages. No. 1520 became No. 260 in 1907 and No. 209 had begun life as No. 1402. No. 1520 is in full MR crimson, No. 209 in LMS lined black. Note the change in position of the cab spectacle (to accommodate the Belpaire firebox) and the variations in smokebox — particularly the lamp iron positions. No. 1520 (as No. 260) was withdrawn round-topped in 1931, No. 209 late in 1932.   *David White Collection & Authors' Collection*

2-4-0 PASSENGER ENGINE

Fig. 11. ED13 was issued in 1910 to cover this small group of 6 ft 6 in engines and shows the class with an intermediate type of Deeley front-end modification.   National Railway Museum

111 CLASS *(included in '1282' class — see Table 8)*

Summary

Built at Derby 1880.

Original MR numbers 111-115. 6 ft 6 in wheels. 17½ x 24 in cylinders.

1907 numbers 217-221, all to LMS in 1923.

Officially paired with 2950 gallon tenders.

These locomotives received 18 in cylinders between 1894 and 1899.

The '111' and '1282' classes were alike in all significant respects but it seems that two diagrams (ED 12/13) were issued to cover the tender differences. One (No. 20219) was given an LMS 1934 series duplicate number, carrying a Belpaire boiler by now) and was the last withdrawal in 1943.

Plate 81. '111' class 2—4—0 No. 220 shows one of this small group of five engines in LMS service c.1930. It took up this configuration c.1910 and remained thus (livery excepted) in late 1932.
Authors' Collection

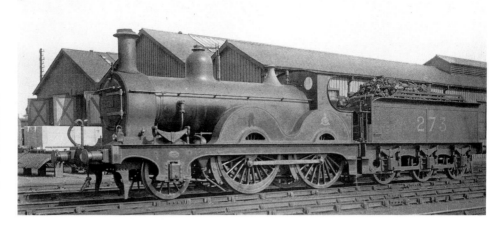

1492 CLASS

Summary

Built at Derby 1881.
Original MR numbers 1492-1501. 7 ft wheels, larger cylinders than '101' class.
1907 numbers 272-281, all to LMS in 1923.
Officially paired with 2950 gallon tenders.

The '1492' class differed from its predecessor solely in the matter of initial cylinder size. When the 7 ft 0 in series all carried 18 in cylinders, it was only the tender size which called for the maintenance of two diagrams.

The '1492' class was the first complete sub-group of Johnson 2−4−0s to become extinct. All but one had gone by the end of 1931 and the last survivor (No. 276) only lasted until 1933. By then, like most of the '1492' class, it had a Belpaire boiler.

Plate 83. '1492' class No. 276 (originally No. 1496) had a similar history to No. 273 (*Plate 82*) save that in its Belpaired condition it lasted a few years longer, until late 1933. It is seen here stored out of use in LMS black livery — whether lined or not is impossible to say. *Authors' Collection*

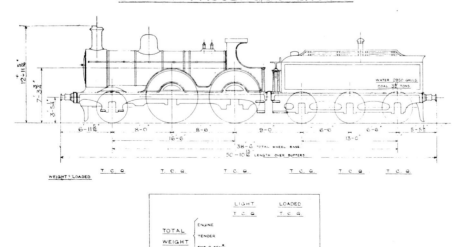

2−4−0 PASSENGER ENGINE

Fig. 12. ED18 was issued in 1910 to cover the ten 7 ft 0 in 2−4−0s of the '1492' class. By this time they differed from the '101' class solely in the matter of officially allocated tender size. The diagram shows the final Deeley front end.
Authors' Collection

Plates 84, 85 & 86. These views show cab interiors (all post-Johnson period) of the following 2—4—0 classes: No. 184 — '1282 class originally No. 1309, 6 ft 6 in series, first batch. No. 219 — '111' class, originally No. 113, 6 ft 6 in series, last batch. No. 271 — '1400' class, originally No. 1531, 6 ft 9 in series, last engine built. Note the slight variations in detail between all three cabs.

National Railway Museum

Plate 87. The original Midland 4—4—0s remained in basically their original condition throughout their lifetime. This late 1890s picture of No. 1320 at rest emphasises their graceful outline. It was built by Kitson in 1877, became No. 308 in 1907 and was withdrawn in 1928.

National Railway Museum

CHAPTER FIVE

THE JOHNSON 'SLIM BOILER' 4–4–0s
(INCLUDING SATURATED REBUILDS)

Plate 88. '1327' class 4–4–0 No. 1343, built in 1877 by Dübs & Co. and shown here in green livery, makes an interesting comparison with *Plate 89* overleaf.

NOT so long after he took over affairs at Derby, Johnson introduced, in 1876, the first of a long line of 4–4–0 engines. By the standards of the mid-1870s, they were big engines and from them was spawned a whole evolutionary family which, in a sense, was not completed until the LMS itself built the last of the compounds and class 2 superheated 4–4–0s, over fifty years later.

The 4–4–0 was to become the archetypal Midland passenger tender engine and, by the time the story reached its climax, the picture was immensely complicated both visually and in terms of variation between the different series. The only way to disentangle the various elements is to break the series into constituent parts, and, in this and the next chapter, an attempt is made to do so for the smaller locomotives (which in due course would be classified 1 and 2), all of which started their long lives in what we have chosen to call their 'slim boiler' form — the classic Johnson engine configuration with all its elegance of line so beloved of both contemporary and present day enthusiasts.

Before analysing each separate class of 4–4–0s in detail, it will therefore be useful to review the whole series 'as built'. The story is summarised in Tables 9 & 10 and the next few paragraphs, along with *Plates 87-99*, describe the evolutionary sequence.

The line of development started in 1876 with ten '1312' class engines (*Plate 87*), a 6 ft 6 in design with 17½ in x 26 in cylinders. A year later, the 7 ft 0 in version appeared with 18 in cylinders, the '1327' class. Twenty were built and these thirty pioneer Johnson 4–4–0s were never substantially altered, remaining slim-boilered until the LMS finally scrapped the last survivors.

In 1882 a third driving wheel diameter was introduced of 6 ft 9 in (officially 6 ft 8½ in). This series, the '1562' class, had 30 members and similar motion/cylinder components to the 7 ft 0 in '1327' class. They were probably the most visually harmonious of all the first three series, the balance between driving wheel size, splashers and boiler being about right (*Plate 90*).

The next to appear in 1884 were ten engines, reverting to 7 ft 0 in wheels, but now with 19 in cylinders and Joy's valve gear, the '1667' class (*Plate 91*). A little 'over cylindered', these engines were fairly soon rebuilt (in 1886/8) with replacement 'B' boilers, having 1261 sq ft heating surface and 160 lbs pressure, compared to 1142 sq ft and 140 lbs pressure of the originals. However, they were still not considered to be satisfactory and so between 1896-1901 they were renewed in similar form to the '150' class (below).

The fifth series of 4–4–0s, the '1738' class (*Plate 92*) were all but identical to the '1667' class series but reverted

Plate 89. In comparing this study of No. 1338 with the previous picture, it is interesting to note the variation in placing the brass numbers on the cabside. Compare also the shape of the domes, No. 1343 has a dome much 'thinner' than that fitted to No. 1338 and has a taller safety valve bonnet but in due course received the 'fatter' version (see *Plate 102*). Another rather subtle point is the different shape of the splasher between the driving wheels. No. 1338 has a continuous 'sweep' whereas No. 1343 shows a flattening between the wheels. The early Johnson 4—4—0s copied the 2—4—0s in this respect (see page 51). Their splashers were originally all in the style of No. 1343, later altered to the style of No. 1338; this variation is believed to have been confined to the two series of 4—4—0s ('1312' and '1327' classes) built alongside the 2—4—0s, plus the immediately succeeding '1562' class. When built they had wrought iron wheels, later to be replaced with cast steel with improved balancing. There are also livery changes to note, No. 1338 having the later style of tender lining, presumably at the start of the move to simplicity. No. 1343 shows the early form of lining on the crimson livery before the fully 'decorated' period. No. 1343 became No. 325 and was withdrawn in 1928 while No. 1338 was to become No. 320. *Collection Bernard Mathews*

to 18 in cylinders and Stephenson motion. Built during 1885-6, the twenty-strong class became very well known as a result of the last example, No. 1757, being exhibited at the Saltaire Jubilee Exhibition of 1887, carrying the name *Beatrice*, one of only two Midland engines to be named (see Volume 1. *Plates 208 & 209*).

The Midland could never quite decide on the proper wheel diameter for its express engines so, not surprisingly, another 6 ft 6 in series then appeared — the '1808' class built to the tune of 25 examples in 1888 and 1891 (15 and 10 respectively) — *Plate 93*.

Although out of date sequence, it should be noted that a final batch of 8 ft 6 in wheelbase locomotives was built by Beyer Peacock in 1900, the '2581' class, described as 'like M & GN C class' and virtually the same as the '1808' class — somewhat unusual since by now the company had adopted a 9 ft 6 in driving wheelbase for its 4—4—0s.

Returning to the story in date order, a reversion to 7 ft wheels came in 1892 with the '2183' class (*Plate 94*).

This was, to all intents and purposes, a 9 ft wheelbase development from the '1738' class but, in consequence, could accept the longer firebox of the 'D' boiler, rather than the 'B' series of the earlier examples. (For boiler types

see Volume 1, p. 56). They could also be identified visually by the frame extension between smokebox and leading splasher which projected above the running plate. Twenty-five were built.

Thus far, all the *smaller* wheeled Johnson 4—4—0s had an 8 ft 6 in coupled wheelbase, but with the next series, the '2203' class of 1893 (*Plate 95*), the coupled wheelbase of the 6 ft 6 in engines was also increased to 9 ft. These engines, like the '2183' class, had 'D' boilers and all had deeper frames visible above the running plate. The series totalled 45 examples, built in batches down to 1895 and was numerically the largest of the original slim boiler classes.

After the building of the '2203' class, a 7 ft wheel version with 9 ft coupled wheelbase and *piston* valves appeared in 1896. This was the '150' class and had much in common with the later series of 4—2—2s (Chapter 7), which were also coming into service at the same time, including the necessarily much more prominent front frames (to accommodate the valves) below the smokebox (*Plate 96*). This feature, which quite suited the 'singles', did not look as well on the 4—4—0s for some reason. Forty of the '150' class were built, of which ten were regarded as renewals of the earlier '1667' class (above). These ten

Plate 90. '1562' class 4−4−0 No. 1666 in almost its original Johnson condition. Reboilered with an 'H' boiler in 1907, the locomotive became No. 357 in 1907 and was withdrawn in the style of Engine Diagram 37 in January 1926. Seen here in fully decorated crimson lake livery style, immaculately turned out, the only significant change from its 'as built' state is the 'newer' splasher shape (see also *Plates 88/9*).

Collection Roger Carpenter

Plate 91. No. 1673 shows the '1667' class as built. As a class they lasted until 1901. It could be argued that Derby did not fully understand the workings of Joy valve gear and this may have been part of the problem which finally led to them being rebuilt. It is pictured here in almost fully decorated crimson lake livery; however, there is no lining on the guard irons or the framing beneath the smokebox. The brake-hangers are lined and the tops of the splashers appear to be red. The lack of 'MR' on the tender suggests a date in the early 1890s and 'transitional' seems a good word to use for its decorative state.

Collection Bernard Mathews

Plate 92. Built at Derby in 1886, '1738' class 4–4–0 No. 1751 received an 'H' boiler in 1906 and the following year became No. 371. This locomotive did not receive a Belpaire boiler and was withdrawn in its 'H'-boiler condition in 1927. It is seen here in full crimson lake livery. *Collection Bernard Mathews*

Plate 93. This broadside view of '1808' class 4–4–0 No. 1816, taken during the early 1890s, once again reveals the immaculate lines of a Johnson engine in its prime. Built in 1888, the engine received an 'H' boiler in 1904 and a saturated Belpaire boiler in 1909. It was withdrawn in 1931. *Authors' Collection*

Plate 94. '2183' class No. 2185 in original condition. This picture displays a locomotive in the early full crimson lake livery — a condition, we believe, all to have carried initially. It received an 'H' boiler in 1906, became No. 405 in 1907 and was renewed as a '483' class in 1914. Note the damaged paintwork on the firebox. *C. M. Doncaster*

Plate 95. No. 233 of the '2203' class is seen here in original condition in fully decorated crimson lake livery. Note, for example, the lining on the cab front around the spectacle plates. This locomotive was built in 1895 and received an 'H' boiler in 1906. The following year it was renumbered 466 and in 1914 it was renewed to '483' class. Scrapped by British Railways in 1949, it was withdrawn without being renumbered.   *Collection Bernard Mathews*

Plate 96. We used this picture in Volume One but much more can be said about the subject matter. Taken at Leeds in 1907, the picture illustrates '150' class 4−4−0 No. 2434 in original condition and still wearing 'decorated' livery. Soon to become No. 516, it received an 'H' boiler the following year and in 1912 it was renewed to '483' class and lasted until 1950 when it was withdrawn as British Railways No. 40516. Note the front frame shape − characteristic of the Sharp-Stewart batch.   *J. H. Wright*

Plate 97. No. 1670 was a renewal of the '1667' class to '150' class in 1901 and received an 'H' boiler in 1908. Four years later in 1912 this locomotive, which had become No. 486 in 1907, was renewed to '483' class and was withdrawn in 1957. This picture, taken in 1907, shows a move towards the Deeley simplified livery, with no lining apparent on the guard irons, brake hangers, framing below the smokebox or the sandboxes. However, all boiler bands are lined and the tender was undoubtedly lettered 'MR' and probably lined round the panel edging. Note the front frame shape compared with *Plate 96*. *Collection Bernard Mathews*

Plate 98. Johnson '60' class 4—4—0 No. 806 is seen here in a form of the crimson lake livery which preceded the full simplification of the Deeley period. Note the lining on the framing below the smokebox. The guard irons, however, are still lined out but the tender panels have been painted in the later style. Photographed at Holbeck in 1906, this locomotive was rebuilt with an 'H' boiler the same year, became No. 544 the following year, was renewed to '483' class in 1914 and withdrawn, still carrying its LMS number, in 1949.

Collection Bernard Mathews

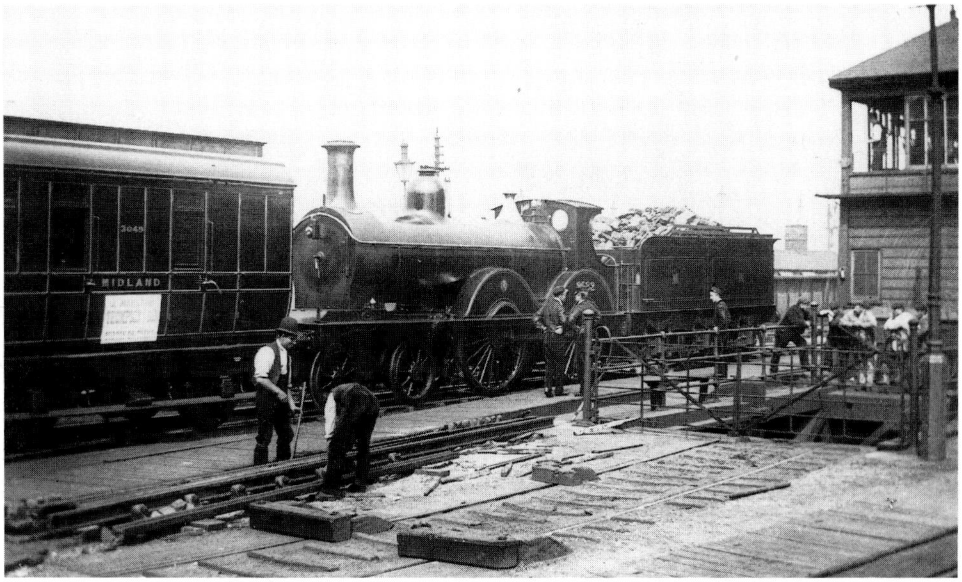

Plate 99. We conclude this survey of the 'slim-boilered' Midland 4–4–0s in their original condition with this picture of No. 2582 at St. Pancras. Recorded by Ahrons as '1808 class (1900)', this locomotive should be compared with '1808' class No. 1816 in *Plate 93*. Becoming No. 474 in 1907, two years after it had received an 'H' boiler, it was to last until 1925 when it was withdrawn by the LMS. Five of the ten members of this, the '2581' class, were renewed to the '483' class configuration but No. 474 was not one of them.
Collection Bernard Mathews

renewals could be identified visually from the original slide valve version by the deep front frame which, of course, they now displayed (*Plate 97*).

By now the Johnson 'slim boiler' 4–4–0 was pushing to the limits of its development and the last series of all, the '60' class, rather showed it (*Plate 98*). The 'E' boiler was used for the first time on a 4–4–0, and the coupled wheelbase therefore went up to 9 ft 6 in (the eventual MR standard for inside cylinder 4–4–0s), the driving wheel diameter was 7 ft and the front frames were of a really massive nature. Forty were built between 1898 and 1901 and, although they could not really be described as badly proportioned, they lacked the sheer elegance of the earlier series, rather as did the contemporary final series of 4–2–2s (Chapter 7). It cannot be denied that this a subjective view and open to debate, but a comparison of *Plates 93 & 98* should indicate the point that we are trying to make. There was a sort of 'grossness' about this final series, not shared by the earlier classes.

Scarcely had the last of the 'slim boilers' made its appearance in 1901 than the Midland embarked upon its great 4–4–0 upgrading programme. It began, of course, with the building of new Class 3 and Class 4 engines (see Chapters 8 & 9) but pretty soon the smaller 4–4–0s came in for attention and from now onwards in this chapter, each specific class will be treated separately.

TABLE 9: 4–4–0 SMALL BOILER LOCOMOTIVES
8' 6" COUPLED WHEELBASE ENGINES

1903 Diagram Page No.	Order No. or Class	Built by	Qty. built	Date of building	Pre 1907 numbers	1907 renumbering	Cylinders	BOILER Centre Line	BOILER Diameter	BOILER Length	BOILER Tubes	BOILER Diameter	Working Pressure	FIREBOX Length	FIREBOX Grate Area in sq. ft.	Total Heating Surface in sq. ft.	WHEELS Leading	WHEELS Driving	WHEELS Tyres	ENGINE WEIGHT Empty	ENGINE WEIGHT Loaded	REMARKS
20	F	Kitsons	10	1876/7	1312-1321	300-309	18" × 26"	7' 2½"	4' 2"	10' 6"	246	1⅝"	140 PSI	5' 11"	17.5	1260	3' 3"	6' 6"	2¾"	36.8.0	41.19.1	1312 CLASS. Built with 17½" × 26" cyls. Never rebuilt with a larger boiler.
19	G	Dübs	20	1877	1327-1346	310-327	18" × 26"	7' 3½"	4' 2"	10' 6"	246	1⅝"	140 PSI	5' 11"	17.5	1260	3' 6"	7' 0"	2¾"	39.11.0	42.19.1	1327 CLASS. Two locomotives were withdrawn before 1907. Never rebuilt with larger boilers.
18	370 400 430	Derby Derby Derby	30	1882/3	1562-1571 1572-1581 1657-1666	328-357	18" × 26"	7' 2"	4' 2"	10' 6"	246	1⅝"	140 PSI	5' 11"	17.5	1260	3' 6"	6' 8½"	2¾"	38.11.0	41.19.1	1562 CLASS. All to H boiler. Afterwards many to saturated Belpaire. Some to 483 class
Rebuilt by 1903	444	Derby	10	1884/5	1667-1676	Re-newed 1896-1901	19" × 26"	7' 3½"	4' 2"	10' 6"	175	1¾"	140 PSI	5' 11"	17.5	1142	3' 6"	7' 0"	2¾"		42.16.0	1667 CLASS. This series was not listed in their original condition in the 1903 Diagram Book. All were renewed as 150 class between 1896-1901. Details of other alterations are given in the class chapter.
17	554 615	Derby Derby	20	1885/6	1738-1757	358-377	18" × 26"	7' 3¾"	4' 2"	10' 6"	246	1⅝"	160 PSI	5' 11"	17.5	1260	3' 6"	7' 0"	2¾"	39.11.0	42.19.1	1738 CLASS. Class history generally as 1562 class above.
16	678 734 920	Derby Derby Derby	25	1888/91	1808-1822 80-7, 11 & 14	378-402	18" × 26"	7' 3"	4' 2"	10' 6"	246	1⅝"	160 PSI	5' 11"	17.5	1260	3' 3"	6' 6"	2¾"	38.8.0	41.19.1	1808 CLASS. Class history generally as 1562 class above.
11	Like M & GN C	Beyer Peacock	10	1900	2581-2590	473-482	18½" × 26"	7' 4"	4' 2"	10' 6"	244	1⅝"	160 PSI	5' 11"	17.5	1252	3' 3"	6' 6"	2¾"	40.12.0	44.0.1	2581 CLASS. Ahrons refers to them as 1808 class (1900). All to H Boiler then five to 483 class. *Principal Source 1903 Midland Railway Diagrams*

Plate 100. This view shows the '1312' class 4—4—0 type No. 1318 as built with a 3-piece chimney, inside spring tender and a pronounced 'flattening' of the splasher between the driving wheels. Engines of this class would have been in this form at the start of the 'red' period. As No. 306, this one became the last survivor (*Plate 102*). Note the original works plate position. Later it was moved when the heraldic emblem went onto the leading splasher.

Authors' Collection

1312 CLASS

Summary

Built by Kitson & Co. 1876-1877. Class F.
Original MR Nos. 1312-1321.
1907 Nos. 300-309.
Six to LMS in 1923.
Class extinct 1930.
Allocated to ED 23 in 1910 and coupled to 2950 gallon tenders.

Although six of the class lasted to become LMS stock, so far as is known, only Nos. 305, 306 and 308 carried the LMS crest.

When Samuel Waite Johnson came to Derby in 1873 to take up his new appointment as Locomotive Superintendent he left two 4—4—0s under construction at the Stratford Works of the Great Eastern Railway. These locomotives, which entered traffic in 1874, may be regarded as the prototypes for the Midland Railway 4—4—0s built from 1876 onwards to Johnson's designs. As far as we can deduce, the '1312' class ran the full gamut of MR liveries (see Volume 1) from 1883-1923 and, of course, they entered service in green and remained thus for a few years. Like the contemporary 2—4—0s (see Chapter 4), the early 4—4—0s were built with a 'flattened' centre section between the splashers, later altered to a full reverse curve some time during the 1890s — precise time not known.

Plate 101. No. 301 in Midland livery with a Deeley front end. Originally No. 1313, it was withdrawn in 1920. Note the change in splasher shape compared with *Plate 100*.

Collection Bernard Mathews

Plate 102. No. 306 in LMS livery. Compare with *Plate 99.* Note also the difference in the dome from that of No. 301; No. 306 seems to have a 'narrower' version. Originally No. 1318, this locomotive was the final survivor of the class. *Authors' Collection*

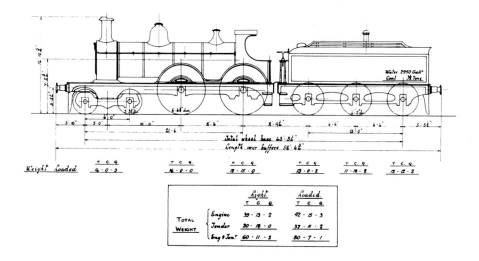

Fig. 13. ED23 was the original 1910 engine diagram for the first ten locomotives, Nos. 300-309, but when a new drawing was produced in 1919, these locomotives were included on ED 1/27. This later composite diagram is illustrated in *Fig. 15.*
National Railway Museum

1327 CLASS

Summary

Built by Dübs & Co. 1877. Class G.

Original MR Nos. 1327-1346.

1907 Nos. 310-327 (Nos. 1332 and 1336 scrapped in 1904).

No. 1346 was renumbered 1336 in 1904.

Ten to LMS in 1923.

Class extinct 1934.

Although, as we have pointed out several times, the Midland never totally standardised a wheel diameter for its express engines, building batches for certain routes with varying wheel diameters, it did build rather more 7 ft 4—4—0s than any other wheel size and, of course, the '483' class renewals perpetuated this wheel dimension; so perhaps the 7 ft 4—4—0 can be considered the most characteristic form. If so, the '1327' class started it all off when these 20 engines were built in 1877. As with the '1312' class, these 7 ft engines also (originally) had a flattened centre section to the splashers, later altered.

One locomotive, No. 323, was rebuilt with extended smokebox and new frames in 1909 (see *Fig. 16*) and four more were also given new deeper frames at various dates. This series of engines was originally allocated to ED 26 (3250 gallon tenders) and later to composite diagram ED 27 (2950 gallon tenders) in 1910. As far as we know, the 7 ft 0 in engines carried the 3250 gallon type, and the 6 ft 6 in '1312' class the smaller version.

This series was little altered during their lifetime and, apart from receiving the inevitable Deeley 'front end', remained in what was basically Johnson condition until withdrawal. They carried the full range of MR passenger liveries, including green, from 1877-1923.

Plate 103. '1327' class 4—4—0 No. 1343 photographed at Hellifield c.1896. While not quite 'as built' (see *Plate 88*), this locomotive typifies the pioneer 7 ft 0 in 4—4—0 series in the pre-decorated crimson lake livery. Note the absence of 'MR' on the tender and the generally restrained lining below the footplate. The engine still retains the 'early pattern' splashers.   *Collection R. S. Carpenter*

4—4—0 PASSENGER ENGINE

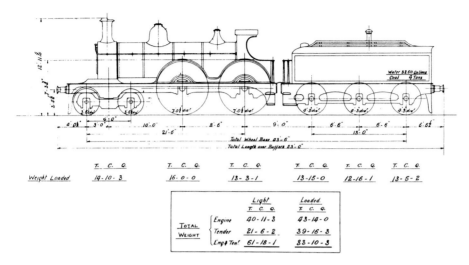

Fig. 14. ED26 was the 1910 Midland diagram for the '1327' class when coupled to a 3,250 gallon tender, believed to be normal for the 7 ft 0 in series of engines.   National Railway Museum

Fig. 15. ED 1/27 was the Midland Railway 1919 composite diagram for the whole series of locomotives Nos. 300-327. However, it is in effect the 1910 diagram for the series 310-327 if coupled to a 2,950 gallon tender. We do not think that many of the 7 ft 0 in series were so paired.   National Railway Museum

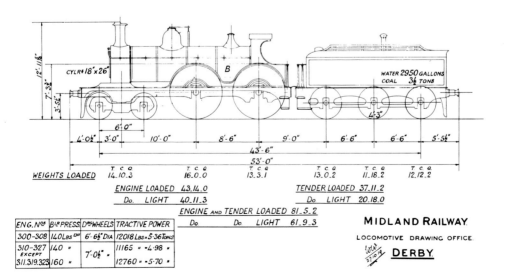

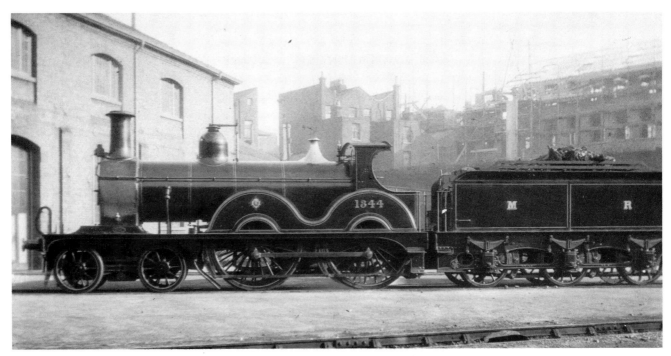

Plate 104. This view of '1327' class engine No. 1344 (later No. 326) shows the type c.1904/5, now with new splashers. The tender lining is now at the panel edge but there is still much decorative embellishment. No. 326 was scrapped in 1928. *Authors' Collection*

Plate 105. This view of No. 313 is a most interesting picture and shows a locomotive running with its 1907 number, earlier crest on the cabside and Johnson front end. The power classification number is visible on the cabside panel. Built as 1330 in 1877, No. 313 was withdrawn in 1920 and is seen in Deeley simplified livery. *Authors' Collection*

Plate 106. '1327' class No. 319 (formerly No. 1337) seen here in Midland livery, was withdrawn at the end of 1924 and so probably never carried LMS insignia. Note the smokebox door − it is of the dished type but is without a horizontal handrail. The small vertical handle was kept on those engines which retained the continuous handrail across the top of the smokebox and was somewhat more common on engines with a flat door.   *Authors' Collection*

Fig. 16. Laurie Ward's drawing for No. 323 with an extended smokebox should be used in conjunction with the dimen-sions given with Fig. 16 — ED 1/27. The engine had helical springs on the leading coupled axle, not the leaf springs as drawn.

L. Ward

Plate 107. Formerly No. 1341, No. 323, seen here at Kings Norton on 21st August 1912, was the single example rebuilt with an extended smokebox and in this condition was allocated to ED27A (see *Fig. 16*). Note the bright metal work on the smokebox door, which (c.f. *Plate 106*) is a flat one with separate handrail.

W. L. Good

Plate 108. No. 1577 (later No. 343) at Bradford around the turn of the century in full but not decorated livery. It now has the modified splasher shape. It received an 'H' boiler the same year that it was renumbered and was scrapped in that condition in 1926.

Collection W. T. Stubbs

1562 CLASS

Summary

Built at Derby 1882-1883.
Original MR Nos. 1562-1581, 1657-1666.
1907 Nos. 328-357, all to LMS in 1923.
The 1903 diagrams suggest that they were running with 3250 gallon tenders, but we believe that other size tenders had previously been used.

The '1562' class was the oldest series of slim boiler Johnson 4—4—0s to undergo the full rebuilding treatment, a process which began in 1904. In consequence, during their slim boiler period, they mostly displayed the full finery of MR decoration. They emerged from Derby almost at the time of the livery change from green to red and some were red when new. We cannot identify the 'split', but thereafter they were all given the early crimson livery (during the 1880s) and many of them subsequently received the later embellishments of the full and 'decorated' period. Their intermediate wheel size (6ft 9 in) probably gave them

a visual 'edge' over the 6 ft 6 in and 7 ft 0 in types, and *Plate 90* is a particularly good example of this.

The 'H' boiler rebuilding rather wrecked their superb lines (*Plates 112/3*) and this was emphasised by the new, more austerely decorated Deeley livery. The bulk of them seem to have received their new Deeley livery (and transferred tender numerals) at the time of rebuilding with 'H' boilers, but there were doubtless a few exceptions.

For some of these engines the 'H' boiler period was quite short and quickly gave way to the 'saturated Belpaire' version with extended smokebox (*Plate 114*). Somehow, this even more aggressively-shaped rebuild seemed rather more visually acceptable and about half of them were so treated. All came to the LMS in one or other of these two saturated rebuild states, retaining their original wheelbase, but a handful were totally renewed as '483' class engines in 1923, bearing no resemblance to their original state. At 1st January 1923 the breakdown was as follows, using the 1907 numbers:

Plate 109. The '1562' class engines were, as far as we know, the last Johnson 4—4—0s to be built with the flattened centre section to the splashers. This otherwise rather indifferent view of No. 1564, later No. 330, clearly shows this. A somewhat better left-hand side view of the 'as built' condition of the '1562' class will be found in Volume One, *Plate 204*. No. 1564 received an 'H' boiler in 1906, a saturated Belpaire in 1909, and was scrapped in 1932. *Authors' Collection*

To LMS with 'H' boilers — 331/2/3/5/41/3-5/8/52/3/4-5/7 (14)
To LMS with saturated Belpaire boiler — 328-30/4/6/7/8-40/2/6-7/9-50/51/56 (16)
Rebuilt to '483' class in 1923 — 332/7/51/3/6

When rebuilt with 'H' boilers between 1906-1908, they were allocated to ED 37. Those which were later rebuilt with extended smokebox Belpaire boilers between 1909-11 were put on ED 63 and the few renewed to '483' class were put onto ED 69.

The 'H' boiler rebuilds became extinct by 1928 and the Belpaire boiler rebuilds (other than '483' class renewals) became extinct in 1937.

Plate 110. '1562' class 4—4—0 No. 1665 (later No. 356) in, as far as can be judged, the full crimson livery of the pre-decorated period c.1893. *National Railway Museum*

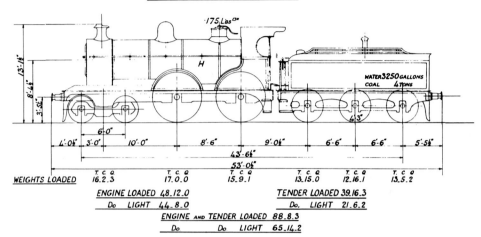

Fig. 17. ED 1/37. This Midland Railway 1919 diagram was intended to cover all the H-boilered 4—4—0s still in service at that date but it is in fact the 1910 diagram for the old '1562' class as running with 'H' boilers and renumbered between 328 and 357.   *National Railway Museum*

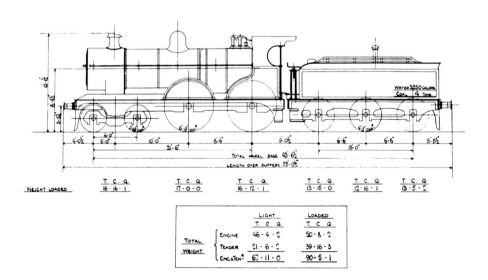

Fig. 18. ED63 was the 1910 Midland diagram for the '1562' class in saturated Belpaire boiler condition.
                                                                      Authors' Collection

Plate 111. No. 336 (previously No. 1570), almost certainly photographed in 1907, is one of relatively few of the class to receive new Deeley number and livery *before* receiving its 'H' boiler (also in 1907). The combination of Deeley smokebox door and Johnson chimney is a bit unusual. No. 1665 (*Plate 110*) may well have been similar at this time, not having received an 'H' boiler until 1908.

National Railway Museum

Plates 112 & 113. Transformation of an engine. These views show '1562' class No. 1567 (later No. 333) before and after the 'H' boiler conversion of 1906. The views taken at Leeds and Derby in 1905 and 1920 respectively, graphically symbolize the visual transformation which took place during the Deeley period. The engine was scrapped in 'H' boiler form in 1926. *Collection W. T. Stubbs and Collection Bernard Mathews*

Plate 114. No. 328, in Deeley period Midland livery at Leeds Wellington, is a saturated Belpaire conversion of a '1562' class 4—4—0 with new frames visible at the front end. Note the Ramsbottom safety valves and the flat smokebox door with horizontal handrail. As an ex-footplateman, one of the authors feels that the fireman (facing to the rear) is adopting one of the most common attitudes to be displayed by this member of the crew when not actually working a train! Note the slaking pipe hanging over the cabside. No. 328 was withdrawn in 1928, having started life as No. 1562, the class pioneer itself in 1882.

Authors' Collection

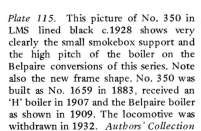

Plate 115. This picture of No. 350 in LMS lined black c.1928 shows very clearly the small smokebox support and the high pitch of the boiler on the Belpaire conversions of this series. Note also the new frame shape. No. 350 was built as No. 1659 in 1883, received an 'H' boiler in 1907 and the Belpaire boiler as shown in 1909. The locomotive was withdrawn in 1932. *Authors' Collection*

Plate 116. Cab interior of rebuilt '1562' class 4−4−0 No. 336 (ex-1570) in saturated Belpaire condition. The 'slim boiler' version of this engine is shown at *Plate 111.*

National Railway Museum

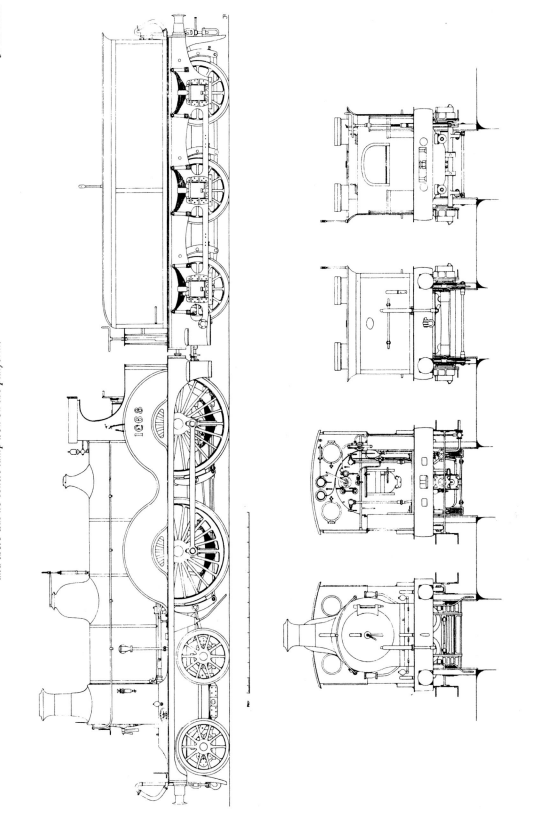

Fig. 19. This drawing of No. 1668, reproduced by courtesy of the HMRS, shows the Joy valve gear '1667' class as built in 1884. They only lasted for some 10-15 years in this form before being renewed as members of the '150' class with piston valves and Stephenson valve gear. However, as drawn, the smokebox waist is about 2 in. too wide above the frames and there was no centre lamp iron on the platform.

J. Rowland

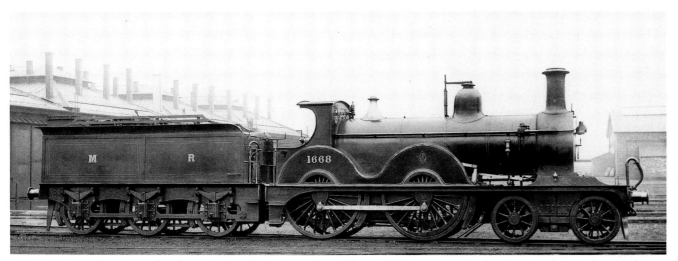

Plate 117. No. 1668 was renewed as early as 1896 but is seen here as built with lined brake hangers, unlined guard irons and no lining on the framing beneath the smokebox.

Collection Bernard Mathews

1667 CLASS

Summary

Built at Derby 1884.

Original MR Nos. 1667-1676.

Renewed between 1896-1901 (in actual fact the renewals were virtually new locomotives which took the old numbers and as such are covered within the '150' class on page 121).

The '1667' class showed an interesting use (for the MR) of Joy valve gear and overhead slide valves, but the appearance of the engines was little changed. They also had 19 in x 26 in cylinders which overtaxed their (relatively) small

boilers of the standard 'B' type. In consequence, they tended (to use contemporary phraseology, by Ahrons and others) to 'run out of breath'. Hardly surprisingly, in their original '1667' class form, the engines lasted only for about 12-15 years, being renewed between 1896-1901, having already received new boilers, with an increased heating surface and higher pressure, well before this wholesale renewal as members of the '150' class. We cannot say how much of the original remained; the wheels, with their rectangular spokes, were retained even though the '150' class had a longer wheelbase. At this date new wheels had oval cast steel spokes.

Plate 118. This semi-close-up view of '1667' class 4−4−0 No. 1674 is included to give more detail of these well-proportioned engines in their original state. No. 1674 was renewed in 1901.

C. M. Doncaster

1738 CLASS

Summary

Built at Derby 1885-1886.

Original MR Nos. 1738-1757.

1907 Nos. 358-377, all to LMS in 1923.

When rebuilt with 'H' boilers 1906-7, they were allocated to ED 39. Some were rebuilt with Belpaire boilers with extended smokebox and in this condition were allocated to composite ED 64.

A few were renewed to '483' class (ED 69).

All fitted with 3250 gallon tenders.

ED 39 class extinct 1927.

ED 64 G7 boiler examples extinct 1940.

The '1738' class was, in effect, a smaller cylindered version of the '1667' class, with Stephenson link valve gear and visually little different from any of the previous 7 ft series (*Plate 118*). The front frames below the smokebox were a fraction deeper, but essentially all these earlier 7 ft 4—4—0s were very similar and on some railways might well have been regarded as being of the same class.

During the slim boiler period, these engines, which were always red, almost certainly displayed both the full and 'decorated' versions of the elaborate 19th century livery (see Volume 1). Being new and generally employed on some of the most important trains, like most of the new Johnson engines of the 1880s and 1890s, they would receive 'most favoured' treatment as, for example, *Beatrice* (see Volume 1, plates 208/9). 'H' boilers began to be fitted to this group just before the 1907 renumbering, but generally after the change to Deeley livery with its simplified lining (*Plate 122*). Like the earlier '1562' class, many of them fairly speedily exchanged this for the saturated Belpaire boiler with extended smokebox (*Plate 126*) and it was in this form that half of them reached the LMS. There were, again, relatively few complete renewals to the '483' class and the engines concerned were modified to this form during 1922-4. The breakdown at 1st January 1923 was as follows:

To LMS with 'H' boiler — 359/360/2/4/7/71/3/5/7*

To LMS with saturated Belpaire boiler — 358/61/3/5-6/8-9/72/4/6

To LMS as '483' class — 370

* Converted to '483' class in 1923 — 359, 362, 377
  Converted to '483' class in 1924 — 364

Plates 119 (opposite) & 120 (right)
These two excellent and almost identical views of '1738' class Nos. 1755/6 (later Nos. 375/6) show the engines in two forms of the full crimson livery. The most obvious difference is that No. 1756 has a one-piece chimney, coal rails and 'MR' on the tender, making it a later view. At the same time, No. 1755, on close scrutiny, has somewhat more embellishment below the footplate (sandboxes, wheel centres). The original of this picture is almost panchromatic in quality and there is no doubt where the black and red areas fall. For example, the centres of the wheels clearly have a black inner disc surrounded by a red band. Both engines were built in 1886 and received 'H' boilers in 1907. No. 1756 (as 376) received a saturated Belpaire boiler in 1911 but No. 1755 stayed 'H' boilered until scrapped (1926) as No. 375. No. 376 lasted until 1935.
Authors' Collection

Plate 121. No. 1746 (later No. 366) at Kentish Town is seen here in full crimson lake livery. Note the additional circle on the bogie wheels around the axle ends. There appears to be black beading on the tender and lining both below the flare and above the horizontal beading. The sandboxes carry full lining and the style is bordering on 'fully decorated' having an 'SE shaded' heraldic emblem. The engine received an 'H' boiler in 1906, saturated Belpaire in 1911 and was scrapped in 1931. We illustrated No. 1757 *Beatrice* in Volume 1 *Plates 208 & 209* but failed to mention that while the rest of the class were fitted with gravity sanders, this locomotive was built with steam sanders.
Collection Bernard Mathews

Plate 122. No. 1739 with an 'H' boiler and a flat smokebox door. Built in 1885 at Derby, No. 1739 received its 'H' boiler in 1906 and became No. 359 in 1907. In 1923, under LMS ownership, it was renewed as a member of the '483' class and was finally withdrawn as BR No. 40359 in 1954.
Collection Roger Carpenter

Plate 123. The more common 'H' boiler conversion was with dished smokebox door, seen here on No. 373, formerly No. 1753 and converted to this form in 1906. It was scrapped in 1925 without further rebuilding.
Collection W. T. Stubbs

Plate 124. This cab interior of No. 375 with an 'H' boiler dates from c.1911 and provides readers with the opportunity to study the controls on a locomotive of this type. Note the slaking pipe on the left below the sight feed lubricator. At least the fireman had a reasonable seat — which is more than one can say for the driver!
National Railway Museum

Plate 125. This view shows 'H' boiler '1738' class No. 360 (formerly No. 1740) on a southbound express and taking water at Dillicar troughs (LNWR). This picture was clearly taken during the short period when the MR ran a daily service from Leeds via Low Gill and the LNWR. No. 360 was scrapped in 1926, still with its 'H' boiler. *Authors' Collection*

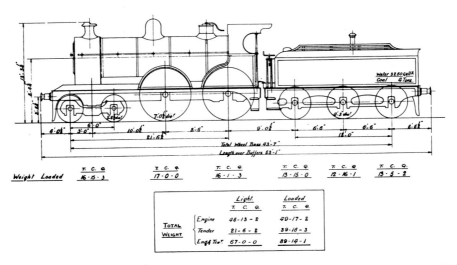

Fig. 20. ED39 was the Midland Railway 1910 diagram for the 'H'-boilered rebuilds of the old '1738' class which had become Nos. 358-377 in 1907.
National Railway Museum

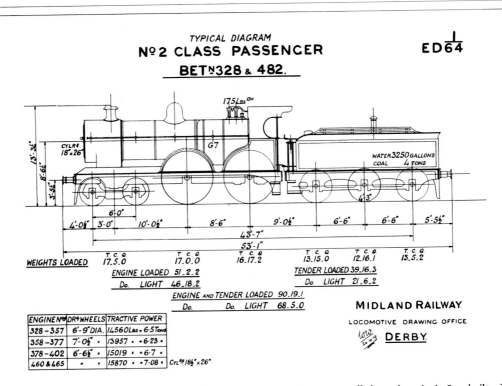

Fig. 21. ED 1/64 was a 1919 Midland Railway composite diagram professing to cover all the various 4—4—0s rebuilt with saturated Belpaire boilers, i.e. other than the '483' class renewals. In fact it re-used the 1910 drawing for the old '1738' class locomotives which, subsequent to rebuilding with 'H' boilers, were again rebuilt with Belpaire saturated boilers. This diagram should, therefore, only be considered as applying to the '1738' class rebuilds and not the full number series mentioned on the diagram itself, 1907 Nos. 358-377.
National Railway Museum

Plates 126 & 127. Front and rear views respectively of '1738' class engines in saturated Belpaire condition with new frames. They were both in Deeley livery but No. 372 has LMS markings. As No. 1741, No. 361 was built in 1885 ('H' boiler 1907, Belpaire 1910) and scrapped in 1929. No. 372 began as No. 1752 in 1886, received its 'H' boiler in 1906 and Belpaire in 1911. It lasted until 1940 to become one of the last of the large wheeled saturated Belpaires to be scrapped.   *Authors' Collection*

Plate 128. The '1808' class engines were, according to Ahrons, one of the more renowned series of Midland 4—4—0s and this picture of No. 1814 shows their elegant lines. The engine is seen here in full crimson lake livery with a built-up cast iron chimney. The reader's attention is drawn to the tool boxes on the tender rear and lack of them on the bulkhead. It was not until 1904 that instructions were issued to move rear-mounted tool boxes forward. No. 1814, built in 1888 at Derby, received its 'H' boiler in 1904, thereby assuming the form that was later to be known as ED34; but by the year these diagrams were issued, it had received a Belpaire G7 boiler and so was now identified with ED64. It had, of course, been renumbered to 384 in 1907 and was withdrawn by the LMS in 1925.   *Collection Bernard Mathews*

1808 CLASS

Summary

Built at Derby 1888:
Original MR Nos. 1808-1822
1907 Nos. 378-392

Built at Derby 1891:
Original MR Nos. 80-87, 11 & 14
1907 Nos. 393-402, all to LMS in 1923.
Both series coupled to either 2950 or 3250 gallon tenders.

Well over ten years after the pioneer Johnson 4—4—0 had appeared, the Midland decided it needed more 6 ft 6 in engines and the '1808' class was the result. As usual, they were superbly proportioned and a comparison of *Plates 87 & 93* will reveal how similar they were to the pioneer '1312' class. Twenty-five were built in two batches and all had the full livery from new. It is likely that the majority also displayed various forms of decorative embellishments during the later 1890s as was usual at this time. The second batch had slightly deeper front frames (see *Plates 129 & 130*).

The 'H' boiler conversion began quite early with this series (1904) and all received this feature prior to the change of number and livery (*Plates 131/132*). In our judgement, the 'H' boiler conversion of the 6 ft 6 in 4—4—0s

was visually rather better than the similar conversion of the 6 ft 9 in and 7 ft series, retaining, as it did, a graceful Johnson-styled double splasher, albeit devoid of the smaller connecting rod splasher at the running plate — but see also the '2183' class variation, page 109.

In due course, the 'H' boilers gave way to the saturated Belpaire type, but this conversion was confined almost entirely to the first fifteen engines (second Nos. 378-92). All fifteen of these were converted to Belpaire plus one only (No. 393) of the second batch, and again a rather neat design resulted. Some sources refer to this sub-group as the '378' class (*Plate 136*). The remaining nine (Nos. 394-402) remained either 'H' boiler or went straight to the '483' class form. We can only surmise that this almost pure division of the two series of '1808' class (when rebuilt) had something to do with the original date of build.

Interestingly, the official drawing of the Belpaire '378' type rebuild, on which *Fig. 25* is based, specified a 9 ft coupled wheelbase, whereas the original '1808' class had 8 ft 6 in wheelbase. This change necessitated new frames and coupling rods of the now standard 'fluted' pattern to be fitted in place of the old plain section rods. The '378' series all emerged in standard Deeley livery with post-1907 numbers, but for a while three were paired with high-sided tenders (*Plate 135*). They became, by a long way, the last of the *saturated* ex-MR 4−4−0s to survive, three reaching BR (Nos. 383/5/91) of which only No. 383 was renumbered by the addition of 40000 to its 1907 Midland and LMS number.

The 'H' boilered engines did not last long into LMS days unless renewed as '483' class. Most of them were, and only Nos. 398/9 remained 'H' boiler until scrapping. They were all rebuilt with 'H' boilers 1904-1905 and then in 1910 they were allocated to ED 34. The few renewed to '483' class were put on ED 69. Those not renewed to '483' class which received Belpaire boilers (i.e. the '378' type) were allocated to ED 64 in 1910 and this class was extinct in 1952.

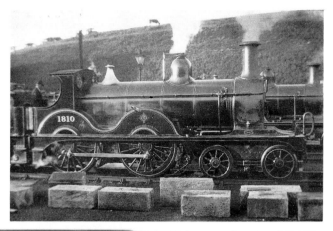

Plates 129 & 130. These two views of '1808' class 4−4−0s allow comparison to be made between the 1888 batch (engine No. 1810, later No. 380) and the 1891 build (engine No. 82, later 395). Superficially, both are the same and both carry full livery, but on No. 82 the front frames between smokebox and splasher can just be seen to project a little above the running plate − presumably there was felt to be a need to make them deeper and stronger than as first built. No. 1810 received an 'H' boiler in 1905, assumed '378' type configuration in 1911, and was scrapped in 1932, whereas No. 82 was given 'H' boiler in 1904 and renewed as a '483' class engine in 1922.

Authors' Collection and National Railway Museum

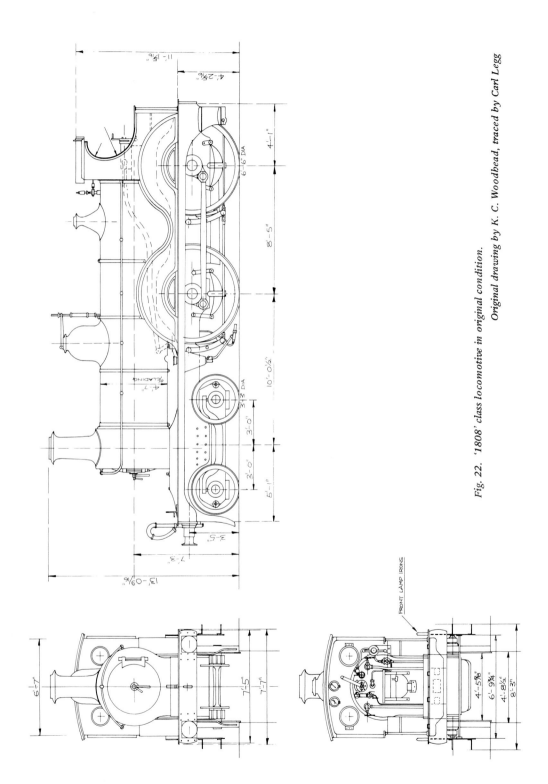

Fig. 22. '1808' class locomotive in original condition.

Original drawing by K. C. Woodhead, traced by Carl Legg

Plate 131. '1808' class No. 11 at Leeds Wellington c.1906. Built in 1891 at Derby, an 'H' boiler was fitted in 1905 and in 1907 the number became 401. In 1922 the locomotive was renewed as a member of the '483' class. It was withdrawn as No. 40401 in 1953.   *J. H. Wright*

Plate 132. This close-up of No. 85, photographed at Heysham in August 1905, illustrates the simple lines of these 'H' boiler rebuilds and shows the lining details. This locomotive was built at Derby in 1891 and received its 'H' boiler in 1904. Becoming No. 398 in 1907, it was withdrawn in this condition in 1926.
Collection Bernard Mathews

Plates 133 &134. When rebuilt to 'H' boiler form, the '1808' class still revealed the front frame differences (see *Plates 129/30*). No. 1818 (later No. 388) got its 'H' boiler, as did all of this series, still with the old number and livery in 1905. Its 1888 origin is revealed by the lower frame depth behind the smokebox. It became a '378' type Belpaire in 1909 and was scrapped in 1930. Note the flower-pot chimney. No. 394 (ex-No. 81) shows the deeper frames ahead of the splasher. This engine has a proper Deeley front end and chimney and also received its 'H' boiler in 1905. It was renewed to the '483' class configuration in 1923.   *Authors' Collection and Bernard Mathews' Collection*

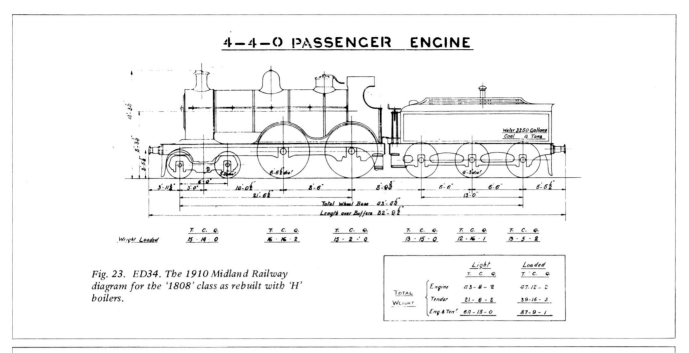

4—4—0 PASSENGER ENGINE

Fig. 23. ED34. The 1910 Midland Railway
diagram for the '1808' class as rebuilt with 'H'
boilers.

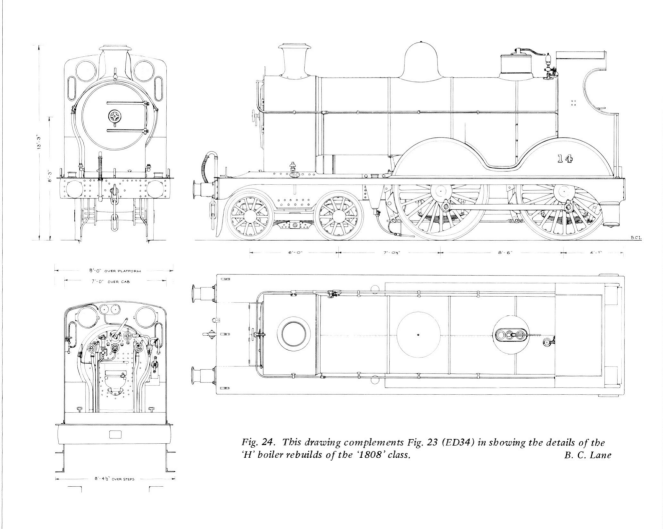

Fig. 24. This drawing complements Fig. 23 (ED34) in showing the details of the
'H' boiler rebuilds of the '1808' class.   B. C. Lane

Plate 135. As mentioned on page 100, three '378' class locomotives had their tenders rebuilt with straight sides, and this picture of No. 386 in works grey illustrates one of them. Built as No. 1816 in 1888, it received an 'H' boiler in 1904. It was, of course, renumbered in 1907 and in 1909 it was rebuilt in the form as shown. Withdrawal was in 1931. Two of the straight-sided tenders were coupled to the new 0—6—0s Nos. 3835/6 when they were built in 1911 and the 4—4—0s from which they came reverted to the normal type for the class.

Authors' Collection

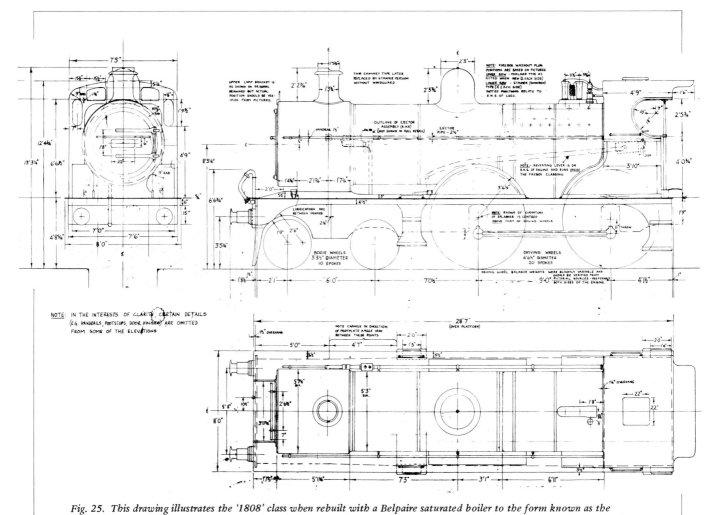

Fig. 25. This drawing illustrates the '1808' class when rebuilt with a Belpaire saturated boiler to the form known as the '378' class. However, the drawing should show slightly curved ends to the buffer planks (see pictures).   *D. Jenkinson*

Plate 136. No. 384 entered traffic in 1888 being built at Derby as No. 1814. In 1904 it received an 'H' boiler and was rebuilt with a G7 boiler with an extended smokebox, as illustrated, in 1910. This locomotive was involved in an accident at Hope in September 1925 and was withdrawn from service. These 6 ft 6 in engines were probably the best proportioned of all the saturated Belpaire rebuilds.

Collection Bernard Mathews

Plate 137. This interesting LMS period view of No. 379 shows clearly the differences in the level of the footplate of the locomotive and the tender. Note the water control valve for the injector just beneath the driver's right heel. A Derby-built locomotive of 1888, numbered 1809, it received an 'H' boiler in 1904, became No. 379 in 1907, was rebuilt with a saturated Belpaire boiler in 1911, and withdrawn in 1937. Note the replacement Stanier chimney.

Collection Roger Carpenter

Plates 138 & 139. '2183' class 4−4−0s Nos. 2189 and 2193. At first sight these two locomotives appear to be identical but close examination will show that No. 2193 has extra lining, for example, on the axle ends of the bogie. There are also variations in treatment of tender springs. It is likely that the pictures were taken at different stages during the move to the fully decorated style. No. 2193 was built by Sharp Stewart in 1893. In 1907 it was renumbered 413 and received an 'H' boiler, in 1918 it was renewed as a member of the '483' class and it was withdrawn as BR No. 40413 in 1959. No. 2189 received an 'H' boiler in 1906 and became No. 409 the following year. Renewal to '483' class was in 1919 and in this form the locomotive lasted until 1957 when it was withdrawn as British Railways No. 40409.

National Railway Museum

2183 CLASS

Summary

Built by Sharp Stewart 1892. Class L.
Original MR Nos. 2183-2202.
156-160 built at Derby 1896.
1907 Nos. 403-422, 423-427, all to LMS in 1923.
All ran with 3250 gallon tenders.

The '2183' class was a development of the 7 ft series with the 'D' class boiler and a new 9 ft wheelbase. They were very handsome engines with a slight visible frame extension from smokebox base to leading splasher (see page 72).

The engines appeared in 1892 at about the time when the MR livery was beginning to show distinct signs of flamboyance in its decoration and we used examples of the series in Volume 1 (Plates 206-7) to illustrate the move from the full to the decorated styles. We feel fairly safe in asserting that all engines came out in full livery, probably with some additional embellishments (*Plates 138/9*) and that most of them are likely to have received the full 'Weatherburn' (or similar) treatment before their 'H' boiler rebuilding, which began in 1906 and was completed by 1908. The second series of five only (Nos. 156-60) probably had more elaborate liveries right from the start.

With this class the 'H' boiler rebuild differed slightly, in visual terms, from that of the previous 7 ft rebuilds of the '1738' class. The '2183' class rebuilds retained a double splasher (*Plate 142*) which, whilst not, perhaps, as graceful as the 6 ft 6 in version, was not as 'brutal' in looks as the earlier engines with their separate splashers. It is all very subjective, of course, but we feel there was a nice 'high-stepping' quality to the Deeley version, even if the Johnson gracefulness had gone.

Many of the 'H' boiler rebuilds received their new style carrying the old numbers and a few probably received the older livery as well. The rebuilding absolutely straddled the change in numbering and livery and all that can positively be stated is that they all ultimately appeared in the manner of *Plate 144*.

Between 1914 and 1922 the MR renewed them again as '483' class engines and none reached the LMS other than in this configuration. They represented the oldest class of Johnson 4−4−0 to undergo total renewal in the '483' configuration without any saturated survivors. When rebuilt with 'H' boilers 1906-1908, they were allocated to ED 40 and when later renewed to '483' class, they were put on ED 69.

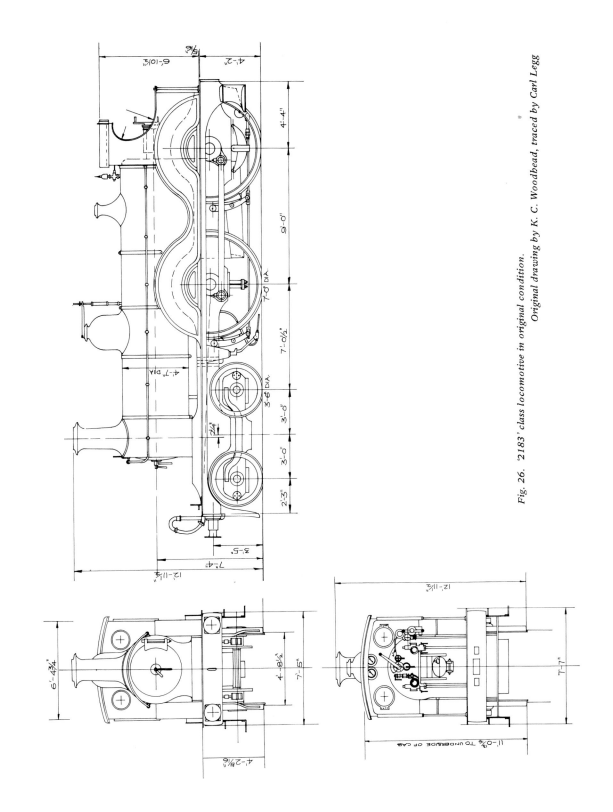

Fig. 26. '2183' class locomotive in original condition.

Original drawing by K. C. Woodhead, traced by Carl Legg

Plate 140. This view of '2183' class No. 159 (later No. 426) shows one of a batch of five built three years after the main series and, in some sources mistakenly attributed to the '150' class. This view clearly reveals No. 159 as a slide valve engine with shallow front frames. The picture is probably dated 1904/5 (note the panel edge lining on the tender, introduced in 1904). Rebuilt with 'H' boiler in 1906, this engine was renewed as a '483' type in 1916. *Authors' Collection*

Plate 141. This view, taken in 1907, shows the pioneer '2183' class engine No. 403, immediately after renumbering and shortly before rebuilding with 'H' boiler the same year. The engine is a bit scruffy, but clearly shows the use of the 'old' livery with new number in brass figures and power class markings on the upper cabside. The tender is likely to have been finished as per *Plate 140.* No. 403 was renewed to '483' class in 1920. *Authors' Collection*

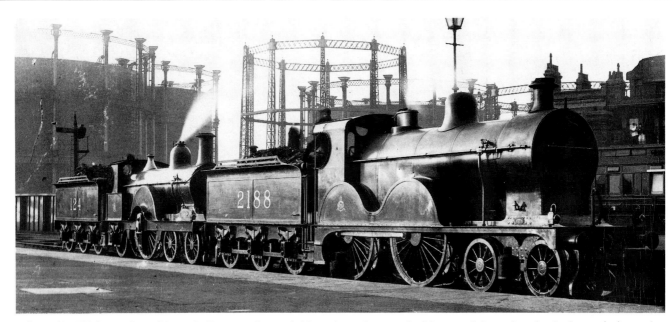

Plate 142. This interesting pairing at St. Pancras, taken probably as the engines were backing out of the station after having worked a southbound train, shows 'H'-boilered rebuilt '2183' class No. 2188 (later No. 408) and '115' class 4—2—2 No. 124 (see Chapter 7) both carrying old numbers with the new Deeley livery and heraldic emblem. The picture must have been taken in 1906, the year No. 2188 received its 'H' boiler. The engine was renewed to '483' type in 1914.   *Collection W. T. Stubbs*

Plate 143. An 'H'-boilered rebuilt '2183' class locomotive to ED40 is shown in this picture of No. 157. Built as one of the final batch at Derby in 1896, it assumed this form in 1906, probably the date of this photograph, and in 1907 it was renumbered 424. 1914 saw it renewed to '483' class and 1951 was the year it was withdrawn by BR as No. 40424. Interestingly (see *Plate 144*) this engine carried the old heraldic emblem, yet there is evidence that some engines at least (e.g. the '860' series Belpaires) had the newer emblem in 1905! It seems likely that both were in use simultaneously c.1905-6, possibly using up old transfer stocks.   *National Railway Museum*

Fig. 27. ED40 is the 1910 Midland Railway diagram for the '2183' class when rebuilt with 'H' boilers. Authors' Collection

Plate 144. This example of rebuilt '2183' class to ED40 in Midland livery at Manchester Central shows the type with its proper 1907 number. No. 414 was built in 1892 by Sharp Stewart as No. 2194 and received an 'H' boiler in 1906, becoming No. 414 the following year. In 1914 it was renewed to the '483' class and was withdrawn by British Railways in 1957 as No. 40414. Note, compared with *Plates 142 & 143*, that the engine now has a dished smokebox door, thus probably dating the view c.1909.   *Collection Bernard Matthews*

Plate 145. This works grey picture of No. 2217 is noteworthy insofar as it suggests two yellow lines separated by a black band on the base of the dome. This feature was quite rare; however, it can be seen on No. 196 (*Plate 146*). Note the lining on the sandboxes, confined to base only, not on the sides proper. Note also the brakeblocks, these have been lined but of course they never were treated in this manner when in traffic. This view gives a very clear example, brakeblocks apart, of this full crimson lake livery in non-decorated form. No. 2217 received an 'H' boiler in 1905 and became No. 442 in 1907. Withdrawal was in 1926 when still in 'H' boiler condition, a somewhat less common fate for the '2203' class, most of which were renewed to '483' type. *National Railway Museum*

2203 CLASS

Summary

Built by Sharp Stewart 1893. Class O.
Original MR Nos. 2203-2217.
1907 Nos. 428-442, all to LMS in 1923.

Built at Derby 1894-1895.
Original MR Nos. 184-199, 161-164, 230-239.
1907 Nos. 443-472, all to LMS in 1923.
All series ran with 3250 gallon tenders.

Built in several batches between 1893 and 1895, the '2203' class was the largest (numerically) of the Johnson slim boiler 4—4—0 series. All told, 45 were constructed and all had the extended 9 ft coupled wheelbase to accept the 'D' boiler — the first MR 6 ft 6 in 4—4—0s to do so. This feature was quite clearly evident on a side view of these 6 ft 6 in engines (*Plate 146*) where the sweeping downcurve between the wheel splashers was altogether more gentle than on the earlier 6 ft 6 in engines.

There is every reason to suppose that a substantial majority of these engines probably displayed some form of livery embellishment from the outset (sandboxes, brake hangers, guard-irons, bogie side frames, etc.), but such pictures as survive tempt the view that the first fifteen (Nos. 2203-17, built 1893) may have (just) preceded the more decorated period. Comparison of *Plate 146* with *Plate*

147 will indicate the evidence on which this conclusion is based and *Plate 95* reinforces this supposition.

All were rebuilt with 'H' boilers from 1904-6 and quite a few retained old style cabside numerals and livery (in rebuilt condition) for a few years — even with new 1907 numbers. However, all eventually became turned out in the standard Deeley style with transfer numerals. After the 'H' boiler phase, only two received saturated Belpaire boilers before the '483' class renewal commenced. These two exceptions were Nos. 460 and 465 which, as rebuilt in 1910, became almost identical to the so-called '378' class (see page 100). At the same time, because these two already had a 9 ft coupled wheelbase, they retained their original plain section side rods and were not given new fluted ones (*Plate 152*) — just one of those silly things guaranteed to cause modellers to trip up, as one of us actually did. But, as with the '378' class, they were given new frames.

The '483' class renewal began in 1914 and, thereafter, the bulk of the '2203' class were so treated. Relatively few went to the LMS in 'H' boiler form and, of these, only four further renewals took place after the 1923 grouping. The 'H' boiler survivors at 1st January 1923 were as follows: 428-9/31/5/8/9/40-2/5/9/50/1/7/67/9/72 of which Nos. 438/9/50/72 were the examples renewed to '483' type after the 1923 grouping.

The 'H' boiler rebuilds were put on ED 36, while the '483' class renewals were, of course, to ED 69.

THE JOHNSON 'SLIM BOILER' 4—4—0s

Plate 146. Writing in *Midland Style*, George Dow records the Weatherburn practice of painting the undersides of the boilers yellow to reflect light downwards to assist drivers oiling the valve gear between the frames. While a number of singles were thus treated, no 4—4—0 examples were given. At first we believed this picture of No. 196 was an exception. However, it would seem that the pale underside of the boiler is light reflected off the running plate. Built in 1894 at Derby, No. 196 received an 'H' boiler in 1905 and became No. 455 in 1907. As such it was renewed as a member of the '483' class in 1916 and was withdrawn as No. 40455 in 1954. Note the two yellow lines on the base of the dome, double lining on the wheels etc. – clearly a decorated engine. *Authors' Collection*

Plate 147. No. 2203 itself at rest, probably at Derby. Receiving an 'H' boiler in 1905 and being renumbered 428 in 1907, it is seen here in its original condition. There is apparently no lining on brake hangers, but there is quite a lot of elaboration when put under magnification. This engine, too, served out its time in 'H' boiler form, being scrapped in 1927. *Authors' Collection*

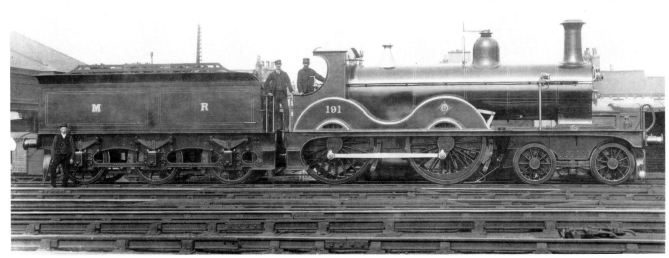

Plate 148. No. 191, built in 1894, probably came into service much as seen here. The lining is not quite so lavish as that on No. 196 (*Plate 146*), but there is still plenty of it. The engine received an 'H' boiler in 1906, was renumbered 450 in 1907 and renewed to '483' configuration in 1923. *Authors' Collection*

Plate 149. 'H' boiler '2203' class rebuild No. 2209 has the new livery with old heraldic emblem, new Deeley smokebox door and flower-pot chimney. It got its 'H' boiler in 1906, became No. 434 in 1907 and was renewed as a '483' in 1916. *Authors' Collection*

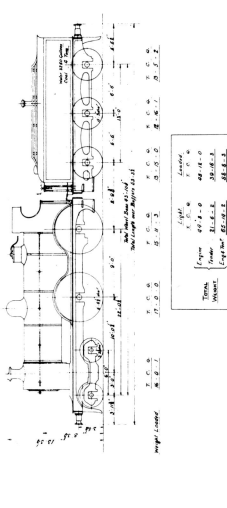

Fig. 28. ED36 is the 1910 Midland Railway diagram which depicts
the '2203' class when rebuilt with 'H' boilers.   Authors' Collection

4—4—0 PASSENGER ENGINE

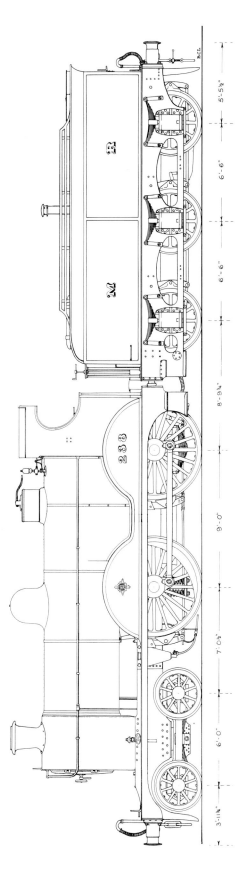

Fig. 29. This drawing depicts a Derby-built engine of the '2203' class after rebuilding with an 'H' boiler. For an
appropriate end elevation see Fig. 24, page 105.

Plate 150. This unidentified example of an 'H' boiler '2203' class 4—4—0 has the *new* emblem but retains the older pattern smokebox door. Unlike No. 2209 (*Plate 149*) it also carries a power class figure on the cabside, so was probably photographed later in time. Note, too, in both plates the retention of polished brass splasher beading with the new livery — a common practice c.1906-10.

Authors' Collection

Plate 151. '2203' class No. 441 (formerly 2216) in final Midland livery, now with black splasher beading, 'dished' door and Deeley chimney. This locomotive was not renewed to '483' class, being withdrawn in this condition towards the end of 1925.   *Collection W. T. Stubbs*

Plate 152. Although the majority of the '2203' class were renewed to '483' type and the bulk of the rest were scrapped with 'H' boilers, two of them (Nos. 460/5) received saturated Belpaire boilers, putting them into the '378' type of configuration (see page 100). No. 465 is seen in this form at Bentham. The picture is not of the best quality, but it does reveal the plain section side rods retained by these locomotives from the slim boiler and later 'H' boiler periods. The remainder of the '378' series received new 'fluted' side-rods at the time they were fitted with saturated Belpaire boilers which coincided with the increase in wheelbase from 8 ft 6 in to 9 ft. No. 465 began as No. 232 in 1895, received an 'H' boiler in 1904, Marshal valve gear (!) in 1907 and assumed '378' style in 1910. It was scrapped late in 1931.

Authors' Collection

Plate 153. The very last '150' class 4—4—0 which was classified as class R (other than the '1667' class renewals, see *Plates 117-8*) was No. 2440, later No. 522, built by Sharp Stewart in 1899. By this time 'full' crimson livery was normal although there are few signs of extra decoration. The engine is depicted here about 1903; note the lamp iron positions. The 'Sharp Stewart' interpretation of the front frames should be compared with the 'Derby' version at *Plate 154*. No. 2440 received an 'H' boiler in 1907 and was an early renewal to '483' type in 1912.

Authors' Collection

Plate 154. When photographed, '150' class 4—4—0 No. 207 was in its original condition as built in 1897 at Derby, having the 'Derby' frame shape with a 'D' boiler. The engine is in full livery with some added embellishments, e.g. double lining on the wheel centres, 'all round' sandbox lining, etc. It received an 'H' boiler in 1906, was renumbered 500 in 1907 and renewed as a '483' class locomotive in 1912.

Authors' Collection

150 CLASS

Summary

Built at Derby between 1896-1901, this series included the renewal of the '1667' class rebuilds (see page 93).
Original MR Nos. 1667-1676, renewed 1896-1901. 150/153-155, 204-209. Built 1897.
1907 Nos. in this order (all to LMS in 1923): 483-492, 493-496, 497-502.
Built by Sharp Stewart 1899 with D boilers. Class R.
Original MR Nos. 2421-2440.
1907 Nos. 503-522, all to LMS in 1923.
Both series had 3250 gallon tenders.

The '150' class of 7 ft engines was noteworthy for being the first new slim-boilered Johnson 4—4—0 to employ piston valves and this immediately imparted a changed visual appearance at the 'front end', the engines having deeper frames above the running plate (*Plate 154*). The Sharp Stewart 'build' displayed a slight variation in this deep frame shape ahead of the smokebox, having a 'cusp plus concave' curve rather than the reverse curve of the Midland-built series. In this, they rather matched the contemporary '115' class 4—2—2s which also showed two frame styles (see Chapter 7).

Included in this series were the 'renewals' of the old '1667' class (page 93) which, on re-appearing, also displayed the 'Derby' frame shape (*Plate 157*) and, as such, were indistinguishable from the parent type. This altered front end shape in either form made the engines somewhat more bulky in appearance than their ancestors and conceivably a bit less elegant. *En passant*, it seems likely that the first few '1667' class renewals came out slightly ahead of the 'built new' series but the whole group took its designation from the first *new* example.

Given their quite late appearance, there can be little doubt that most, if not all, displayed the more decorative variants of the full MR livery but one can never be 100% certain. Rebuilding to 'H' boiler form was a little later than for some of the 4—4—0 series (not much) and this undoubtedly explains why some of them received a new Deeley 'front end' while still in slim boiler form, occasionally including a new style repaint with old number and emblem (*Plate 157*). Renumbering seems to have taken place close to the date of 'H' boiler conversion — or, in a few instances, at the actual date of rebuilding.

The 'H' boilered version of the '150' class displayed the separate splashers of the '1738' class rebuilds (see page 95) rather than the combined splashers of the rebuilt '2183' class series (see page 109) and it rather seems that this separate splasher arrangement was adopted a little later in time.

Unusually, this group were all renewed very rapidly to the '483' class between 1912 and 1914 and none of them received the intermediate 'saturated' Belpaire boilers. It was, of course, one of this series which, when 'renewed', gave its number to the new superheated type (see also Chapter 6).

The 'H' boiler rebuilt version of the '150' class was given ED 41, renewals to '483' class going onto ED 69.

Plate 155. The '1667' class renewals to '150' class form were spread over the 1896-1901 period and No. 1670 was one of the last four in 1901. This view shows that, as renewed, the 'Derby' frame shape was adopted. It also reveals the final early 20th-century interpretation of the full (but *not* decorated) crimson livery. No. 1670 became No. 486 in 1907, received 'H' boiler in 1908 and was another early renewal to '483' class in 1912.

Authors' Collection

Plate 156. This view of one of Sharp Stewart series of '150' class known as class R engines, piloting an unidentified Belpaire from the '840' series (see Chapter 8), is of particular interest in giving a few visual clues to Midland locomotive matters c.1905. The engine, No. 2424 (later No. 506) has its number painted on the front buffer plank between the coupling and the 'R', along with the name of its home base Nottingham. This is a new variation to us. As the tender is lined at the panel edges (1904 and later) and the engine received an 'H' boiler in 1906, the picture must have been taken c.1904-6. If the buffer plank numbering shown here was an experiment, then the choice of smokebox numberplates which appeared in 1905 was obvious!
Authors' Collection

Plate 157. '1667' class renewal No. 1672 shows an interesting combination of pre-1907 number with large tender numerals and old emblem, together with a Johnson 'front end', chimney and continuous handrail plus a flat Deeley smokebox door. Note the power class 1 on the cabside, the rivets on the smokebox and lack of lining on the ends of the axles. Built at Derby in 1896 as one of the early renewals, it became No. 488 in 1907 and the following year received an 'H' boiler. Four years later this locomotive became a member of the '483' class and lasted until 1950 when it was withdrawn by BR as No. 40488.
National Railway Museum

Plate 158. Rebuilt '150' class No. 509 at Leicester on 28th December 1909 with both horizontal handrail and vertical handle on the slightly dished smokebox door. Built by Sharp Stewart in 1899 as class R No. 2427 (note the front frame shape), it received an 'H' boiler in 1906 and six years later was renewed to '483' class. As such it survived until 1957 when it was withdrawn by British Railways as No. 40509. Note also the position of the top lamp iron, c.f. *Plate 159*.   *V. R. Webster*

Fig. 30. ED41 was the 1910 Midland Railway diagram for the 'H' boiler rebuilds from the '150' class.

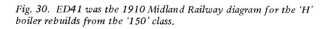

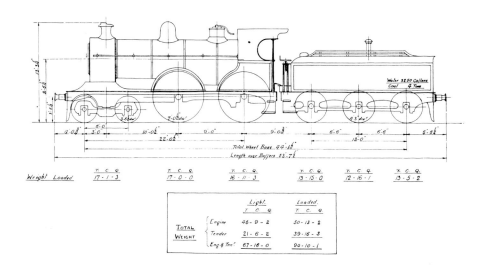

4-4-0 PASSENGER ENGINE

Plate 159. This view of 'H'-boilered '150' class No. 505 piloting 4—2—2 No. 646 (see Chapter 7) c.1909, makes a fascinating comparison with *Plate 156*, the latter taken only a few years earlier, and reveals how quickly the Midland's 'face' changed during the Edwardian period. No. 505 (ex-No. 2423), a Sharp Stewart engine of 1899, was given an 'H' boiler in 1908 with a flat door (c.f. *Plate 158*), but lower position for the upper lamp iron! Clearly, much experimentation was taking place at this time. The engine ran for only four years in this form, being renewed as a '483' type in 1912. *Authors' Collection*

Plate 160. Taken at Birmingham New Street on 21st August 1912, this picture of No. 498 shows an 'H'-boilered locomotive prior to being renewed as a '483' class locomotive the following year. Built in 1897 as '150' class No. 205, it received an 'H' boiler in 1906. Note the retention of the 'Derby'-shaped front frames and the later lamp iron position on a slightly dished door (see *Plates 158/159*). *W. L. Good*

Plate 161. '60' class 4—4—0 No. 63 seen here in works grey livery in 1898. This picture suggests two lines on the base of the dome, lining on the bottom of the sandbox and lining on the inside of the guard irons. Note the suggestion of black on the beading on the tender sides. No. 63 was fitted with an 'H' boiler in 1906, the year before it became No. 526. Renewal to '483' class was in 1913 and withdrawal as British Railways 40526 was in 1956.

National Railway Museum

Plate 162. '60' class No. 2591 also in works grey livery as built in 1901. This locomotive received an 'H' boiler in 1907, the year it was renumbered 553. In 1914 it was renewed to '483' class and lasted until 1958 when it was withdrawn as British Railways No. 40553. If the works finish is accurate, it rather demonstrates that this batch was given the fully lined paint scheme when first built. Note, for example, the sandboxes *vis-à-vis Plate 161.*   *Collection Bernard Mathews*

60 CLASS

Summary

Built at Derby 1898-1901.
Original MR Nos. 60-66, 93, 138-9, 151-152, 165-169, 805-809, 2636-2640.
1907 numbers 523-552, all to LMS in 1923.
Built by Neilson Reid & Co. 1901.   Class T.
Original MR Nos. 2591-2600.
1907 Nos. 553-562, all to LMS in 1923.
Both series coupled to 3500 gallon tenders.

The final slim-boilered Johnson 4−4−0s to enter service before the inevitable enlargement of the principal passenger locomotives were this series of 4−4−0s. Although roughly contemporary with the 'Princess of Wales' bogie singles, the '60' class engines were in fact the 4−4−0 equivalent of the '115' class 4−2−2s (Chapter 7) sharing the same 'E' boiler. The front framing was somewhat out of balance visually and it is surprising how a substantially similar frame shape could produce such elegance on a 4−2−2 yet appear rather clumsy on the 4−4−0 equivalent. Wheelbase went up again to 9 ft 6 in and this caused the downward sweep of the splashers between the driving wheels to have a much larger radius — very obvious in full side elevation, e.g. *Plate 162.* Like the '115' class singles, the '60' class 4−4−0s had

curved 'levers' to the Salter safety valves — a nice detail touch.

There is little doubt that all of them came out bedecked in the full final flowering of the Johnson Midland lake livery and, since they just preceded the introduction of the massive bogie tenders, the overall effect was not displeasing and nothing like as unfortunate as was the case with the final 4−2−2 series. However, the 3500 gallon tenders were, visually, still rather big in relation to the engines.

The whole series of 40 engines received 'H' boilers during the confused livery/numbering changeover and a few undoubtedly kept the old numbers with new style and livery (*Plate 167*). Funnily enough, with the 'H' boilers, the deep front frames gave a good visual balance to the engine, in spite of repeating the separate wheel splashers. In fact they were really quite handsome in this form. None received the short-lived saturated Belpaire boiler.

Like the preceding '150' class above, these engines were early candidates for the '483' type renewal which mostly took place during 1913 and 1914. No. 523 was the last to be renewed as a '483' class in 1915. Since this particular series of Johnson engines did at least have the same wheelbase as the '483' class, it seems possible that there may have been a bit more genuine rebuilding than was usual in this conversion to superheated form.

The 'H' boiler version was allocated ED 42, the '483' renewals to ED 69.

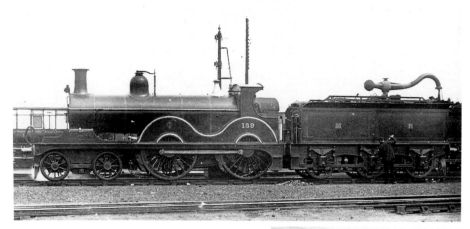

Plate 163. This picture of '60' class No. 139 (later No. 532) is not ideally clear, but nevertheless reveals, in service, the sort of embellishments suggested by *Plates 161/2.* The dome base carries a double line as do the wheel ends. The sandbox treatment cannot be verified but tender springs (*and* hangers) are fully lined. With this engine (built 1898) the 'H' boiler conversion was 1906, renewal to '483' type being in 1913.

Collection W. T. Stubbs

Plate 164. '60' class 4—4—0 No. 151 in original condition. Built in 1899, it was reboilered in 1907, the year it was renumbered 536, and six years later it became a '483' class member. It is seen here in a transitional stage to the Deeley livery with lining round the edge of the tender panels and some simplification below the footplate.

Authors' Collection

Plate 165. This view of No. 2596 (later No. 558 and built in 1901) shows a '60' class engine in a not uncommon transitional style c.1905-6. There are no significant anatomical changes but the engine has the new Deeley livery with old number and heraldic emblem. The boiler bands may be lined (this is unclear) and the number spacing is rather wide for the 'proper' Deeley livery (see Chapter 8, page 184) so we feel disposed to date this view as mid-1905. The engine received 'H' boiler in 1907 and was renewed to '483' class in 1913.

National Railway Museum

Plate 166. '60' class 4—4—0 No. 169 at Leeds Wellington. Unlike No. 2596 (*Plate 165*) this locomotive is in a hybrid physical condition — mostly Johnson but with the flat Deeley smokebox door. Becoming No. 542 in 1907, it received an 'H' boiler in 1908, and was renewed to '483' class in 1913 and withdrawn in 1959 as British Railways No. 40542. It is seen here with all boiler bands lined but otherwise in Deeley's simplified livery.   *J. H. Wright*

Plate 167. No. 2600, seen here in new Deeley livery, was, when new in 1901, the final slim-boilered Johnson 4—4—0 to be built. It was reboilered as pictured in 1907 and became a member of the '483' class in 1913. Its 1907 number was 562 and withdrawal was in 1955. Note the flat door compared with *Plate 168.*

National Railway Museum

Fig. 31. ED42. This 1910 Midland Railway diagram depicts the '60' class in 'H' boilered condition.

National Railway Museum

Plate 168. Rebuilt '60' class No. 525 with an 'H' boiler, photographed at Bristol Temple Meads. Derby-built, in 1898, as No. 62, this loco-motive received an 'H' boiler in 1907, the year it also became No. 525. In 1913 it was renewed as a '483' class member, and withdrawn by British Railways in 1957.

Collection Bernard Mathews

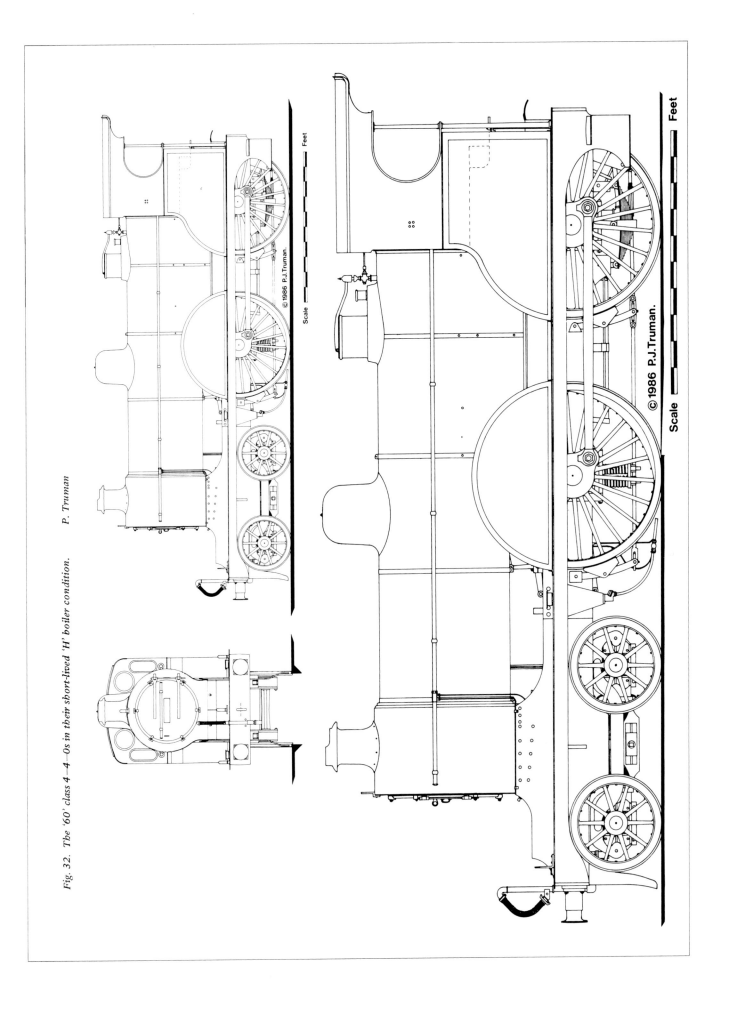

Fig. 32. The '60' class 4–4–0s in their short-lived 'H' boiler condition.   P. Truman

© 1986 P.J.Truman.

Scale ▬▬ Feet

©1986 P.J.Truman.

Scale ▬▬ Feet

2581 CLASS

Summary

Built by Beyer Peacock 1900.
Original MR Nos. 2581-2590. In 1907 they were renumbered 473-482.
All to the LMS in 1923.
Built with 3250 gallon tenders.

Throughout their life this batch of 10 locomotives were frequently referred to as 'like the M & GN C class engines' although Ahrons refers to them, quite correctly, as '1808 class (1900)'. This apparent backward step was one of necessity; in 1899 there was a great shortage of locomotives and Derby Works had no spare capacity. It would seem that it was quicker to add 10 more locomotives to an order

being built for the M & GN by Beyer Peacock than to get Beyers to build locomotives to what would have been to them a new design, so this is what happened. Therefore, at a time when the Midland Railway was building piston valve locomotives with a 9 ft 6 in driving wheelbase, an older and somewhat smaller design was built new by Beyer Peacock.

In due course five were renewed to '483' class after all had first been fitted with 'H' boilers. On 1st January 1923, five were in the '483' configuration, while the other five carried 'H' boilers. These five 'H'-boilered locomotives were all withdrawn between 1925 and 1927.

As far as livery is concerned, the available evidence suggests that when built they carried the full Crimson Lake livery and, with rebuilding to 'H' boiler commencing in 1904, they probably carried full livery until their next repaint, then assuming the Deeley simplified style.

Plate 169. Ten locomotives were built by Beyer Peacock in 1900 and No. 2588 was one of this series. Only five years later it assumed 'H' boiler form as seen here, still with essentially the 'old' livery, save for revised tender lining. Note the 'flower-pot' chimney (not always approved by contemporary observers) and the Johnson-style smokebox door. The engine became No. 480 in 1907 and was renewed as a '483' type in 1922.

National Railway Museum

Plate 170. In *Plate 99* we illustrated their original condition and in due course all were renewed, first to 'H' boiler and then five to '483' class as typified by this picture of 477 (originally MR No. 2585). Photographed at Holbeck in late Midland livery, this locomotive was to remain in service until 1951 when it was withdrawn as BR No. 40477. As such this '483' class renewal picture provides an introduction to Chapter 6 where we follow the story of the 'slim boiler' 4—4—0s in their final superheated form.   *Authors' Collection*

CONCLUSION

Having surveyed this incredible series of Johnson 4—4—0s and many of their subsequent ramifications to the end of the MR period, one is tempted to ask all sorts of questions, some of them a bit peripheral since it is all of no great consequence now! But it does strike us that of all the classes covered in this volume, this series of 4—4—0s poses the most queries.

Why, for example, did the company go to so many minute variations? There surely cannot have been all that much difference even between the first and last class, particularly compared with the great leap forward with the Compounds and Belpaires. Increasing the wheelbase, the change to piston valves and some of the 19th century boiler improvements probably made sense; but why such obsessive concern over the odd half-inch in wheel diameter, not to mention an apparent degree of indecision about what basic size the wheels should be? It is, of course, a marvellous detective story to unravel — assuming we have even got it right at all points — but one cannot but feel that, stripped of the minutiae, the MR could have probably got away with but four series of these engines, viz., 6 ft 6 in and 7 ft wheels with slide valves, repeated later with a long wheel-

base and a change to piston valves. This is, in practical terms, what happened, but Johnson undoubtedly additionally favoured the process of progressive refinement, in the small details. In this he can probably only be compared with Patrick Stirling (an earlier 'artist engineer' on the GNR) who never really favoured big engines, but never ceased to tinker about with every batch of his celebrated 4—2—2s before his successor, Ivatt, had to tackle the problem more fundamentally. The difference was that Johnson does not, intuitively, seem to have been a 'small engine' designer to quite the same degree — but then he may have had the MR Board of Directors to contend with!

The Midland Board in the 19th century, like its successor in the 20th, was concerned with economical operation and this meant the smallest engines which would do the job. The MR became the richest railway in the country so it obviously worked! Thus, Johnson had to work against this background of economical operation, which probably accounts for the style of his work. His mechanical judgement is said to have been superb and it is understood that for some years prior to the 'Belpaires' (Chapter 8), he had pressed the case for larger engines but was refused. The '60' class 4—4—0 was, however, along with the final 4—2—2s (see Chapter 7), about as big as he could get within existing policy and it probably needed even more persuasion before the Board would finally relent and let him 'build big'. When he did, the results were equally noteworthy (Chapters 8 & 9).

On the question of wheel diameter, there was, of course, in the 19th and early 20th centuries, a very strong 'horses for courses' philosophy which Johnson may have shared. The LNWR, for example, often built separate classes, differing mostly in driving wheel size, the smaller-wheeled versions being, ostensibly, for working north of Crewe. Generally, however, these classes were built in larger batches than was the case on the Midland — and the LNWR had in any case developed a sort of 'general utility' concept quite alien to Derby. Even if the Midland's idea had been to use the smaller-wheeled engines on the steeper graded sections (e.g. the 6 ft 6 in '2203' class for the Dore and Chinley line), it did not always work out that way since the 7 ft engines regularly worked over both the Peak Forest and the Settle-Carlisle as, indeed, did the even larger wheeled 4-2-2s in the former case.

Then there is the 'H' boiler business. There can be little doubt that these boilers 'beefed up' the inside cylinder 4-4-0s, yet they were frequently changed again long before many of them were life expired, sometimes for a saturated Belpaire version, and often for the far more expensive superheated '483' class renewal. However, the reduced royalty payable to the Superheater Co. for the rebuilt engines may have helped speed this process!

Not knowing the whole story, we mention these points in the hope that readers may feel sufficiently stimulated to let us know anything further which will help our understanding. After all, in the last analysis, a railway built its engines (in the case of the MR with infinite variety) not to delight enthusiasts, but to move traffic economically. Changes cost money so the MR (generally regarded as a well organised and profitable system) must have been convinced of its policy — and when commercial considerations are brought to bear on technical design, it is often the latter which suffers. Of course, it could also have been that as years went by the many and often seemingly quite trivial alterations which Johnson felt he had to make began to look progressively more inappropriate when their implications were viewed commercially. If so, this might just explain why Johnson, at last, was given some freedom to build the 'Belpaires'. It would also account for some of Deeley's activities and also, paradoxically, explain some of the stagnation of the Fowler period once a few reasonably successful and more powerful types had been developed. From about 1914 to 1932, there was not much sign that Derby wanted to do anything bigger or better if existing types would suffice, any more than it had done in the 1890s. A repeat of the Johnson era? Who knows?

All we can say is that it adds to the fascination if not always to the full understanding of those far off times. Meantime, we conclude this chapter with a brief class by class summary of the position in 1923 when the LMS inherited them and the next chapter takes a closer look at the '483' class renewal programme.

SUMMARY OF FORMER 'SLIM BOILER' 4-4-0s as at 1st January 1923

(to be read in conjunction with Tables 9 & 10)

Original Class	1907 Nos.	No. Built	No. at 1st January 1923 and remarks
1312 class	300-309	10	6 to LMS, all much 'as built'
1327 class	310-327	20	10 to LMS, all much 'as built'
1562 class	328-357	30	14 to LMS ('H' boiler)
			16 to LMS (saturated Belpaire)
1738 class	358-377	20	9 to LMS ('H' boiler)
			10 to LMS (saturated Belpaire)
			1 to LMS ('483' class renewal)
1808 class	378-402	25	4 to LMS ('H' boiler)
			16 to LMS (saturated Belpaires)
			5 to LMS ('483' class renewal)
2183 class	403-427	25	All to LMS as '483' class renewals
2203 class	428-472	45	17 to LMS ('H' boiler)
			2 to LMS (saturated Belpaire)
			26 to LMS ('483' class renewal)
2581 class	473-482	10	5 to LMS ('H' boiler)
			5 to LMS ('483' class renewal)
150 class	483-522	40	All to LMS as '483' class renewals
60 class	523-562	40	All to LMS as '483' class renewals

1923 Totals:

'Original' condition	16
'H' boiler (various classes)	49
Saturated Belpaire	44
'483' class renewals	142
	251

TABLE 12

DERBY ORDERS FOR 4-4-0 'H' BOILER to 'G7' SATURATED BOILER REBUILDS

Order No.	Date	Quantity	1907 Engine Nos.	
3462	1909	25	378-402	Not all rebuilt.
3544A	1909	30	328-357	Not all rebuilt.
3544B	1909	20	358-377	Not all rebuilt.
3602	1909	45	428-472	Only 460/5 rebuilt. Contemporary reports refer to them as 'Baby Belpaires'.

Source: S.L.S. Journal

TABLE 10: 4−4−0 SMALL BOILER LOCOMOTIVES
9' 0" COUPLED WHEELBASE ENGINES

1903 Diagram Page No.	Order No. or Class	Built by	Qty. built	Date of building	Pre 1907 numbers	1907 renumbering	Cylinders	BOILER						Working Pressure	FIREBOX		Total Heating Surface in sq. ft.	WHEELS			ENGINE WEIGHT		REMARKS
								Centre Line	Diameter	Length	Tubes	Diameter			Length	Grate Area in sq. ft.		Leading	Driving	Tyres	Empty	Loaded	
14	L	Sharp Stewart	20	1892	2183-2202	403-422	18½" × 26"	7' 4"	4' 2"	10' 4"	236	1¼"	160 PSI	6' 6"	19.5	1240	3' 6"	7' 0"	2¾"	41.17.1	44.19.0	2183 CLASS. All to H boiler. Then all to 483 class.
	1458	Derby	5	1896	156-160	423-427																Sometimes referred to as 156 class.
13	O	Sharp Stewart	15	1893	2203-2217	428-442	18½" × 26"	7' 4"	4' 2"	10' 4"	236/ 240	1¼"	160 PSI	6' 6"	19.5	1223	3' 3"	6' 6"	2¾"	39.17.1	42.19.2	2203 CLASS. All to H boiler. Then many to 483 class.
	1235	Derby	10	1894	184-199	443-462																
	1276	Derby	10	1894	161-164																	
	1410	Derby	10	1895	230-239	463-472																
15	1460	Derby	5	1896/7	1672, 1675, 1668, 1667, 1676	488, 491, 484, 483, 492	19" × 26"	7' 7"	4' 2"	10' 4"	236	1¼"	160 PSI	6' 6"	19.5	1205	3' 6"	7' 0"	2¾"	41.10.2	44.17.3	150 CLASS. All to H boiler. Then all to 483 class.
	1597	Derby	10	1897	204-209 150/3/5	493-502																Nos 1667-76 officially renewals of 1667 class, see table 9, but were in effect new engines which carried the old numbers.
	1707	Derby	2	1898	1669/1671	485, 487																
	2072	Derby	3	1901	1670/73/74	486, 489, 490																
10	R	Sharp Stewart	20	1899	2421-2440	503-522	18½" × 26"	7' 7"	4' 2"	10' 4"	236	1¼"	170 PSI	6' 6"	19.5	1205	3' 6"	7' 0"	2¾"	41.17.1	44.19.0	2421 CLASS. All to H boiler. Then all to 483 class. Ahrons recorded them as a variant of the 150 class and we treat them as such in the class summary.

9' 6" COUPLED WHEELBASE ENGINES

12	1635	Derby	10	1898	60-66, 93, 138/9	523-542	See remarks	7' 8½"	4' 2"	10' 6"	236	1¼"	170 PSI	7' 0"	21.3	1233	3' 6½"	7' 0½"	3"	42.3.2	45.14.2	60 CLASS. Ahrons records them all built with 19½" × 26" cyls. The diagrams show 166-169 with 19" × 26". All to H boiler then all to 483 class
	1834	Derby	10	1899	67-69, 151/2, 165-169																	
9	T	Neilsons	10	1901	2591-2600	553-562	19" × 26"	7' 8¾"	4' 2"	10' 6"	230	1⅛"	170 PSI	7' 0"	21.3	1205	3' 6½"	7' 0½"	3"	43.14.1	47.4.0	"2591 CLASS" but regarded by Ahrons as 60 class as indeed we do in the class summaries.
	2041	Derby	10	1901	805-809 2636-2640	543-552																Summaries. Principal Source 1903 Midland Railway Diagrams

TABLE 11: 4−4−0 H BOILER REBUILDS OF THE 6' 6" COUPLED WHEEL LOCOMOTIVES

1903 Diagram Page No.	Order No. or Class	Driving wheelbase	Date of rebuild	Number of engines	Pre 1907 numbers	1907 renumbering	Cylinders	BOILER						Working Pressure	FIREBOX		Total Heating Surface in sq. ft.	WHEELS			ENGINE WEIGHT		REMARKS
								Centre Line	Diameter	Length	Tubes	Diameter			Length	Grate Area in sq. ft.		Leading	Driving	Tyres	Empty	Loaded	
83	2675 rebuilds	8' 6"	1904	25	11, 14, 80-87, 1808-1822	378-402	18" × 26"	8' 3"	4' 8"	10' 5¹³⁄₁₆"	258	1¾"	175 PSI	7' 0"	21.1	1427.9	3' 3"	6' 6"	2¾"	43.2.2	47.12.2	
84	2675A rebuilds	8' 6"	1904	10	2581-2590	473-482	18½" × 26"	8' 3"	4' 8"	10' 5¹³⁄₁₆"	258	1¾"	175 PSI	7' 0"	21.1	1427.9	3' 3"	6' 6"	2¾"	43.8.2	47.12.2	
85	2676 rebuilds	9' 0"	1904	45	184-199, 161-164, 203-239, 2203-2217	443-462 463-472 428-442	18½" × 26"	8' 3"	4' 8"	10' 5¹³⁄₁₆"	258	1¾"	175 PSI	7' 0"	21.1	1427.9	3' 3"	6' 6"	2¾"	44.7.3	48.6.1	
																							Midland Railway Derby works orders.

NOTE: The next order shown in the Diagram Book was 0/3021 for engines Nos. 156-160, 2183-2202 but regrettably no dimensions were recorded and readers are referred to the Diagrams of H boiler rebuilds, saturateds and Belpaire boiler rebuilds within the class chapter. However, many years ago the SLS Journal published details of Derby works order rebuilds and this information is given below. It covers all the remaining 'slim boiler' Johnson locomotives which were to receive H boilers.

Date of order	Qty	Order No	Pre 1901 Eng Nos	1907 Eng Nos	
1903	30	2676A	1562-81 1657-66	328-357	To H boiler.
1903	20	2676B	1738-1757	358-377	To H boiler.
1906	40	3021A	1667-76,150/3-5 204-9, 2421-2440	483-522	To H boiler. To H boiler.
1906	40	3021B	60-66, 93 138/9 67-69 151/2 165-9, 805-9 2591-2600 2636-2640	523-562	
1905	30	3021	2183-2202 156-160	403-427	

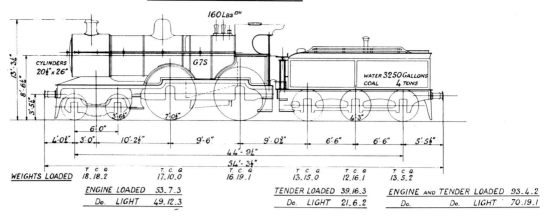

N⁰ 2 CLASS SUPER^{HTR} PASSENGER
BETⁿ N⁰S 403−562

160 LBS □''

CYLINDERS
20⅛" x 26"

G7S

WATER 3250 GALLONS
COAL 4 TONS

13'-3¾"
8'-6"
3'-5¾"

3'-6½"
7'-0⅜"
4'-3"

6'-0"
4'-0½" 3'-0" 10'-2½" 9'-6" 9'-0½" 6'-6" 6'-6" 5'-5½"

44'-9½"
54'-3¾"

| WEIGHTS LOADED | T C Q 18.18.2 | T C Q 17.10.0 | T C Q 16.19.1 | T C Q 13.15.0 | T C Q 12.16.1 | T C Q 13.5.2 |

ENGINE LOADED 53.7.3   TENDER LOADED 39.16.3   ENGINE AND TENDER LOADED 93.4.2
Do. LIGHT 49.12.3   Do. LIGHT 21.6.2   Do. Do. LIGHT 70.19.1

Fig. 33. ED69 was raised in 1919 for the '483' class renewals. It obviously preceded the decision to renew Nos. 328-402 and does not allow for the 3,500 gallon tenders fitted to Nos. 523-62. Otherwise, in conjunction with Fig. 34, it gives an accurate representation of this familiar type.

National Railway Museum

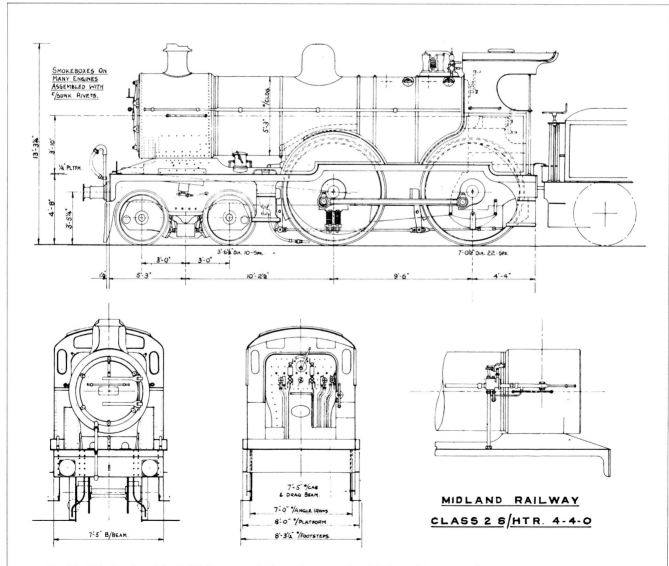

SMOKEBOXES ON
MANY ENGINES
ASSEMBLED WITH
C/SUNK RIVETS.

⅝"CLDG
5'-3"

13'-3¾"
3'-10"
¼ PLTFM.
4'-8"
3'-5¼"

3'-6½" DIA. 10-SPK.   7'-0⅜" DIA. 22-SPK.

3'-0" 3'-0"
1½" 5'-3" 10'-2½" 9'-6" 4'-4"

7'-5" B/BEAM.

7'-5" º/CAB
& DRAG BEAM.
7'-0" º/ANGLE IRONS
8'-0" º/PLATFORM
8'-3½" º/FOOTSTEPS.

MIDLAND RAILWAY
CLASS 2 S/HTR. 4-4-0

Fig. 34. This drawing of the '483' class renewals shows them in their original condition. Later the Ramsbottom safety valves were exchanged for Ross Pops, the bogie brakes were removed and they acquired Stanier and British Railways replacement chimneys.

K. C. Woodhead

CHAPTER SIX

FOWLER '483' CLASS 4-4-0 RENEWALS

Plate 171. At the time this photograph was taken, No. 483 was a rebuilt '150' class with an 'H' boiler. It was a pioneer member of the '150' class series and became the locomotive to give the new class of superheated locomotives their identity, even though it was not the first of the class to be renewed (see text). Indeed it could be considered to date back to the '1667' class, its pre-1907 number 1667 was a 'renewed' member of that class (see Chapter 5, page 121). *Authors' Collection*

THE Fowler era of the Midland (and early LMS) is not often given a particularly good press and there may be some sort of rough justice in this retrospective view, but in one respect it was significant. It saw the introduction of superheating on quite a number of the passenger engines and thus enabled the Midland to carry on with smaller locomotives than might otherwise have been the case — doubtless to the satisfaction of the company accountant, and fully in accordance with traditional MR practice of not building over-large locomotives.

Trials on many railways during the early part of the 20th century had revealed the economic benefits of superheating, coupled with enhanced output. It is not, therefore, altogether surprising that in the fiercely competitive environment of the pre-group period, the beneficial effect of superheating was applied first to the 'flagship' operations rather than the 'bread and butter' tasks. This was certainly true of the Midland which clearly regarded superheating as more relevant to its passenger operations than on the freight side where, until the class 4 0-6-0 began to be built in quantity towards the end of the pre-group period, saturated steam ruled the roost.

In consequence, and from about the end of the Edwardian period, the Midland commenced the superheating of its fleet of passenger engines. Attention was confined entirely to the 4—4—0s, the 2—4—0 and 4—2—2

arrangements being presumably regarded as obsolescent if not obsolete and, moreover, often incapable of accepting bigger boilers; but there appears to have been a degree of half-heartedness about the whole business, which is rather strange in retrospect. It is possible that increased boiler maintenance costs and problems of cylinder lubrication could also have played their part. For example, the superheating of the Compounds and Belpaires (see Chapters 8 & 9) went on well into LMS days and took rather longer to achieve than one feels would have been the case if the Midland was *totally* convinced of its virtue. But the smaller inside cylinder 4—4—0s, discussed in the previous chapter, were treated differently.

From 1912 onwards, commencing with No. 494, the Midland, under Fowler's directions, embarked upon what amounted to a total reconstruction of its 'second line' 4—4—0 stock to the superheated form. By 31st December 1922 (at the start of the first full year of the LMS), no fewer than 142 out of 251 engines had been renewed (see Vol. 1, page 51) a far more rapid and drastic programme than was ever carried out in the more powerful (and prestigious) Class 3 and Class 4 engines. One can only wonder why this was so.

The answer would seem to be found in the economics of the railway itself. The company had embarked on its great structural shake-up in 1907 (control, reporting, rationalisa-

Plate 172. Class 2 4-4-0 No. 534 at Kentish Town in July 1921. Built at Derby in 1899 as '60' class in 1913. Withdrawal was in 1959 by British Railways as No. 40534. it received an 'H' boiler in 1906 and was renewed to the '483' class in

Collection Bernard Mathews

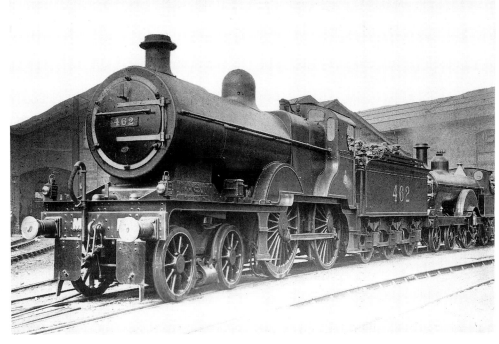

Plate 173. Former '2203' class 4—4—0 No. 462 is seen here in immaculate condition. Built at Derby in 1894 as No. 164, it received an 'H' boiler in 1905 and was renumbered in 1907. Renewal to '483' class was in 1916 and it lasted until 1951 when, as No. 40462, it was withdrawn.
Collection Bernard Mathews

tion of activity, etc.) which, as we have stated more than once, 'spun-off' into the realm of locomotive livery, numbering and decoration. Additionally, it also affected the actual *providing* of motive power as it did also, in succession, on the LMS.

Engines cost money, expenditure eats into profits and profits pay dividends to shareholders. There was, therefore, every incentive to keep engine costs down, so rigid standardisation may well have seemed a cost-effective solution. Deeley more or less started the business, Fowler carried it on and, of course, the LMS (under both Fowler and particularly, Stanier) took it further than on any other system. One of the first fruits of this 'new' approach was, we feel, the '483 class renewal programme amongst the class 1/2 4—0s.

But why start with the *lower* powered engines? The answer, we think, comes back to superheating. If, by superheating the older engines, the company could achieve better economy and performance, it might just get away *without* having to build too many new, bigger and more powerful engines, except for the really heavy jobs. It is a matter of history that this is precisely what happened. The 'little and often' policy of the MR passenger operations has frequently been commented upon by many observers and it is not too fanciful to postulate that the '483' class helped to make it possible in the early 20th century, just as Johnson's excellent efforts had done in the 19th.

They were very good and economical engines, given their smallish size, the LMS went on building them (in the form of the standard class 2 4—4—0) and no less an authority than E. S. Cox has written of their surprising economy in

maintenance and so forth. In fact, the cost of maintaining a class 2 was regarded as the 'norm' against which other classes were assessed when Lord Stamp instituted his even tighter accounting procedures on the LMS during the late 1920s.

The '483' class engines were, unquestionably 'accountancy rebuilds' (effectively new locos 'disguised' to gain routine expenditure approval from the board). In other words, they were, in effect, one for one replacements of the earlier Johnson types, and in all significant respects were new machines. They certainly had new frames and cylinders (the basic 'heart' of the locomotive) and since the 'G7S' boiler was, by definition, a new unit, and the cab was of new style, there was precious little of the original left, save for its running number! However, some components could perhaps be re-used, above all the existing tenders; so doubtless economies (on paper) were made. Moreover, as previously stated, rebuilds (however defined) attracted lower royalties to the Superheater Company than new engines.

Be that as it may, there is little doubt that Derby eventually intended to renew the whole series from No. 328-562. Works orders were issued for this renewal, generally based on the old 'class' batches (see Chapter 5) and only the very first of the Johnson 4—4—0s (Nos. 300-27) were exempted; but it was planned to give some of them new frames and all of them, of course, ultimately sported 'standard' Deeley/ Fowler 'front ends'.

It is interesting to list the order in which the various Johnson classes were *intended* to be renewed and this is given overleaf (Table 13).

Plate 174. No. 485 in Midland livery was originally '150' class No. 1669, renewed in 1898, and rebuilt with an 'H' boiler in 1907 before being renewed as a '483' in 1913. Note the bogie brakes and 3,250 gallon tender (see also No. 553 Plate 176).   Authors' Collection

TABLE 13
ORDERS FOR H BOILERS & G7 SUPERHEATED BOILER REBUILDS
(See Table 10 in Chapter 5 for the original building dates)

Derby Order No.	Locomotive Numbers (1907 Nos. used throughout)	Rebuild Details
0/3021A	483-582	To H Boiler
0/3942	483-582	To G7 Boiler (superheated)
0/3021B	523-562	To H Boiler
0/4116	523-562	To G7 Boiler (superheated)
0/3021	403-427	To H Boiler
0/4311	403-427	To G7 Boiler (superheated)
0/2676	428-472 (except 460 & 465)	To H Boiler
0/3602	460 & 465	To G7 Boiler (saturated)
0/2675A	473-482	To H Boiler
0/4476	428-482 (plus S & DJR 67-69 see Vol. 5)	To G7 Boiler (superheated)
0/2670A	328-357	To H Boiler
0/3544A	328-357	To G7 Boiler (saturated)
0/2670B	358-377	To H Boiler
0/3544B	358-377	To G7 Boiler (saturated)
0/2675	378-402	To H Boiler
0/3402	378-402	To G7 Boiler (saturated)
0/5664 superseded 0/4476	328-482	To G7 Boiler (superheated)

From this list several conclusions can be drawn. Firstly, the renewals were roughly in reverse order to the original 'build' regardless of subsequent 'H' or 'G7' (saturated) boilers. This may have reflected a genuine wish to rebuild, especially in the case of the newer engines, rather than to completely renew. Secondly, it infers that even with 'H' boilers, the newer Johnson designs were not quite 'up to it', thus reinforcing Johnson's apparent desire to build bigger engines at an earlier time. Thirdly, it suggests that even though the basic 'engine' part was often older, those which had received saturated Belpaire boilers were probably better than the 'H' boiler versions and this was borne out in fact. The 'G7' boiler was only a few years newer than the 'H' type but those engines so fitted lasted considerably longer, no doubt due to the availability of replacements.

It is, of course, a matter of history that this renewal programme was not completed by the end of MR days and at page 134 in Chapter 5 we have already given the 'state of play' in 1923. What does seem rather surprising to us is that having brought the '483' programme to a conclusion in 1924, it was another four years before the LMS decided to start again with a series of *new* engines of broadly the same type (eventually LMS Nos. 563-700). Given the 'accountancy' mind of the LMS, it might have been more logical to 'renew' all the remaining saturated engines (some 109 in total at the beginning of 1923) and reduce the 'new' build to considerably less than 100. However, the saturated Belpaire rebuilds, particularly the '378' class, were obviously good enough to keep going for a time with their 'G7'

Plate 175. No. 502 was originally '150' class No. 209 built in 1897, rebuilt with an 'H' boiler in 1906 and renewed as '483' class in 1912, being withdrawn as No. 40502 in 1961. This locomotive was used for royal train working and for some reason did not carry a number on the tender but did carry the royal cypher on the cabside as seen in the picture. We believe the colour of the top half of the buffer plank was white but we are not sure why it was so painted. In addition, it should be noted that the buffer plank does not carry the initials 'MR'.

National Railway Museum

Plate 176. Class 2 4—4—0 No. 553 at St. Pancras. This interesting picture was taken c.1923 and shows neither the initials 'MR' on the buffer plank nor crest on the cabside. Built as '60' class No. 2591 in 1901, it was rebuilt with an 'H' boiler in 1907 and renewed as a '483' class in 1914, being withdrawn as No. 40553 at the end of 1958. This engine was coupled to a 3,500 gallon tender, readily identified by the fact that the horizontal beading below the 'flare' and the top of the 'flare' itself are at a noticeably higher level (relative to the cabside) than on, say, No. 485 (*Plate 174*).

Authors' Collection

Plate 177. No. 419 is seen here in LMS pre-1928 livery. The plates attached to the front buffer plank were to prevent problems encountered when two locomotives working a train picked up water and the leading locomotive's overspill of water 'washed out' the oil on the bogie of the train locomotive! No. 419 was renewed as a '483' class locomotive in 1919 and withdrawn in 1955 after starting as '2183' class No. 2199 in 1892 and receiving an 'H' boiler in 1906.   *Authors' Collection*

boilers; so it ultimately transpired that the 328-482 series never contained a 'full house' of '483' renewals.

For the record, and presuming (as we believe to be the case) that the '483' class renewals mostly retained the original tenders of the Johnson classes, the tender 'split' was as follows.

Engines numbered up to No. 522 — 3250 gallon
Nos. 523-62   — 3500 gallon

So now, at last, we can turn to the engines themselves and their characteristics.

The class took its designation from the lowest numbered engine of the first complete Johnson series to be renewed (Nos. 483-522), although, in fact, No. 494 was the first *actual* renewal in 1912. They were, in effect, if not officially, the last 'new' design of express passenger engine to be built by the MR. The design took the 9 ft 6 in wheelbase of the Johnson '60' class and the slightly more favoured 7 ft driving wheel (in preference to 6 ft 8½ in or 6 ft 6 in) of the Johnson period, married it to a superheated version of the existing 'G7' boiler (already well-regarded) and the result was visually highly predictable. Fowler may have authorised it, but the visual effect was pure Deeley (*Fig. 34*).

The renewal was allocated ED 69 in the 1919 diagram book (*Fig. 33*) which was clearly raised before the decision to renew Nos. 328-402 was taken. As already explained, in the event, not too many engines below No. 403 were, in fact, renewed and the final example, No. 364, emerged in 1924.

Visually, the engines remained astonishingly consistent for the whole of their long lives. They were never, as far as we know, separated from the Johnson pattern 'flared' tenders during the LMS period, although some tender

changes must have taken place from time to time. In BR days it was different; we have recorded 40453/87/504/11/37/40/42, all with straight-sided Fowler tenders. The more significant changes are given at the caption to *Fig. 34* and it only remains to review their basic decorative state.

All of them, before 1923, were given the Deeley red livery, typified by *Plate 173*. During early LMS days this livery was maintained, with the LMS emblem replacing that of the Midland (*Plate 178*), and thereafter (1928 onwards) they gradually assumed the LMS black liveries and the BR continuation thereof. By this time they had been joined by the LMS standard version (page 139) and were regarded as an LMS 'standard' type. As such, more details will be found in our companion volume* and we have no desire to indulge in superfluous 'padding' in the form of repetition here.

The last Midland-built '483' class 4-4-0 did not disappear until 1962. By then steam in general was in its last years, so one might reasonably conclude that for all the criticisms of latter-day Midland locomotive practice, many of them perhaps quite justifiable, the '483' class 4-4-0s did not really qualify for this sort of opprobium. They were pretty good engines and generally earned their keep over a period of some 50 years, even if not in the most puissant category.

---

* *An Illustrated History of LMS Locomotives, Vol. 4.*

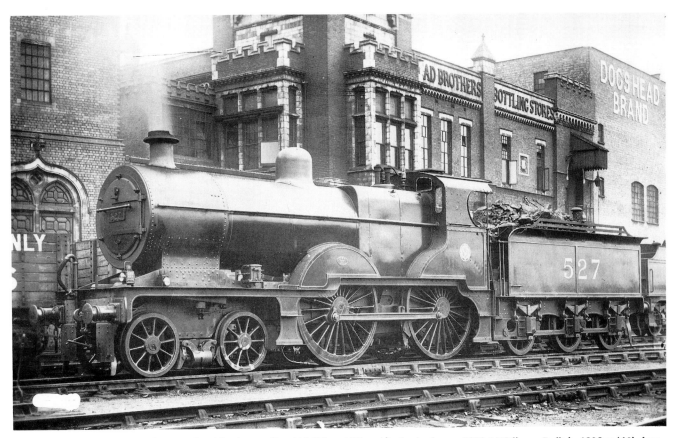

Plate 178. No. 527 shows the opposite side view to No. 419 (*Plate 177*) and is also in the pre-1928 LMS livery. Built in 1898 as '60' class No. 64, an 'H' boiler was fitted in 1906 and the engine was renewed to '483' class in 1913. Withdrawal as BR No. 40522 was in 1956.

Authors' Collection

Plate 179. With an excursion number on the smokebox door, class 2P 4−4−0 No. 554 is seen at Tilbury in 1931 in black LMS livery with red lining. It is worth noting that No. 554 has had a 'bang' on the front left-hand side buffer but is otherwise in good condition. Originally '60' class No. 2592, it was built in 1901 and fitted with an 'H' boiler in 1908, renewed to '483' class in 1913 and withdrawn in 1949.

G. Coltas

Plate 180. This picture, taken at Derby on 11th October 1936, illustrates class 2P No. 495 in immaculate LMS lined black livery with gold characters, shaded red. It can be considered typical for the class during this period. Pop safety valves have now replaced the Ramsbottom type which, together with the chimney with capuchon, but the loss of bogie brakes, all combine to present a late 1930s view of the class. No. 495 started life as '150' class No. 154 in 1897, received its 'H' boiler in 1907, was renewed in 1912 and withdrawn as No. 40495 in 1957.

L. Hanson

Plate 181. Class 2P No. 409 in the late LMS era when equipped with an exhaust steam injector and running with a short Stanier chimney. No. 409 commenced life as '2183' class No. 2189 of 1892, was fitted with an 'H' boiler in 1906, renewed as a '483' class locomotive in 1919 and withdrawn in 1957. The livery illustrated was plain black with yellow characters, shaded red.

Authors' Collection

Plate 182. An early BR view taken at Derby in July 1948, showing class 2P No. 436 running as M436 in plain black livery. Built in 1893 as '2203' class No. 2211, No. 436 received an 'H' boiler in 1905, was renewed to '483' class in 1914 and withdrawn as BR No. 40436 in 1954. Note both the replacement Stanier chimney and flat-topped dome cover. *H. C. Casserley*

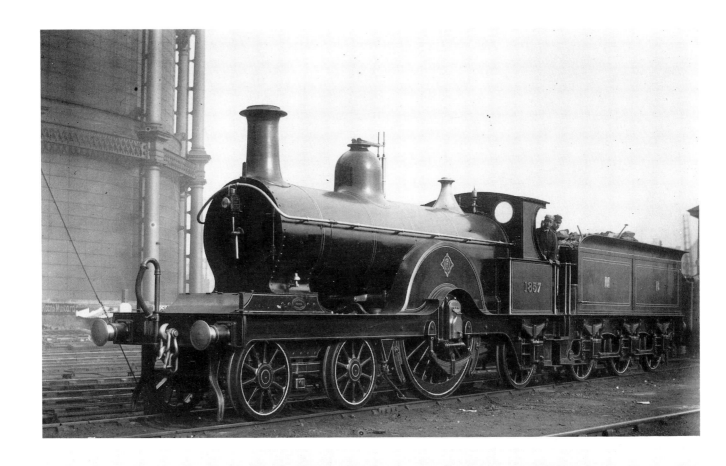

Plate 183. The '25' and '1853' classes compared. No. 1857 (top) is a member of the 7 ft 4 in driving wheel '25' class, while No. 1853 was the pioneer member of the '1853' class, whose driving wheels were two inches greater, and this, together with an extra half-inch diameter on the cylinders, gave rise to a new class description.

Authors' Collection

CHAPTER SEVEN

THE JOHNSON BOGIE SINGLES

Plate 184. 4—2—2 No. 1859 was built in 1889 as a member of the '25' class, becoming No. 616 in 1907. It was scrapped in 1922. This broadside view clearly shows the shallow front frames and underhung driving wheel spring of the first twenty-five Johnson singles.

Collection W. T. Stubbs

BEAUTY, so they say, is in the eye of the beholder, and it would be hard for us to start a review of the Midland's 4—2—2 engines without admitting that, like so many other enthusiasts, we have fallen under the spell of these oh so elegant machines. Mark you, we are in good company. C. Hamilton-Ellis made the point a generation ago, E. H. Ahrons and J. N. Maskelyne did so even further back in time, while in the present day, no less an authority than the Keeper of the National Railway Museum has gone on public record as stating that the preserved MR No. 673 is the 'most beautiful and elegant' of all the engines in the National Collection — and he is a GWR devotee.

However, before coming to the main subject of this chapter, it is perhaps necessary to state why we have chosen to interrupt the 4—4—0 story (Chapters 5 and 6; 8 and 9) with the account of the bogie 'singles'. It is, most certainly, *not* because the Midland chose to number them between the Class 2 and Class 3 4—4—0s in 1907!

The reasons are more fundamental. During the latter part of the 19th century, Samuel Johnson built 2—4—0, 4—4—0 and 4—2—2 designs, all sharing much detail in common; but it was not a simple business of progressing from 2—4—0, 4—2—2 to 4—4—0. In fact, the actual sequence was approximately: 2—4—0, 4—4—0, 2—4—0, 4—4—0, 4—2—2, 4—4—0, 4—2—2, 4—4—0, almost as though the 'old

man' could not quite make up his mind what to do — but we don't really believe this!

Now Johnson was a Yorkshireman as, indeed is one of the authors (!) and the White Rose county is not renowned for its indecision (except during the 1970s and early 1980s on the cricket-field!) and we cannot seriously believe that this great man did not know what he wanted to build. Nevertheless, it is a somewhat curious fact, as has been shown in both Chapters 4 and 5, that for more than twenty years the Midland 'tinkered about' with subtle changes in express passenger tender engines in a manner quite alien to the almost ruthless standardisation it adopted with the passenger tank and freight engine series. It may well be utterly insignificant, but we find it fascinating and consider that it is quite impossible to analyse the Johnson 4—2—2s without relating them to the other designs instigated by the Midland locomotive chief.

The ramifications in the 2—4—0 and the Class 1/2 4—4—0 area have, of course, already been considered, so it seemed to us more logical to consider first the remaining slim-boilered engines of the Johnson era (i.e. 4—2—2s) before going on to the 20th century developments as exemplified by the Class 3 and Class 4 4—4—0s. The Johnson 4—2—2s were undoubtedly part of the 19th century story so it seems best to include them here.

Plate 185. No. 1867 is visually identical to No. 1859 (*Plate 184*) and its 2 in. larger driving wheels, making it '1853' class, are not instantly obvious. No. 1867 was built in 1890, became No. 624 in 1907, and was scrapped in 1922. It was the last of the singles to employ the underhung driving wheel spring.

Collection W. T. Stubbs

The renewal of interest by the MR in the single driving wheel locomotive in 1887 was undoubtedly prompted by the development of steam sanding by the then Derby Works Manager, Mr. Francis Holt. Although Johnson had been one of the first British engineers to embrace the 4—4—0 concept (as early as 1876), one senses that, as we have inferred in Chapter 5, he was, at times, prepared to let his artists and perhaps his own personal inclination take precedence, provided it made engineering sense. There seems no real doubt that he would be more than happy to meet the Board's wish for smallish engines and 'get away with' a single driver provided it could pull the trains. Steam sanding gave him the spur he needed. Moreover, there were a few quite relevant technical considerations too — and at this

Plate 186. This view clearly demonstrates the visual changes in the next series of 35 singles, starting with No. 1868 (later 625) and ending with No. 178 illustrated, later No. 659. The heavier front frames and coil springs to the driving wheel immediately differentiate the series from the '25' and '1853' class engines; yet the later series was still officially '1853' class. This is the style we have referred to as 'modified 1853' class. The view was taken at Nottingham in 1906, just prior to renumbering and shows some simplification of lining compared with the pre-1904 days. No. 178, as No. 659, was withdrawn in 1925. It had been built in 1893 as the last slide valve single.

Collection W. T. Stubbs

Plate 187. The '179' class 4–2–2 saw the introduction of piston valves on the singles, ten engines being built to this variation. No. 181, illustrated, built in 1893, became No. 662 in 1907 and lasted until 1926. The engine is carrying full, but not decorated, crimson livery, the date of the picture being c.1905.

Collection W. T. Stubbs

Plate 188. '115' class No. 123 (later No. 677) shows off to perfection the balanced lines of the second piston-valve series of 4—2—2s. Note the changed front frame shape compared with the '179' class. The engine carries a full Deeley livery with the old type heraldic emblem, a state it probably displayed c.1905-7.

Authors' Collection

point a slight digression into locomotive power output and associated matters seems relevant.

The power of a steam locomotive, in the sense of its tractive effort, has nothing to do with the *number* of driving wheels, merely their size in relation to cylinders and boiler pressure. Thus, for example, the first Ivatt 4—4—2s, for the GNR, were no more powerful (nominally) than some of the preceding singles! However, it is no good developing power at the cylinders if the wheels lack adhesion; so by the later Victorian period, many engines had adopted coupled wheels, so that the greater adhesive weight possible on multiple axles would enable power to be transferred more effectively to the rails.

There was, however, a price to pay.

Patrick Stirling (on the GNR) had, to put it simply, somewhat eschewed the coupled wheel concept because he felt the engine, constrained by coupling rods, tended to run like a man with his 'breeks doon', as he is alleged to have put it. He was worried about the loss of efficiency in the necessarily increased number of bearing surfaces. Moreover, metallurgy was, as yet, fairly unsophisticated. The speed of a locomotive is governed by the rate of revolution of its driving wheels and the larger these latter features are, the fewer revolutions needed (in a given time span) to produce a desired speed. Each revolution of the driving wheel is

achieved by one 'to-and-fro' action of the piston within the cylinder so a large driving wheel involves less 'to-and-fro' movements in a given time within the cylinder to produce a particular speed, for a given piston stroke.

Now in the later 19th century, cylinder lubrication was quite a serious problem, as were stresses within metal itself — so it was considered worthwhile to try and keep piston speeds down. However, the operators wanted to increase train speeds, so the natural tendency was to increase the size of the (often single) driving wheels to keep the piston speeds down. The operators, however, also wanted to increase loads, and the single driver type then began to meet adhesion problems, regardless of speed, thus leading to the 4-coupled philosophy at the expense of sheer wheel size. This fact, of course, had long been appreciated on the freight side, but there, of course, speeds were much lower so it was acceptable.

However, and there is no reason to suppose that Johnson thought differently from his contemporaries, there was always the underlying 'feeling' that a single driver engine was a more free-running machine if only it could 'keep its feet'. Steam sanding must, therefore, have seemed a well worthwhile idea and, in consequence, the Midland, under Johnson, resumed the building of 'singles' after a gap of more than twenty years since Kirtley had built his final

2—2—2 engines. It would undoubtedly suit the MR Board's policy (see Chapter 5, page 133), the boilers, cylinders and motion could be to modern standards, yet the free running capability of the single could be exploited in terms of lower piston speeds and fewer moving parts. Driving wheels could be made a little larger without serious loss of power provided the engine could 'grip' the rails) so it probably all seemed most logical. What is known is that the MR removed the coupling rods from some four-coupled locomotives in 1885 to try out the steam sanding, and it seems to have worked.

We should, perhaps, apologise to those who have a good engineering background for the above excursion outside the realms of pure Midland matters; but one of us is an ex-engineman, the other has to explain these things for a living, and there may just be a few readers who have wondered,

like ourselves, why these things happened — so we hope we may be forgiven for offering a simple explanation.

It is, of course, nigh on 100 years ago that these considerations were uppermost in the mind of the Midland Railway Company and its Locomotive Superintendent, so we can never be sure precisely *why* Johnson elected to build his sublime series of engines. Let us just be thankful that he did and, moreover, even more thankful that one has survived for us to see. Collectively, they surely represent one of the aesthetic high-points in British engineering — and they weren't bad engines either!

Their building began in 1887 and continued until 1900, by which time, 95 were in service. They were introduced, intermixed with the contemporary 4—4—0s and shared many points in common. Eventually five varieties were represented, each a development of the previous version;

Plate 189. The last series of ten 4—2—2s, the so-called 'Princess of Wales' or '2601' class, had a 'drop' to the front buffer plank and the dome set centrally over the driving wheels. No. 22 was the penultimate example, becoming No. 693 in 1907 and being scrapped in 1921. The first appeared at the end of 1899 and the rest were built in 1900 and had a relatively short life. No. 22 is finished in full, but non-decorated crimson livery.   *National Railway Museum*

but, as with the 4—4—0s (see page 133), one sometimes wonders why some of the more minor variations were countenanced.

Essentially, as with the 4—4—0s, there were two main groups, the slide valve and the piston valve series. This obviously made engineering sense once a piston valve could be adequately lubricated, but the divisions within this two-fold categorisation are a bit more subtle. Two or three varieties, depending on definition, existed within the slide valve engines and three in the piston valve continuation. Examples of each of the series are shown at *Plates 184-189.*

At this point, and before summarising each series separately, a brief preliminary note is necessary for the slide valve batches (1907 Nos. 600-59). Many sources divide them into two classes, the '25' class (with 7 ft 4 in wheels and 18 in cylinders) and the '1853' class (7 ft 6 in wheels, 18½ in cylinders). This seems reasonable enough, but within the latter group, Nos. 625 upwards displayed markedly changed anatomy which made them visually more different from the '1853' class prototype than the latter was from the original '25' class. Moreover, this differentiation was reflected in the MR 1907 renumbering. In consequence we have chosen to put the '25' and '1853' classes together, as indeed did the Midland Railway (see Table 14), being visually almost indistinguishable, and to regard the engines from No. 625 upwards as modified '1853' class. We hope that our analysis will clarify the issue and at Table 14, a preliminary summary is given.

TABLE 14: JOHNSON BOGIE SINGLES

1903 Diagram Page No.	Order No. or Class	Built by	Qty. built	Date of building	Pre 1907 numbers	1907 renumbering	Cylinders	BOILER Centre Line	BOILER Diameter	BOILER Length	BOILER Tubes	BOILER Diameter	Working Pressure	FIREBOX Length	FIREBOX Grate Area in sq. ft.	Total Heating Surface in sq. ft.	WHEELS Leading	WHEELS Driving	WHEELS Trailing	WHEELS Tyres	ENGINE WEIGHT Empty	ENGINE WEIGHT Loaded	REMARKS
5	655	Derby	5	1887	25-29	600-604	18″ × 26″	7′ 5½″	4′ 2″	10′ 4″	244	1⅝″	160 PSI	6′ 6″	19.6	1240	3′ 6″	7′ 4″	4′ 2½″	2¾″	40.7.2	43.9.3	25 CLASS. Slide valves. Start of drumhead smokebox construction by MR. Plate spring to driving axle.
	745	Derby	3	1888	30-32	605-607																	
	796	Derby	5	1889	1854-1857	610-614																	
	809	Derby	5	1889/90	37, 1858-1862	615-619																	
5	745	Derby	2	1889	1853, 34	608-609	18½″ × 26″	7′ 6½″	4′ 2″	10′ 4″	244	1⅝″	160 PSI	6′ 6″	19.6	1240	3′ 6″	7′ 6″	4′ 4″	2¾″	40.7.2	43.9.3	1853 CLASS. Modification of 25 class with larger cylinders and driving wheels. However, the MR did not place these engines onto a separate diagram. Plate spring to driving axle.
	809	Derby	5	1889/90	1863-1867	620-624																	
4	935	Derby	5	1891	1868-1872	625-629	18½″ × 26″	7′ 6½″	4′ 2″	10′ 4″	240/244	1⅝″	160 PSI	6′ 6″	19.6	1240	3′ 6″	7′ 6″	4′ 4″	2¾″	41.1.0	44.3.0	MODIFIED 1853 CLASS. As 1853 class but modified by coil spring suspension to driving axle and altered framing at the front end.
	998	Derby	10	1892	8, 122, 20, 145, 24, 33, 35, 36, 38, 39	630-639																	
	1080	Derby	10	1892	4, 16, 17, 94, 97, 98, 99, 100, 129, 133	640-649																	
	1094	Derby	10	1893	149, 170-178	650-659																	
3	1124	Derby	5	1893	179-183	660-664	19″ × 26″	7′ 7″	4′ 2″	10′ 4″	240	1⅝″	160 PSI	6′ 6″	19.6	1223	3′ 6″	7′ 6″	4′ 4″	2¾″	41.1.3	44.4.0	179 CLASS. First use of piston valves on locomotives on the MR. Coil spring to driving axle.
	1454	Derby	5	1896	75-77, 79, 88	665-669																	
2	1474	Derby	5	1896/7	115-119	670-674	19½″ × 26″	7′ 10″	4′ 2″	10′ 6″	236	1⅝″	170 PSI	7′ 0″	21.3	1233	3′ 9½″	7′ 9″	4′ 4″	2¾″	43.14.3	47.2.1	115 CLASS. Enlargement of 179 class. Coil spring to driving axle.
	1659	Derby	10	1899	120-121, 123-128, 130-131	675-684																	
1	1926	Derby	10	1899/00	2601-5, 19-23	685-694	19½″ × 26″	8′ 1″	4′ 1⅞″	10′ 6″	228	1⅝″	180 PSI	8′ 0″	24.5	1217	3′ 10″	7′ 9½″	4′ 4½″	3″	46.13.1	50.3.0	2601 CLASS. Final development. Fitted with bogie tenders when built. Coil springs to driving axle. Originally 19-23 were 2606-10 but were renumbered in 1900.

NOTE: Tender allocation in 1903 shows 3250 gallon 600-669 (1907 nos given for clarity). 3500 gallon for 670-684, and 4000 gallon bogie type with equalised beam suspension. These tenders were later rebuilt to six-wheel high-sided Deeley pattern Type D1—see footnote to Table 16. Class 3 Belpaires Chapter 8 for further details.
No 118 preserved in National Collection with its final tender—2950 gallon capacity.

Principal source 1903 Midland Railway Diagrams

Plate 190. This broadside view affords an interesting comparison of both anatomy and livery between the '25' class proper (No. 1856, later 612) and the '1853' class variant with 2 in. larger driving wheel (No. 1853, later 608) featured overleaf in *Plate 191.* We are dashed if we can see any significant differences in locomotive shape! No. 1856 carries a form of decorated livery, almost certainly a 'Weatherburn' finish – note sandbox, heraldic emblem, driving wheel spring anchorage, bogie wheel centres – whereas No. 1853 (in works grey) shows the 'normal' arrangement of the full livery. *Authors' Collection*

25 and 1853 CLASSES

Summaries

25 Class
Built at Derby 1887-1890.
Original MR Nos. 25-32. 1854-1857. 37. 1858-1862.
1907 Nos. 600-607. 610-619.

1853 Class
Built at Derby 1889-1890.
Original MR Nos. 1853. 34. 1863-1867.
1907 Nos. 608. 609. 620-624.
ED 47
Tender size 3250 gallons was the official size when built and on the 1903 engine diagrams.

The '25' class was introduced in 1887 with a batch of five engines which mechanically and chronologically sat between the '1738' class and '2183' class 4—4—0s (Chapter 5). They combined the 18 in cylinders of the '1738' class with the 'D' boilers which were to be fitted to the '2183' class and they created something of a sensation at the time – an impression never subsequently diluted. Hamilton Ellis*

* The Midland Railway – Ian Allan 1953 et seq.

says of them: 'there was something magical about the spectacle of one of these engines at speed. They seemed to pour themselves towards those who watched them . . . It was the effect of the big driving wheels turning without visible connecting rods . . . they swept along in quite a different way. They seemed to be so effortless!'

Indeed they did, and during the next two years orders were issued for another 20 engines of the same type, all of which had been built by 1890. However, within this build, a modification was incorporated in some seven examples (1907 Nos. 608-9/20-4). This group had enlarged cylinders and 7 ft 6 in wheels and the first of them was built in 1889 as No. 1853 (later No. 608). It was sent to the Paris Exhibition in 1889 where it won a gold medal, and, in some references, gives its nomenclature (rather misleadingly) to *all* the remaining slide valve 4-2-2s. In fact, the '1853' class as such should only refer to the seven engines above mentioned, the remainder of the 600-24 series being '25' class, and Nos. 625 upwards being to a third variant (below).

In point of fact, it was well nigh impossible, visually, to distinguish the '25' class and the true '1853' class engines apart, as a comparison of *Plates 190 & 191* will reveal.

In due course, all this group received Deeley pattern front ends (e.g. *Plate 199*) but it was impossible (as with all

Plate 191. '1853' class variant No. 1853 in works grey. *Authors' Collection*

the other 4–2–2s) to fit the 'H' boiler, so the engines mostly remained recognisably 'Johnson' until scrapping. There was, however, one exception – the pioneer member No. 600. In 1917 this engine received a Deeley pattern cab and vacuum control regulator for working with the General Superintendent's Saloon (*Plates 201 & 202*). From then on, it led a somewhat cossetted existence in both MR and early LMS days, and, possibly for this very reason, became the last of all the Midland 4–2–2s to be withdrawn, late in 1928, the preserved No. 673 ('115' class – below) having been withdrawn a few months earlier. No. 600 was allocated ED 46A (*Fig. 37*).

Decoratively, the engines were always regarded, as indeed were all the 4–2–2s, as something 'special'. We have explored this subject already in Volume One and the several additional pictures should help give a more comprehensive understanding. In effect they always carried full or decorated liveries in the 1890s until, from about or just before the time of the 1907 renumbering, they began to assume the Deeley style. Only two of them (Nos. 600/614) reached the LMS and they were both withdrawn before the LMS 'black' period commenced after 1928. No. 614 was withdrawn in 1925, the last to run in basically original state (smokebox and chimney excepted).

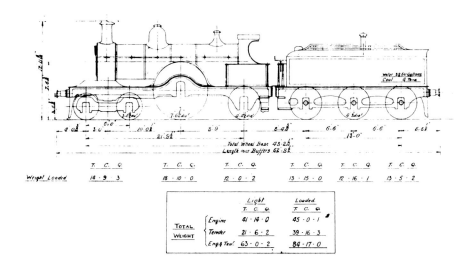

Fig. 35. This shows Engine Diagram 47 which, in general terms, applied to engines 608/9 together with 620-659, but we believe was specifically applicable to the modified '1853' class. Compare with the table of dimensions; note the extra half-inch wheel diameter – thicker tyres have now been fitted. *Authors' Collection*

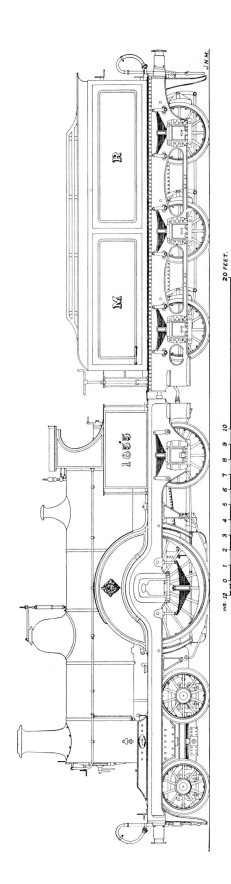

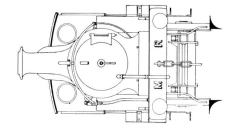

Fig. 36. This drawing by J. N. Maskelyne appeared in the HMRS Journal and has been reproduced by courtesy of that society. It shows old No. 1855 (later 611) in its original condition.

Plate 192. No. 26 was built in 1887, became No. 601 in 1907 and was withdrawn in 1919. It is in perfectly normal livery for the pre-1907 period, with little evidence of 'extra' decoration.

Collection Bernard Mathews

Plate 193. No. 1856 at St. Pancras in 1895 in what is clearly the full crimson livery (see also *Plate 190*). This locomotive became No. 612 in 1907 and was withdrawn in 1921. Note particularly the lining arrangement on guard irons, bogie frames and on the front of the sandbox.

C. M. Doncaster

Plate 194. This picture of No. 1860 at St. Pancras illustrates a '25' class single in the 'London' or 'Weatherburn' livery. Note the panel on the splasher, double circle on the bogie wheels around the axles and lining on the cabfront around the spectacle plate opening. On close examination the inside of the guard iron is seen to be lined. This was probably a 'Weatherburn' addition since many other pictures show the inside of the guard irons normally to be black. Note also the lining on the bracket which runs across the frames ahead of the driving wheels. This is edged black and fine lined yellow. Dome and safety valves are lined in the normal way but not the chimney base. It appears that the underside of the boiler is yellow, and note the serif 'MR' on the front buffer plank. No. 1860 was built in 1889 and, becoming No. 617 in 1907, was withdrawn in 1921.   *Collection Bernard Mathews*

Plate 195. No. 1859 displays a less ornate style than No. 1860 (*Plate 194*), having no splasher panel or extra circles on the bogie wheel centres. There is, however, lining on the top of the bracket between the frames on this locomotive although the sides do not appear to be lined. Finally note the way in which the front coupling links are arranged (see also No. 1860). This method was very common with Midland locomotives which had a three-link front coupling. No. 1859, built in 1889, became No. 616 in 1907 and was withdrawn in 1922.

National Railway Museum

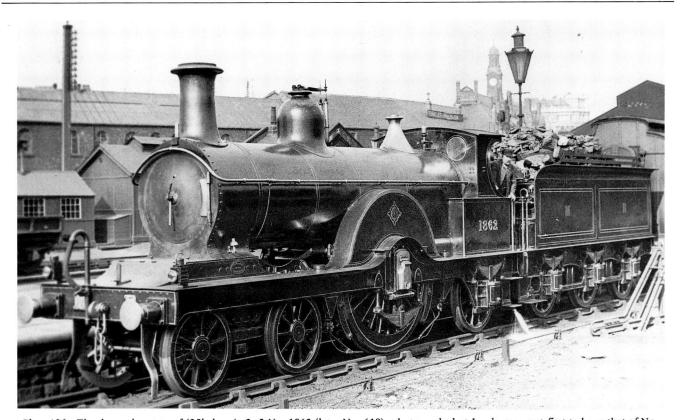

Plate 196. The decorative state of '25' class 4—2—2 No. 1862 (later No. 619), photographed at Leeds, seems at first to be as that of No. 1856 (see *Plate 193*). However, it is clearly a 'London' area job (with a 'yellow' belly) and carries additional detailing (e.g. cab spectacle glasses and front sandboxes) in the manner of *Plate 194*. However, it only has one circular line on the bogie wheel centre and there is no panel on the splasher top — who would be a model maker? (!)   *J. H. Wright*

Plate 197. No. 34 (later No. 609) was one of the seven '1853' class variants of the first twenty-five 4—2—2s. This is not the best of pictures but it shows more decorative peculiarities like double lining on the sandbox side and a separate 'panel' on the cabside, inside the normal edge lining. This seems likely to have been a 'local' variation, possibly from Bristol or Leeds.

Authors' Collection

Plate 198. No. 1867 (later No. 624) was the last of the seven '1853' class variants and also the last 4–2–2 fitted with leaf springs to the driving wheels. Built in 1890, it is seen at Holbeck, almost certainly in 1906-7, in the new Deeley livery but bearing its old number and still in 'pure' Johnson condition.

J. H. Wright

Plate 199. Photographed at Liverpool in Deeley livery. No. 623 shows the '1853' class (7 ft 6 in wheel) variant as it appeared in its final years, before withdrawal in 1921. Starting life as No. 1866 in 1890, by now No. 623 has a Deeley front end.   *Authors' Collection*

Plate 200. No. 608 at Elstree on 21st September 1917. Originally No. 1853, the Gold Medal winner at Paris in 1889, this locomotive did not survive to become LMS property, being withdrawn in 1921. The reader's attention is drawn to the 'tender cab', almost certainly a wartime fitting.   *A. G. Ellis*

Plates 201 & 202. Two contrasting views of No. 600 (with the rounded eaves cab) in Midland and early LMS livery. Built in 1887 as No. 25, the underslung cantilever spring to the driving axle can be clearly seen. Note, on the top view (in Midland livery) the vacuum control gear on the side of the smokebox. No. 600 seems destined for a long day's work in the LMS picture — judging from the coal piled high on the tender! It could have been that the engine and carriage were starting out on a several day duration tour of inspection. *Authors' Collection*

Fig. 37. Engine Diagram 46A dated March 1923 applied only to No. 600 after it received the Deeley rounded eaves cab.
Authors' Collection

4-2-2 PASSENGER ENGINE

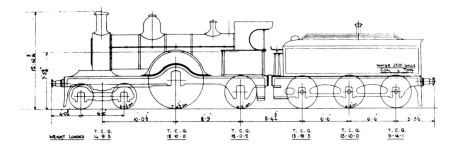

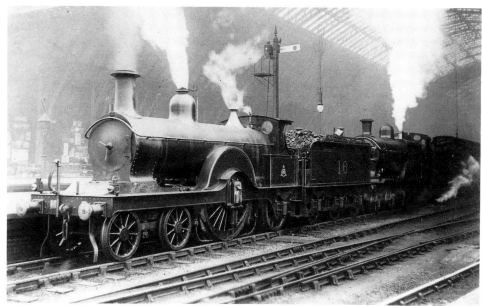

Plate 203. This view shows a Midland single from the 'modified 1853' class in service. No. 16, later to become No. 641, and not withdrawn until 1927, was photographed here as an assisting engine at St. Pancras c.1906. Note the Deeley simplification of paint scheme. The revised front frame shape and coil springs to the driving wheel are readily apparent.
Authors' Collection

MODIFIED 1853 CLASS

Built at Derby 1891-1893
Original MR Nos. 1868-72. 8. 122. 20. 145, 24. 33. 35. 36. 39. 4. 16. 17. 94. 97. 98. 99. 100. 129. 133. 149. 170-178. 1907 Nos. 625-659.

ED – Believed put on ED 47, see Fig. 35
Tender size – 3250 gallon was the official type in 1903 and indeed the size they were built with.

These 35 engines are often regarded as part of the '1853' class, but we have coined our own expression to describe them. They were built during 1891-3 and kept the 'D' boiler, 18½ in cylinders and 7 ft 6 in wheels of the '1853' class. However, they displayed heavy coil springs to the driving wheels and a somewhat more massive frame (with a rearward extension to the splasher) below the smokebox and were, therefore, quite distinctive visually.

It would have been convenient had the Midland defined them as '1868' class after the first one built, later No. 625, but we have found no evidence of this. In purely practical terms, of course, they can have been hardly any different from the first 25 engines and there would be a good case for lumping them all together as one single class of 60 locomotives.

Our remarks on the '25'/'1853' class engines (regarding livery and structural change etc.) apply equally well to this group so there is little need to say more than can be revealed by the appended pictures. Quite a number reached the LMS, the last withdrawals being in 1927. They were, of course, always painted red and our picture selection deliberately concentrates on the later period, having covered most of the earlier styles in the '25'/'1853' class section.

Plate 204 (Top right). This less than perfect view shows 4–2–2 No. 35 (later No. 636) on duty near Cheltenham. It is of principal interest in showing the first stage of 20th-century lining simplification – the tender is lined on the edge beading only.
Authors' Collection

Plate 205 (Right). 4–2–2 No. 94 at Cheltenham shows an early modification with a Johnson chimney and flat Deeley smokebox door. Note the 'extra' screw coupling carried on the front drawbar hook. Although not yet renumbered, the locomotive is in the simplified livery c.1906 for this class (no circles on the bogie wheel centres and no lining on the framing beneath the smokebox), but still carries the older heraldic emblem on the cabside. It became No. 643 and was withdrawn in 1925. *Collection Bernard Mathews*

Plate 206. Taken at Leeds in July 1909, this picture of No. 655 shows a single with a new smokebox, flat Deeley smokebox door and Deeley chimney. No. 655, originally No. 174, was withdrawn in 1925. Note the absence of lining on bogie axle ends and frames beneath the smokebox, typical of the Deeley livery, now with 'proper' heraldic emblem.

Authors' Collection

Plate 207. No. 640 in final Midland condition. This picture provides a good view of the 'front end' and in particular the cylinder cover plates. Originally No. 4 built in 1892, this locomotive was withdrawn in 1927. Note that on this version of the Deeley livery, the splasher beading is painted black (compare *Plate 206*).

Authors' Collection

Plate 208. This beautiful picture of No. 644 in LMS service is displaying the pre-1928 LMS livery. Originally No. 97, this locomotive was withdrawn in April 1926. *Authors' Collection*

Plate 209. This interesting picture shows No. 632 inside Brunswick MR shed on 27th September 1924 retaining MR livery. No. 632 was originally No. 20, built in 1892, and was renumbered 132 in 1900 and then 632 in 1907 before being withdrawn in 1926. The front frame shape of this series is clearly visible in this view. *Authors' Collection*

Plate 210. This ex-works view of No. 183 (later No. 664) gives a works grey interpretation of the full livery on the '179' class, devoid of some of the 'local' embellishments. *Authors' Collection*

179 CLASS

Summary

Built at Derby 1893 & 1896.

Original MR Nos. 179-183 & 75-77. 79. 88.

1907 numbers 660-669.

Class extinct 1927.

All had 3250 gallon tenders, and the 1903 engine diagrams show them all coupled to 3250 gallon tenders.

The '179' class came into service in two batches (five each) during 1893 and 1896. The driving wheels remained the same 7 ft 6 in size but 19 in cylinders and piston valves were fitted. They slightly preceded the '150' class 4–4–0s, but the two types obviously had much in common (see Chapter 5).

The heavier framing, consequent upon the piston valves, the first use of such by the Midland Railway, gave a much more purposeful front end 'look' to this series and, on average, they probably had a slightly longer life than any other group of 4–2–2s. All went to the LMS and scrapping took place from 1925-7.

We feel safe in asserting that this series of engines all carried full or decorated crimson liveries during the first ten years or so of their lives. Thereafter the simpler Deeley treatment was adopted, usually at or close to the time they received Deeley pattern front end fittings. All remained red throughout their lives and some got LMS markings (*Plate 215*).

Plate 211 (Right). This picture of '179' class No. 76 is particularly interesting in that it shows the elaborate lining inside the cab, including the base of the reversing gear and the locker behind it. Note also the double lining on the south-east side of the crest and the rear of the rear sandbox. However, in spite of having an obviously 'decorated' livery, the engine is coupled to a tender bearing the newer style simplified lining on the panel edge. No. 76 was built in 1896, renumbered 666 in 1907, and withdrawn in 1925.

National Railway Museum

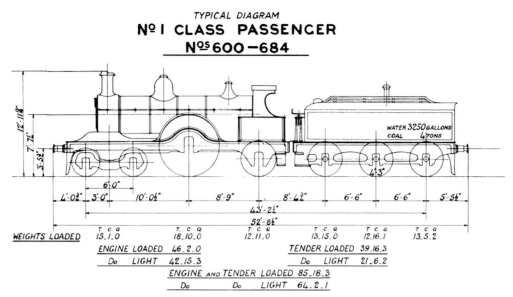

TYPICAL DIAGRAM
Nº I CLASS PASSENGER
Nºs 600 – 684

WATER 3250 GALLONS
COAL 4 TONS

WEIGHTS LOADED	T. C. Q 15.1.0	T. C. Q 18.10.0	T. C. Q 12.11.0	T. C. Q 13.15.0	T. C. Q 12.16.1	T. C. Q 13.5.2

ENGINE LOADED 46.2.0   TENDER LOADED 39.16.3
Do   LIGHT 42.15.3   Do   LIGHT 21.6.2
ENGINE AND TENDER LOADED 85.18.3
Do   Do   LIGHT 64.2.1

Fig. 38. *This 1919 diagram ED 1/48 was the 1919 diagram issued by the Midland Railway to encompass all the class 1 locomotives but in fact it was based upon the 1910 diagram which was intended to cover the series of ten '179' class locomotives only. The diagram shows the Deeley front end and specifies a 3,250 gallon tender.*

Plate 212. No. 79 in a simplified form of the 'old' livery without circles on the bogie wheel centres or lining on the framing beneath the smokebox. The locomotive is not in immaculate condition, so it is not possible to see if the brake hangers, sandboxes or guard irons are lined — they appear not to be. Built in 1896, this locomotive became No. 668 in 1907 and was withdrawn in 1925.

National Railway Museum

Plate 213. '179' class No. 669 in Midland livery at Tamworth in May 1923. At this date the locomotive was allocated to Saltley and is probably working a Derby-Birmingham passenger train. No. 669 was originally No. 88 and was withdrawn in 1927.

Authors' Collection

Plate 214. No. 662 in final Midland condition. Built in 1893 as No. 181, this locomotive was withdrawn in 1926 and makes an interesting comparison with *Plate 187* showing the same engine in earlier condition.   *Collection Bernard Mathews*

Plate 215. Two '179' class engines, Nos. 663/5 (formerly Nos. 182 and 75) at Kentish Town during May 1924. Both were withdrawn in 1926, but No. 665 had received an early form of LMS markings. No. 663 (at the rear) still carries the MR emblem.   *H. C. Casserley*

Plate 216. This picture of No. 119 at Bedford displays a '115' class single in full crimson lake livery. Built in 1897, this locomotive became No. 674 in 1907 and was withdrawn in 1925. An enhancing detail variation, usually to be seen on the '115' class and featured here, was the graceful down curve of the Salter safety valve 'levers'.

Coll. Bernard Mathews

115 CLASS

Built at Derby 1896-1899.
Original MR numbers 115-121. 123-128. 130-131.
1907 numbers 670-684. Allocated to Engine Diagram 49 in 1910.
Class extinct 1928.
Fitted 3500 gallon tenders.

. . . and so, eventually, came the 'Spinners'. This was a nickname subsequently given to all the 4−2−2s but which, we believe, was first applied to the '115' class − confirm-

ation/denial would be welcome. The driving wheels went up to 7 ft 9 in, the cylinders to 19½ in and the engines were given the 'E' boiler. Like their predecessors, the '179' class, the '115s' were closely related to a Johnson 4−4−0 design, in this case the '60' class. They shared the same front frame shape but in the case of the 4−2−2s, it 'came off' in visual terms. Perhaps the characteristic deep outside frames of the 4−2−2 helped to balance the masses above and below the running plate. Like the '60' class 4−4−0s, they were part of Johnson's attempt to increase power within the 'small engine' policy of the Board.

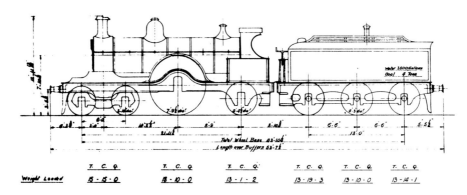

Fig. 39. Engine Diagram 49 was the official Midland Railway diagram issued in 1910 to cover the '115' class series of fifteen locomotives. It actually shows the front frame shape of the last ten examples built to order No. 1659 in 1899.

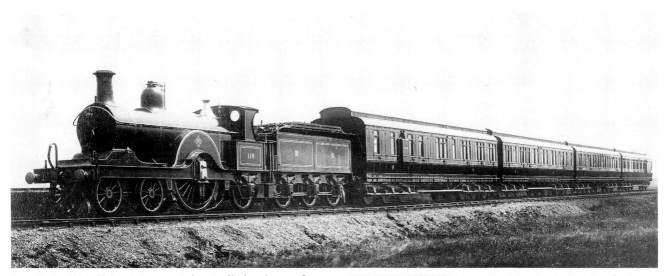

Plate 217. This official picture was taken to display the new four-coach 12-wheel clerestory train introduced in 1897 for the Manchester-St. Pancras service. The engine, '115' class No. 118, is the now preserved No. 673 and was obviously given a special 'paint job' with all the Weatherburn trimmings. Note, additionally the extra cabside panel lining, matching that on the tender.

National Railway Museum

Plate 218. No. 117 is seen here in Weatherburn livery when photographed at Kentish Town. Note the additional lining on the bogie axle ends, on the cabfront around the spectacle plates and, of course, the yellow underpart of the boiler. Built in 1897, this locomotive became No. 672 in 1907 and was withdrawn in 1926.

Collection Bernard Matthews

Plate 219. This is another posed official view (taken in the Peak District) and shows off the superb lines of the '115' class to good effect — this time from the second batch with modified front frame shape. With tired paintwork, the engine appears to be in 'standard' full livery without embellishment. It was renumbered 681 in 1907 and scrapped in 1922.

National Railway Museum

Visually they were a masterpiece generally acknowledged as having the best lines of all the Johnson 4—2—2s. Moreover, they were big engines for the type, as close proximity to the preserved No. 673 will indicate. Within the class, a slight change in the front frame shape was incorporated in the last ten, readily apparent by comparing, say, *Plates 220 & 221.*

They emerged in all the glory of the full red livery and many were the decorations applied to them — including one rather nasty one which we included in Volume One, *Plate 212.* In due course they all received Deeley front ends and simplified livery but even as modified, their essential looks were maintained. It is in this condition that No. 673 is preserved, having been saved in 1928. For nearly fifty years it carried a most peculiar version of the pre-1906 livery with painted numerals and a wooden Johnson chimney on top of the Deeley smokebox. Fortunately, the National Railway Museum put right these obscenities in 1976 and agreed to restore the engine to (limited) working order for participation in the Rainhill commemorations of 1980. Those who saw it gliding effortlessly along with no visible moving parts could well understand how the 'Spinner' nickname arose.

As preserved, No. 673 is coupled to the 2,950 gallon tender with which it ran on the date of withdrawal. However, this smaller tender has the curious effect of enhancing the visual lines, even if somewhat historically

Plate 220. No. 683 at St. Pancras is seen with a flat smokebox door and a ghastly looking tapered chimney. Note the absence of lining on the framing beneath the smokebox. No. 683, withdrawn in 1926, was originally No. 130. The front frame shape should be compared with *Plate 221* to further appreciate the difference between the two series of this class.   *Photomatic*

wrong. (It ran most of its life with a 3,500 gallon tender, being coupled to a 2,950 gallon tender during its final years.) If the '115' class had a fault in appearance, it was probably because the 3,500 gallon tender was visually a bit too big for the engines. Nevertheless, posterity is indeed fortunate that the Johnson era of the Midland is represented by one of these fine machines.

Plate 221. No. 671 when allocated to Birmingham. Built in 1896 as No. 116, it survived until the end of 1926, having been renumbered in 1907. This view gives a good impression of the front frame of the first five engines in the series. Note, too, the replacement (straight) levers to the Salter safety valves.   *Collection Bernard Mathews*

Plate 222. No. 679 in immaculate pre-1928 LMS livery at Farnley Junction on 30th June 1925. Note the LMS works plate on the splasher. This picture typifies their livery during the LMS era of ownership; none of these locomotives were ever black! Originally No. 125, it was withdrawn in 1928. Note also that in LMS days, as indeed in later MR times, the splasher beading was painted black with the Deeley livery (compare with *Plate 220*).

Authors' Collection

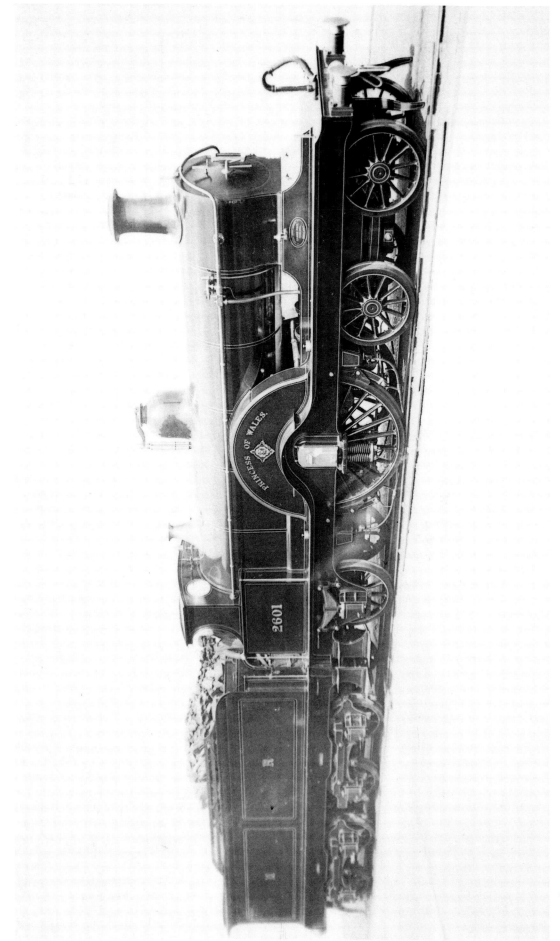

Plate 223. Princess of Wales resplendent in full 'London' decorated livery. Although a less than perfect view, this picture does reveal the care taken in those days.   *Authors' Collection*

Plate 224. No. 2602 on shed. This early view clearly illustrates the 'London' livery. Note the yellow underside of the boiler, double relief on the south-east side of the crest, double lining on the smokebox top just outside the base of the chimney, together with the lining around the smokebox front and the bases of the dome and safety valve. It is not possible to see if the splasher top has been panelled but it probably was. Becoming No. 686 in 1907, it was withdrawn in 1919. *Authors' Collection*

2601 'PRINCESS OF WALES' CLASS

Built at Derby 1899-1900.
Original MR numbers 2601-2610.
2606-10 renumbered 19-23 in 1900.
No. 2601 was named *Princess of Wales* and awarded Grand Prix at the Paris exhibition in 1900.
1907 numbers 685-694.
Allocated to Engine Diagram 52 in 1910.
Class extinct 1922.

Just as he had done a year or two earlier in the 4—4—0 field with the '60' class, Johnson, in trying to keep to his Board's remit, somewhat overreached the 'small engine' philosophy with the final batch of 4—2—2s, the so-called 'Princess of Wales' type introduced late in 1899. The cylinders and wheels were much the same size as the '115' class but the wheelbase was longer and the 'F' boiler was fitted. For this reason this class, uniquely among the 4—2—2s, was put into power class 2, whereas all the others were class 1. The fact is that for an engine this size, the single wheel concept was not wholly appropriate, but as has been stated (page 133), Johnson may have had some difficulty in persuading his Board that what was really needed was bigger engines.

Visually, the engines were extremely imposing, but seemed somehow to lack something of the pure harmony of all the earlier series. This was partly because of the slight drop in the running plate to the front buffer plank and partly caused by the movement of the dome to a position centrally over the driving axle. This 'broke' an imaginary downward line from chimney to cab roof rear which, on all previous batches of 4—2—2s, had just 'touched' each of the boiler mountings and helped contribute to their visual harmony.

However, these are rather minor matters and, of course, somewhat subjective. What really spoiled things was the appearance when viewed side-on, of the new 'water cart' tenders built to a size more suited to a 'Duchess' Pacific! These massive bogie tenders were introduced (because of a lack of water troughs at the time) to give a longer range between stops. They no doubt succeeded but eventually, after the MR had installed troughs, the bogie tenders were converted to a high-sided six-wheel type, and these, when re-attached to the poor old 4—2—2s, were even more of a visual disaster! Deeley style tenders never looked well on those rare occasions when they were attached to a slim-

Plate 225. This view shows the '2601' class to advantage — No. 688 (ex-2604) possibly on a Leeds—St. Pancras express at Harpenden around 1908/9. *Authors' Collection*

Plate 226. No. 689 at Leeds c.1908 with bogie tender, new chimney, flat Deeley smokebox door with horizontal handrail and vertical handle and seriffed 'MR' on the front buffer plank. Note also the screw coupling 'hooked up' behind the buffer plank. Originally No. 2605, built in 1900, this locomotive lasted only until 1922. In our opinion the '2601' class looked at their best when viewed from this semi-frontal position, from which angle, the bogie tenders did not dominate quite so strongly. *Collection Bernard Mathews*

Plate 227. No. 690 (formerly No. 2606, later 19) with a six-wheel rebuilt ex-bogie tender. The unfortunate visual effect is all too obvious. The engine has a Deeley front end with dished door and carries Deeley livery. *Authors' Collection*

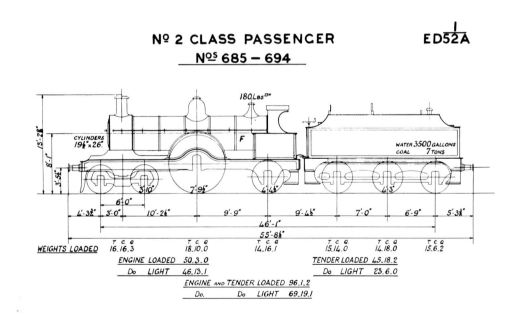

Fig. 40. The original Engine Diagram 52 was used to cover the '2601' class when coupled to 4,000 gallon bogie tenders and was later modified to allow for the changed 'front end' to the locomotive — Deeley smokebox door. Later still, ED52A was issued when the bogie tender had been rebuilt to the straight-sided version seen in Plate 227. The diagram reproduced is the 1919 version of Engine Diagram 52A.

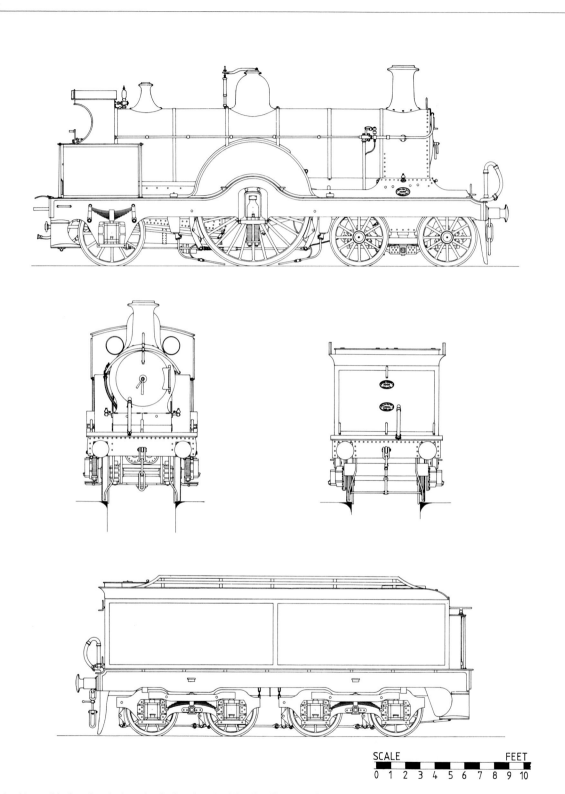

SCALE · · · · · · · · · · FEET
0 1 2 3 4 5 6 7 8 9 10

Fig. 40A. This drawing depicts the final series of Midland Railway singles, the '2601' class (built in 1899/1900), in their 1903 condition with slight modifications to the bogie tender. It closely matches the first version of Engine Diagram 52.

B. D. Hunt

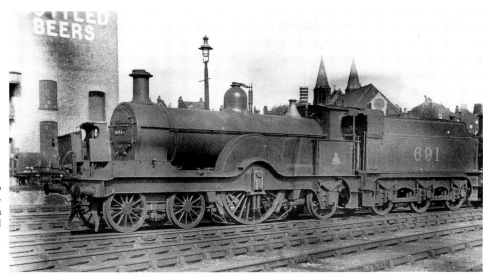

Plate 228. In similar condition to the previous view, No. 691 (formerly 2606, later 20) carries a crude 'tender-cab' of a type fitted during the First World War.
Authors' Collection

boiler Johnson engine. For the record, the rebuilt Deeley tenders were of type D1 — more fully analysed in Chapter 8, page 187.

Princess of Wales herself was only the second MR engine to carry a name and, as was not unprecedented with Midland locomotives of the Johnson era, carried off a major international prize — this time at Paris in 1900. Like all other 4−2−2s, this ultimate series was magnificently turned out and if *Plates 223 & 224* are a reliable guide, many of them received the usual embellishments of the period.

The usual Deeley front end and simplified livery took over in due course, but the engines were the shortest-lived of any of this noteworthy series. It may have been no more than life-expiry of the original boilers (they were never given replacements), but whatever the reasons, all were scrapped between 1919 and 1922, having run for barely twenty years — on average some ten to fifteen years less than the earlier 4−2−2s.

CONCLUSION

How can one best sum up the Johnson bogie singles? Disregarding their self-evident good looks — a point always made in books and which we have repeated — were they good engines? On the whole we think the answer must be 'yes'. They spanned a more than 40 year period (1887-1928) which by any standards was not bad. By accepted Midland criteria, they may have seemed short-lived types, but this is not really a fair assessment. Many of the so-called long-lived Midland engines were virtually rebuilt beyond recognition. In fact one of our acquaintances has likened it to 'jacking-up the numberplate and running a new engine underneath'. This never happened to the 4−2−2s. They were always recognisably the same machines from start to finish — and they had a pretty good innings, twice as long as the 'Deltics' for example!

Happily for posterity and their appearance, they could not accept the new larger 'H' and Belpaire boilers. In this they displayed the characteristics of most single driver engines — i.e. the boiler diameter being severely constrained

by the need to fit it almost 'between' the driving wheels. The single driving wheel engine could never really be developed to meet the 'big engine' philosophy and the '2601' class rather demonstrated this fact. It is, however, remarkable, and to Johnson's credit, that his 4−2−2s managed to hold their own for some 20 years *after* the Midland had at long last perceived that need for larger engines which Johnson had been urging.

However, and striving to be objective, they were nothing like as long-lived as the 2−4−0s and probably, in retrospect, not much more effective and probably less versatile in traffic. Within their dimensional constraints, however, they were economical and efficient — especially with piston valves. A superheated 'Spinner' might have been interesting (!) but this never happened; so perhaps Johnson's noble experiment from 1887-1900 was too little and too late. But who, when they behold No. 673, can regret that he tried?

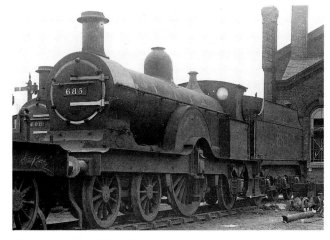

Plate 229. No. 685, still carrying its name, shortly before withdrawal. This picture should be compared with its state at *Plate 223* as No. 2601. By now it has a straight-sided tender rebuilt from a 4,000 gallon bogie tender and looks neglected. Upon withdrawal of the 4−2−2s, these tenders were coupled to newly constructed LMS standard compounds.
H. C. Casserley

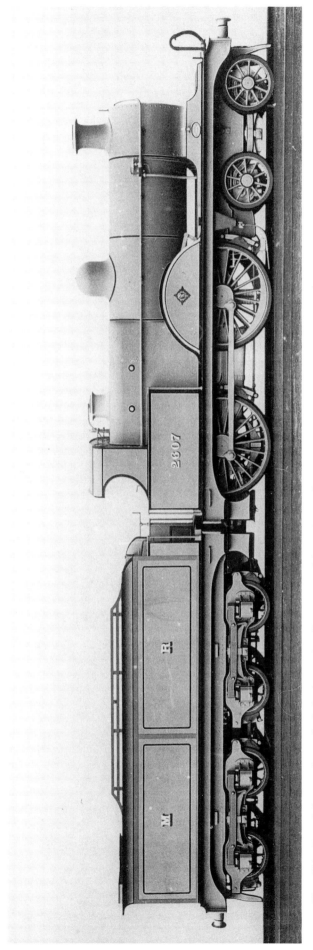

Plate 230. One of the ten pioneer 'Belpaires' No. 2607 (later No. 701) in works grey finish 'as built'. Note the Johnson chimney shape, the neat safety valve casing and the large bogie tender with coal rails terminating some three-quarters distance from the tender front. The 'equalised beam' tender bogies show very clearly in this view as does the lower height bottom rectangular cab panel when compared with later views, e.g. *Plate 231*.

Authors' Collection

JOHNSON/DEELEY CLASS 3 4-4-0s

THE Midland Railway entered the 'big engine' field right at the end of the 19th century when, in September 1900, Johnson designed and introduced a large, Belpaire-boilered 4—4—0 type of a size and visual character quite unlike anything before. Its impact must have been quite something to behold at the time, since there had been no obvious visual clue in any of Johnson's previous designs that he was contemplating such a bold step, although, as we have stated, there is much evidence that he had wanted to move in this direction for some time.

Other than sheer size, amplified by the new design of bogie tender, the most significant departure was the introduction of the Belpaire boiler to the Midland. It is generally considered that Robert Weatherburn had more than a small part to play in this development and had been pressing Johnson for some time to make the change. Johnson was not inclined to rush things and was certainly not against the idea as such; but he chose to wait until he judged the time was right, and in the event his timing was just about perfect. The engines were an immediate success and were quickly referred to as 'Belpaires' by the men — and 'Belpaires' they were called right to the end of their lives,

(which came in 1952) even though the MR (and the LMS) subsequently built little save Belpaire-boilered engines of all shapes and sizes for almost half a century.

The first series of these engines was built for the increasingly heavy and still fairly newly introduced corridor trains to Scotland via the Settle-Carlisle line and they were to be the first of what eventually proved to be a 'class' of 80 similar machines whose building continued into the Deeley period. The word 'class' is used in its broader sense as far as this group of engines is concerned, for the visible variations to be seen within them were considerable. Each batch differed in some way from its predecessors and, given normal Midland policy, one would have expected each change to be regarded as justifying a new class designation. To some extent this was so (see Table 15), but when all 80 engines were renumbered in 1907 as Nos. 700-79, they became lumped together as the '700' class, variations notwithstanding. They were all placed in power class 3 and 'class 3 Belpaire' became another all-embracing term.

To aid understanding, we shall use the phrase 'XXX Series' (using the original pre-1907 numbers) to differentiate the various batches of engines within this anything but

Plate 231. '2781' series 'Belpaire' No. 2783 (later No. 712), the second variety of this class, gives a very characteristic example of the full crimson lake livery as applied to these engines when new. Some (e.g. *Plate 249*) were even more elaborate and, as usual, there were individual variations. For example, compared with *Plate 249*, the lining on the bottom of the frame between the bogies differs with the line going below the bolts (2788) and above (2783). In this view there is no second circle on the centre of the bogie and driving wheel centres, the splasher tops are black, there is no yellow line at the front of the smokebox but there are the same yellow lines at the bottom of the tender side. Note how the slight decrease in bogie wheel size, the lengthened 'bogie to coupled wheel' dimension and the lower height 4,500 gallon tender with 'full length' coal rails, all impart a much better visual balance than on the 2606 series (*Plate 230*). The new style tender bogie is also clearly shown, as is the new and somewhat less pleasing safety valve housing. Nevertheless, it is truly a Johnson engine.
Collection Bernard Mathews

Plate 232. No. 819 (later No. 729) was one of the modified '2781' series with ascending steps ahead of the coupled wheels. Note that the tender coupled to this engine has the shallower valance. No. 819 is illustrated in full crimson lake livery and the view clearly shows all the lining on the right-hand side of the locomotive. As No. 729, this engine received modified ascending steps at a later date (see *Plate 245*).

Collection Bernard Mathews

homogeneous 'class' and, as with the Johnson 2–4–0s (Chapter 4), it is felt helpful to start with a fairly comprehensive review of the complete line of development.

One or two further preliminary comments should also aid understanding. All 80 engines were built in saturated state and it was in this form that they exhibited most visual variety — at least six identifiably different sub-species! Superheating began in 1913 and this, eventually, reduced the visible variations to only four types. Tenders too, added to the confusion. The first 50 were given large bogie tenders, but of several different types, while the last 30 had their own unique versions of the standard Johnson style 3500 gallon six-wheel tender — again in two identifiable styles.

The bogie tenders were intended to give a longer range between water stops, the Midland having no water troughs at the time. However, after troughs were introduced in 1903, the six wheel tender was preferred again and a few years later the bogie tenders were drastically rebuilt to high-sided six-wheel style. Not surprisingly, however, there were two visibly different versions, even after conversion.

Superheating added its own quota to the already chameleon-like characteristics of these popular engines so we have attempted in Table 16 to summarise the whole story as best we can up to the start of the superheated period. The table appears on page 193, immediately before

the detailed series-by-series summaries. However, we start by reviewing the 'as built' condition of the whole class.

THE 'SATURATED' STORY (AS BUILT)

The first ten engines, the '2606' series, renumbered 700-9 in 1907, were always more different from their successors than the later batches were from each other. They were fitted with the new 'GX' Belpaire boiler and, to suit this boiler, the wheelbase came out at 10 ft 2½ in between bogie pivot and leading coupled axle. Driving wheels were 6 ft 9 in at 9 ft 6 in wheelbase and the cab was of somewhat spartan character. It did, however, introduce the 'rounded eaves' profile, later developed by Deeley. The lower cab panel was rectangular in shape but quite shallow in depth, the top edge being several inches below the handrail. The chimney was still very much 'Johnson', albeit nothing like as tall as previously, and the new style safety valve casing (housing Ramsbottom type valves) was of pleasing shape.

The new high-sided bogie tender of 4000 gallon capacity, was recognisably in the Johnson style as were the front end frames of the engine. while the footplate angle (valance) on both engine and tender had the usual graceful Johnson curves. All told, a very satisfactory visual balance was achieved for what was, by 1900 standards, a very big engine

(Plate 230). Subsequent changes to this series of engines in saturated condition are given on page 184.

The next group of ten engines, the '2781' series, renumbered 710-19 in 1907, was conceivably, the most visually well-balanced of them all in terms of 'original' condition. A development of the 'GX' boiler was fitted (classified G8) which was 6 in longer and this was reflected by increasing the wheelbase to 10 ft 8½ in between bogie pivot and leading coupled axle and lengthening the bogie wheelbase from 6 ft to 6 ft 6 in. The cab remained the same but the lower (rectangular) cab panel was deepened to a height where the top edge aligned with the handrail. Other engine details were much as the '2606' series, save for a new style safety valve casing of not quite such harmonious style.

Bogie tenders were again supplied of considerably lesser height but, paradoxically, greater water capacity (4500 gallons). This gave much nicer visual lines between engine and tender which, together with the extra length of the engine itself, imparted a sleek, almost racy 'look' to the ensemble *(Plate 231)*. The tender bogies on this batch had individual springs rather than the equalising beam suspension of those fitted to the '2606' series and the tender coal rails were of 'full length' rather than the shorter style originally provided with the '2606' series. The tender valances were rather deeper than previously.

The third group of ten (1907 Nos. 720-9) were almost identical to the '2781' series save for the introduction of foot steps (between bogie and leading driving wheels), somewhat crudely bolted on, as a sort of afterthought — which they may well have been. In fact, this series could more accurately be referred to as 'modified 2781 type'. The 4,500 gallon tenders of this batch had shallower valances than the previous 4,500 gallon type.

The next batch of Belpaires, the '820' series, numbered 20 engines all told and, starting with No. 820 (1907 No. 730), retained the dimensional characteristics of the '2781' series, but with a few more visual changes. Most noticeable was the new 'flowerpot' shape chimney which has been much criticised by many observers in terms of its visual quality. It looked pretty awful when fitted to some of the smaller Midland engines (e.g. *Plate 131*), but was not totally offensive on the 'Belpaires' *(Plate 233)*. This chimney became standard for all subsequent Belpaires when first built.

Another, more subtle change was a slight reduction in depth of the side valances on the engine, the foot steps being retained as on the modified '2781' series. The bogie tenders were little changed save for a reduction to 4,100 gallon capacity from No. 825 onwards.

This build of twenty '820' series engines concluded the use of the bogie tender with the Class 3 Belpaires. The next

Plate 233. This lovely view of '820' series 4-4-0 No. 827 (later No. 737) was taken at Holbeck (Leeds) and gives a very clear impression of the first examples fitted with 'flower-pot' chimney. In our opinion it does not look all that offensive with this class of engine. This series also had shallower footplate angle depth, matching that of the 4,100 gallon tender used on 825-839. The 'cranked' shape of the ascending step (to avoid the sandbox) is clearly evident. This was a distinctive feature of many of the 'Belpaires' both before and after superheating. No. 827 became No. 737 in 1907 but was never superheated, being withdrawn in 1925. *Collection Bernard Mathews*

Plate 234. Photographs of the '840' series of 'Belpaires' in their 'as built' condition have proved hard to come by, so we have been forced to utilise this rather indifferent official view of No. 845 (later No. 755). It does, however, give enough detail to reveal the full 'Johnson' livery still in use (1904) and the 'flower-pot' chimney. The new style 3,500 gallon tender is not 100% clear but does reveal the tank ventilation pipes (projecting upwards behind the coal rails). These allowed air to escape from the water tank when filling at speed — the visible indication that the tender was fitted with water pick-up apparatus. This engine was superheated in 1922 and withdrawn in 1956.

National Railway Museum

batch of ten, the '840' series, were almost identical to the '820' build, but were fitted with a Deeley pattern smokebox door and carried a new pattern six-wheel 3500 gallon Johnson style tender (*Plate 234*). This was, in essence, the standard variety, but with footplate was raised in height by some 5¾ inches (to line up with the engine footplate) and fitted with a decorative valance to harmonise with the locomotive. Once again it produced a most pleasing visual combination and this style of tender was exclusively fitted to the Belpaires. These ten engines (1907 Nos. 750-9) were also the last new passenger tender engines to carry the full Johnson livery and were in fact built during the first year of Deeley's term of office, albeit still basically Johnson in style.

Although Johnson's direct involvement with the Belpaires had ceased with the completion of the '820' series, it was not until the final twenty Belpaires were built that Deeley's modifications became really obvious. Once again, two groups of ten can be distinguished, the '850' series and the '860' series (1907 Nos. 760-9; 770-9). Both these latter were fitted with a modified boiler of the 'G8A' type.

Starting with the '850' series, the most obvious change was the adoption of a 'straight-through' running plate, devoid of Johnson's characteristic 'drop' to the leading buffer plank (*Plate 235*). This went with the foot steps now fixed behind the footplate angle in an altogether more tidy fashion. However, the small Johnson cab and Johnson-style tender were retained.

Finally, the full Deeley modifications were applied to the '860' series (1907 Nos. 770-9). Visually, the most obvious was the lengthening of the cab roof by a considerable amount, but the tenders too were slightly changed by the abandonment of the vertical central beading on the tender side. The tenders were otherwise pure Johnson and the change seems to have been occasioned by the new Deeley livery as much as anything else.

No. 860 (later No. 770) is recorded as having been the first *new* MR engine to carry the proper Deeley livery (with large transfer figures etc.). Along with Nos. 861-3, No. 860 was turned out as *Plate 236*. Later, however, the new heraldic emblem was adopted along with 'proper' spacing of the figures (*Plate 237*). The omitted vertical centre beading allowed the new style figures to be placed exactly centrally in the side panel rather than flanking the beading, as was the case with most Johnson tenders when re-liveried.

This final group of ten engines gave the first 'clues' to the ultimate visual style of most of the class, especially after superheating, but, before this took place, quite a few changes had occurred to the earlier saturated engines and these must first be considered.

CHANGES TO THE 'SATURATED' ENGINES

The 80 'Belpaires' were hardly in service before changes began to take place, but fortunately these tended to be 'across the board' rather than confined to one specific series.

As far as the engines were concerned, the principal changes were at the cab and smokebox. Having built the last ten ('860' series) with the extended cab roof, supported by vertical stanchions at the rear, it was not long before some of the first 70 were modified to match. However, the

Plate 235. '850' series 4—4—0 No. 857 (later No. 767) shows an 'as built' example of the first 'proper' Deeley 'Belpaires' of 1905, although this was not its first livery (see *Plate 250*). Note the 'straight through' running plate or platform even though the cab remains 'Johnson'. No. 857 became No. 767 in 1907 and was superheated in 1921. Withdrawal was in 1947. This photograph was taken to illustrate a 'well coaled' tender. This picture of the simplified livery confirms the absence of lining on the dome base and boiler bands when in this style. Also there is no lining on the framing, centres of the wheels, guard irons or brake hangers. Even the lower side frames above the bogie seem unlined — most unusual for this style.

National Railway Museum

Plates 236 & 237. These two excellent official views of the '860' series as built show very clearly both the livery and 'anatomical' changes which took place in the last series of ten 'Belpaires'. No. 863 (later No. 773) clearly shows the new cab roof arrangement and the somewhat curious 'first stage' Deeley livery with widely spaced numbers and 'old' heraldic emblem. The lack of vertical centre beading on the tender side is also apparent, thus allowing the '6' to be exactly central in the main side panel. This official picture of No. 864 (later No. 774), taken in 1906 and depicting the new crest, as well as showing an excellent and crisp works grey rendering of the 'proper' Deeley livery, also gives excellent 'front end' detail of the 'ultimate' saturated Belpaires. The profile of the original 'flower-pot' chimney, the revised cab spectacle plate (basically used again on the superheated development) and the 'straight' ascending steps neatly mounted behind the running plate angle, are all most clearly illustrated. No. 863 (773) was superheated in 1919, withdrawn in 1940, and No. 864 (774), superheated in 1923, was also withdrawn in 1940.   *National Railway Museum*

original Johnson and 'flower-pot' chimneys were replaced on all 80 engines by the more familiar almost 'parallel-sided' style with 'capuchon' (wind guard) at the upper front rim. This usually went with a new Deeley pattern smokebox door on the first 50 engines. On all 80 examples, the original continuous handrail around the smokebox gradually gave way to the separate style. These 'front end' changes were all much in accordance with normal contemporary MR practice and *Plates 238-241* exemplify some of the various alterations.

Another small change was the alteration of the safety valve 'casing' on the first ten engines to match those of the rest of the class.

It was, however, the rebuilding of the bogie tenders, shortly after the great renumbering, which imparted the most fundamental visible change. This procedure was initiated slightly before some of the engine alterations (above) and gave quite a different appearance to the ensemble (*Plate 242*). The rebuilt tenders displayed high, flat sides in a style soon to become familiar in developed form, on both the MR and the LMS well into the 1930s. The rebuilt 'ex-bogies' could, however, always be recognised by their very deep upper panels above the top horizontal beading strip of the main side panel. This upper-side section was reduced slightly in height on the purpose-built

examples, (i.e. those fitted to the Compounds and '990' class 4—4—0s (Chapter 9).

Two variants of the rebuilt bogie tenders were to be seen, most of them having a noticeable 'in-curve' as the bottom of the side panel met the side frames, e.g. *Plate 242*.

Plate 238. This view shows 'modified 2781' series 4—4—0 No. 818 with a flat Deeley smokebox door prior to renumbering in 1907. This locomotive retains the Johnson continuous handrail and Johnson chimney. Note the footstep positioned between the leading driving wheel and rear bogie wheel. These were not fitted to the earlier batch (old Nos. 2781-2790). When photographed, this locomotive was in slightly simplified livery, viz., lining on the tender beading, no lining on the guard irons, wheel centres, framing below the smokebox, brake hangers, etc. Note also the 4,500 gallon bogie tender with shallower valances (see text and *Plate 232*). No. 818 was renumbered 728 in 1907 and superheated in 1922. Withdrawal as British Railways No. 40728 was in 1952.
National Railway Museum

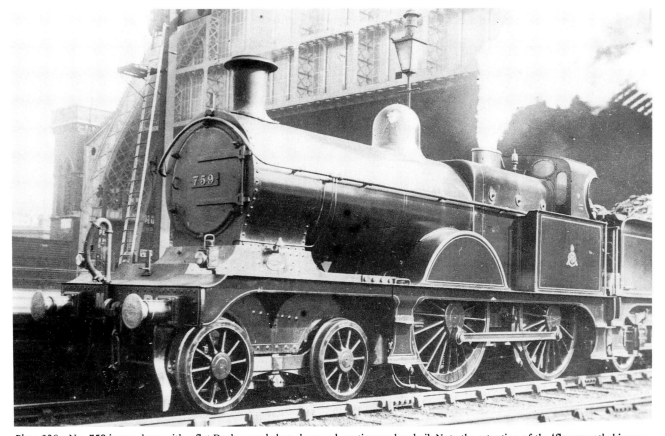

Plate 239. No. 759 is seen here with a flat Deeley smokebox door and continuous handrail. Note the retention of the 'flower-pot' chimney. This picture is useful in providing a clear picture of the inward cranked footstep and the bracket supporting the running plate which is attached to the frames and located above the bogie centre. No. 759 was originally No. 849, built in 1905. It was superheated in 1923 and withdrawn in 1946. The livery of the engine in this view is clearly Deeley style. *Collection Bernard Mathews*

Plate 240. This rather nice train picture shows '2781' series 4—4—0 No. 714 (formerly No. 2785) very much 'as built' at Mill Hill c.1908. The smokebox door has, however, been replaced by one to the Deeley pattern, the cab roof is extended and the livery is pure post-1907 Deeley style. However, the engine retains its 'flower-pot' chimney and bogie tender — a very typical 'intermediate' configuration for the period.
Authors' Collection

Some, however, had a continuous flat valance and a slightly different footstep treatment, e.g. *Plates 262-3*. This latter group were more nearly like the genuinely new Deeley flat-side tenders, but were nothing like as widespread on the Belpaires as the alternative 'turn-under' style.

These engine and tender alterations were all taking place quite rapidly, frequently in association with livery changes too; but before considering the latter subject in detail, it is best to complete the 'anatomical analysis' by first considering the further changes caused by the introduction of super-heating.

THE SUPERHEATED STORY

By the time the first Class 3 Belpaire was superheated in 1913, the whole group of 80 engines had undergone the changes outlined above and were carrying their 1907 series numbers. They will, therefore, be referred to in this section solely by their 7XX series identification. Superheating brought a fresh round of visible changes and, although there was some degree of 'coming together' as far as outward appearance was concerned, the original character of most of the various series of these engines did remain obvious to a greater or lesser degree. Once again, therefore, it is simpler to divide them into their various batches. However, before dealing with the specific changes, it should be mentioned that the superheating of this class was a slow process, not completed until LMS days and even then, some 'Belpaires' were never superheated, being withdrawn by the LMS still in saturated condition. These engines were, of course, the first withdrawals.

The first ten (Nos. 700-9) remained somewhat different, as they had always been. The new G8AS boiler was longer than the GX type, even discounting the characteristic extended smokebox of the superheated version, so the

opportunity was taken to increase the 'bogie to driving wheel' dimension by the requisite six inches to match the rest of the class. This involved new frames and running plate angle and made their visual characteristics quite different. However, the original 'shallow depth' cabside panel remained as a visible identification of their early origins (*Plate 244*). New cab upper panels with roofs of somewhat higher and more rounded profile were fitted, as indeed was the case with all the superheated 'Belpaires', and this also changed the shape of the cab spectacle windows in most cases save for the last batch (see *Plate 237*).

The running plate on Nos. 700-9 was now 'straight through' (copying the original state of Nos. 760-79) and ascending front steps were fitted behind the running plate angle, again as per Nos. 760-79. The upper front frame shape did, however, reveal its 'new' status.

The remaining 70 engines, if and when superheated, were all treated in much the same way when the G8AS boilers were fitted. Those numbered between 710-59 received 'straight-through' footplates and *all* received the new, taller and more rounded upper cabs as per Nos. 700-9. All these new cab roofs were fitted with ventilators. However, since the G8AS boiler was the same length as the previous G8/G8A, there was no need to lengthen the wheelbase, consequently the frames/footplate angle still remained broadly as in the saturated period. This meant that even after superheating the following visible variations existed:

Nos. 700-09   Shallow footplate angle, new front frames, shallow cab panel; rear mounted footsteps as 760-79.

Nos. 710-29* Deep footplate angle, footstep supports (frequently referred to as 'ascending steps') front mounted.

Plate 241. '820' series Belpaire No. 735 is seen here following renumbering in 1907. Originally No. 825, it was superheated in 1920 and in this condition it survived until withdrawal in 1949, still carrying its LMS number. At the time it was photographed, the locomotive was in simplified MR Deeley livery and had received the full Deeley front end modification but, compared with 714 (*Plate 240*), still retained the original cab. *Collection Bernard Mathews*

Plate 242. '2781' series 4—4—0 No. 719 (ex-No. 2790) is seen here with a straight-sided tender with 'turn-under' side panels rebuilt from a bogie tender. When photographed, this locomotive had been fitted with a dished Deeley smokebox door and Deeley chimney. Note the absence of the front ascending footsteps. These were fitted to this series when superheated. This locomotive was superheated in 1921 and lasted until 1947 when it was withdrawn. *Collection Roger Carpenter*

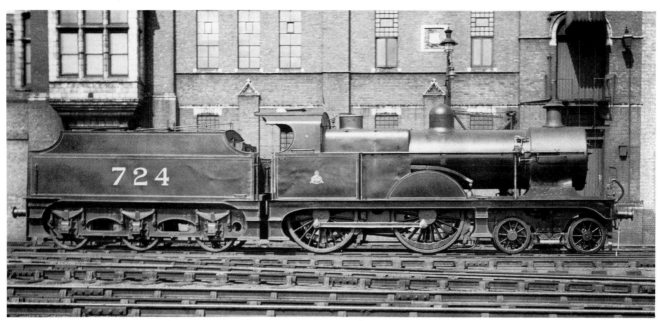

Plate 243. Superheated 'Belpaire' No. 724 started life as one of the '2781' series. In this crisp view, the changed shape is well portrayed. The rebuilt bogie tender is of the 'turn-under' variety (see text) but the deep locomotive footplate valance (plus added ascending steps) is retained, as were the 'cased in' safety valves at this time. Comparison with *Plate 232* reveals how much the superheating plus tender rebuilding changed the visual character of this series.   *Collection Roger Carpenter*

Plate 244. '2606' series No. 706, originally No. 801, was superheated in 1921, so this picture was taken in the last two years of the Midland's existence and well displays the superheated form of this batch of ten engines. Note the retention of 'low' cabside panel, the revised roof profile and cab spectacle plate, the 'turn-under' style of rebuilt bogie tender and the complete transformation of the 'front end' framing consequent upon lengthening the wheelbase to accept the G8AS boiler. The engine is finished in the simplified Deeley livery of this period. The lower edge of the completely new style valance was lined, as indeed were the wheels and footsteps. Note the new ascending steps fixed behind the valance in the manner of Nos. 760-79.   *Collection Bernard Mathews*

Plate 245. Superheated '2781' series Belpaire No. 729 should be compared with *Plate 232*, where it is illustrated as saturated No. 819. Superheated in 1916, this locomotive lasted until 1951 when it was withdrawn by British Railways but still carrying its LMS number. Note the ascending front footstep. On this particular locomotive it was attached behind the valance whereas all the others of this series had them attached in front. We presume that this somewhat maverick variation may have had something to do with either sandbox modification or accident damage. The engine is otherwise much as would be expected in this group.

Collection Bernard Mathews

Nos. 730-59 Shallow footplate angle, ascending steps front mounted.

Nos. 760-79 Shallow footplate angle, ascending steps rear mounted with the support plate entirely vertical, not angled (see pictures).

* No. 729 was an exception regarding the steps (see *Plate 245*).

During the Midland period, the tender distribution remained pretty much as during the saturated phase, but, of course, the tender variations were still present, and increasingly, tender changes began to make things more confusing.

There were a few experimental modifications to the 'Belpaires', e.g. *Plate 247*, and the LMS continued to make further changes after 1923, but we shall cover this period in some detail elsewhere. Suffice to say that tender changing began to be more frequent (and confusing), with, we believe, some tenders receiving LMS standard tanks as well. However, for the record, the following engines were never superheated.

730-59 series: 737/42/9/51
760-79 series: 772/8-9

In spite of the fact that the LMS did not complete the superheating programme and regarded the 'Belpaires' as non-standard, these engines were always very popular, frequently being preferred to newer types. In consequence, withdrawal of the superheated series was quite slow, no

fewer than 22 examples reaching BR, of which the last to be withdrawn was BR No. 40726, late in 1952.

CLASS 3 'BELPAIRE' LIVERIES

Before coming to the series-by-series summaries, a few general remarks about livery seem appropriate. The first examples ('2606' series) came out during the full flowering of the elaborate Johnson livery and, not surprisingly, received considerable attention as far as their finish was concerned. Since the engines were visually so different from the traditional Johnson style, the appearance of the full livery did not look quite the same as it had done. For one thing, the larger external surfaces meant that there were larger red areas between the features which carried lining and decoration, giving a superficial appearance of simplification. In fact, of course, this was not so — all the small detail attention was still present and at *Plates 248 & 249* some of this can readily be appreciated.

The full crimson livery seems to have been used up to and including the '840' series (see page 184), after which the '850' series (later Nos. 760-9 began to display some simplification (*Plate 250*), but not much. It was only the '860' series (built 1905) which came out *from new* in the simplified Deeley style and we have described this process on page 184.

During the period covering the 1907 renumbering, tender rebuilding and the locomotive detail changes, livery

Plate 246. This view of superheated Belpaire No. 757 (formerly No. 847) shows the transformation of the '840' series. The slightly shallower valance identified this group (Nos. 730-59) as also did the Johnson style six-wheel tender on Nos. 750-9. This early LMS view at Kentish Town in September 1926 displays the first LMS livery and bogie brakes (soon removed); but the characteristic water 'splash plates', ahead of the bogie, e.g. *Plate 247*, have already gone. Note, too, the now uncased Ramsbottom safety valves. No. 757, superheated in 1921, was a late survivor (until 1948) but never received its BR number.

H. C. Casserley

variations were considerable (e.g. *Plates 251/252*), but things began to settle down, well before the onset of superheating, to the standard Deeley livery. This version of the red livery was, of course, the only one used on the 'Belpaires' in their superheated form and remained current until 1928 (with LMS ownership markings from 1923-8). Thereafter LMS lined black (1928 onwards), LMS plain black (if repainted c.1940-7), and BR livery were applied in turn. At *Plates 254-8* a small selection of these post-Midland alterations are given.

We conclude this section of the chapter by giving at Table 16 a summary of this complex class, which attempts to cover most of the details mentioned so far in a 'quick reference' form.

Plate 247. Superheated Belpaire No. 768 (ex-No. 858) not only reveals the final condition of most of the last twenty engines, but also shows the arrangement of the Weir feedwater pump applied to one or two examples of the class in late MR/early LMS days. The picture was taken at Kings Norton in 1921 and the bogie 'splash plates' (to protect the bogie from water overspill if running as 'second' engine in a double-headed train passing over troughs) are well featured.

Authors' Collection

Plate 248. This view shows '2606' series 4−4−0 No. 802 which was built in 1901 but not superheated until 1925, the last of the first series of ten locomotives to be altered. In its superheated condition it survived until the end of 1947, outlasting by more than ten years any of the original series. This picture gives a very good idea of the original lining which one would normally expect to see at this date, but there was no excessive decoration.
Collection Bernard Mathews

TABLE 15: 4−4−0 BELPAIRE LOCOMOTIVES AS BUILT

1903 Diagram Page No.	Order No. or Class	Built by	Qty. built	Date of building	Pre 1907 numbers	1907 renumbering	Cylinders	BOILER Centre Line	Diameter	Length	Tubes	Diameter	Working Pressure	FIREBOX Length	Grate Area in sq. ft.	Total Heating Surface in sq. ft.	WHEELS Leading	Driving	Tyres	ENGINE WEIGHT Empty	Loaded	REMARKS
8	1869	Derby	10	1900-01	2606-2610 800-804	700-709	19½″ × 26″	8′ 3″	4′ 8″	10′ 6″	272	1¾″	175 PSI	8′ 0″	25.0	1519	3′ 6½″	6′ 9″	3″	47.11.3	51.17.2	2600 CLASS. Fitted with compensation suspension to the bogies.
7	2135	Derby	10	1902	2781-2790	710-719	19½″ × 26″	8′ 3″	4′ 8″	11′ 0″	262	1¾″	180 PSI	8′ 0″	25.0	1528	3′ 3½″	6′ 9″	3″	47.14.2	53.4.0	2781 CLASS. Second five engines to o/n 2458 weighed 48.8.2 empty and 52.18.1 loaded. Plus all of o/n 2601. All fitted with four point suspension bogies. On this series the distance from the centre of the bogie to the front buffer was increased to 7′ 1″ from the 6′ 10″ employed on o/n 1869.
	2250	Derby	10	1902	810-819	720-729	19½″ × 26″															
	2458	Derby	10	1903	820-829	730-739	19½″ × 26″															
	2601	Derby	10	1903/4	830-839	740-749	19½″ × 26″															
82	2726	Derby	10	1904	840-849	750-759	19½″ × 26″	8′ 3″	4′ 8″	11′ 0″	262	1¾″	180 PSI	8′ 0″	25.0	1528	3′ 3½″	6′ 9″	3″	48.8.2	52.18.1	840 CLASS. *The above information is taken from the Midland Railway 1903 Engine Diagram Book*
	2798	Derby	10	1904	850-859	760-769	19½″ × 26″	8′ 3″	4′ 8″	11′ 0″	251	1¾″	200 PSI	8′ 0″	25.0	1455.5	3′ 3½″	6′ 9″	3″		53.10.2	850 CLASS. Boiler pressure reduced to 180 psi after May 1912
	2918	Derby	10	1905	860-779	770-779																*The information about o/n 2798/2918 taken from 'Derby Works & Midland Locomotives' by J. B. Radford*

		Bogie wheelbase	Bogie centre to leading driving wheel	Coupled wheelbase	Trailing driving wheel to loading tender wheel
The engine wheelbase was:—	O/N 1869	6′ 0″	10′ 2½″	9′ 6″	10′ 4¾″ Bogie tenders
	All others	6′ 6″	10′ 8½″	9′ 6″	10′ 3¾″ (9′ 6¾″ to 6-wheel tender)

TABLE 16: SUMMARY OF CLASS 3 BELPAIRE 4−4−0 SERIES — STYLE VARIATIONS AS BUILT

Note: This table applies to saturated locomotives only; for further changes after superheating see main text analysis—page 188.

Number series Pre-1907	Post-1906	Cab details Panel style	Roof style	Footplate details Style	Valance depth	Front steps	Chimney	Boiler *	Tender Type (see key)	Original livery
2606-2610	700-704	Shallow	Short	'Drop' front	Deep	No	Johnson	GX	B1	Full/decorated
800-804	705-709	Shallow	Short	'Drop' front	Deep	No	Johnson	GX	B1A	Full/decorated
2781-2790	710-719	Deep	Short	'Drop' front	Deep	No	Johnson	G8	B2	Full/decorated
810-819	720-729	Deep	Short	'Drop' front	Deep	Yes	Johnson	G8	B2A	Full/decorated
820-824	730-734	Deep	Short	'Drop' front	Shallow	Yes	Flowerpot	G8	B2A	Full/decorated
825-839	735-749	Deep	Short	'Drop' front	Shallow	Yes	Flowerpot	G8	B3	Full/decorated
840-849	750-759	Deep	Short	'Drop' front	Shallow	Yes	Flowerpot	G8	J1	Full but undecorated
850-859	760-769	Deep	Short	Straight through	Shallow	Yes	Flowerpot	G8A	J1	Simplified Johnson
860-869	770-779	Deep	Long	Straight through	Shallow	Yes	Flowerpot	G8A	J2	Deeley style

* **Note:** GX boilers had different style safety valve casings when built (see text) later altered to match G8/G8A style.
Key to tender types
B1 Bogie 4000 gallon, equalised beam suspension, high sided, deep valance. Wheelbase 5′ 6″ × 5′ 6″ × 5′ 6″   3′ 6″ wheels.
B1A Bogie 4000 gallon, equalised beam suspension, high sided, shallow valance.
B2 Bogie 4500 gallon, individual wheel suspension, lower sides, very deep valance. Wheelbase 5′ 7″ × 5′ 8″ × 5′ 7″   3′ 6″ wheels.
B2A Bogie 4500 gallon, individual wheel suspension, side height as B2 but shallow valance.
B3 Bogie 4100 gallon, individual wheel suspension, side height as B2 but shallow valance as B2A. Wheelbase 5′ 7″ × 5′ 8″ × 5′ 7″   3′ 6″ wheels.
J1 Six-wheel 3500 gallon Johnson type with valance and vertical centre bead.
J2 As J1 but without centre bead.
Tender Rebuilding
When rebuilt, the bogie tenders displayed two forms viz:
D1 Deeley pattern with flat valance below rudimentary 'footplate'—see Plate 243 (believed confined to rebuilds of type B1).
D2 Deeley pattern with pronounced 'turn under' at base of side panel—see Plate 242 (believed to be rebuilds of types B2/B3).
Note: In general, the 'Belpaires' retained the rebuilt version of their **original** type of tender—i.e. type D1 for the 700-9 series, type D2 for the 710-49 series but there were some later changes which became ever more complex in late Midland and early LMS days.

Plate 249. This superb view of '2781' series 4–4–0 No. 2788 shows the full glory of what we consider to be the most visually attractive series of 'Belpaires' in original condition, carrying a fully 'decorated' crimson lake livery. Note the yellow line at the front of the smokebox and the upper cabside and cab roof panels. The three boiler and one firebox lagging bands are lined, together with the angle at the cab front end. The firebox washout covers have a line around them as indeed does the works plate. The heraldic emblem has double lining on the south-east corner and in true Weatherburn fashion the underside of the boiler has been painted yellow. Note also the lining on the tender side, beneath the flare and on top of the top horizontal beading — not to mention the double yellow line on the base of the tender side. There is a lined-out panel on the splasher, the one on the front being clearly visible. A similar panel would have been placed on the rear of the splasher top. The sandboxes were lined on all visible faces. Note, too, the extra circles on the centres of all locomotive wheels and the bogie frames, locomotive frames, brake hangers and guard irons. What a sight it must have been — and still very 'Johnson' — size and configuration notwithstanding.

National Railway Museum

Plate 250. This fascinating picture of '850' series 4—4—0 No. 857 (later No. 767) was also used at *Plate 129,* Volume 1, but we did not exhaust its possibilities! In this present context it reveals the original liveries of the '850' series of 'Belpaires' in 1905 before the assumption of the style shown (on the same engine) at *Plate 235.* This, in essence, was the short-lived period (c.1904-5) when the tender lining went to the panel edges and when there was some slight reduction in general decoration *before* the adoption of what can be called the 'proper' Deeley livery with the large tender numerals. Even so, the springs, axleboxes and guard irons were still fully embellished and, as we have stated elsewhere, the translation of tender lining to the panel edges, rather than the 'traditional' Johnson style did, we feel, harmonise rather more effectively with the structural characteristics of the familiar Johnson tender. Subjective — yes; but we do not apologise!

National Railway Museum

Plate 251. Pioneer 'Belpaire' No. 2606 (later No. 700) at Leeds (Wellington) on 14th October 1905, well exemplifies the Johnson-Deeley livery transition (during the 1904-6 period) which we have several times mentioned. The tender is lined 'round the panel edges', the front 'MR' is seriffed and the safety valve casing has been changed; but the Johnson smokebox door is unchanged, as is the chimney. Below the footplate some lining has been suppressed (brake hangers etc.) but the leading splasher still carries polished brass beading. Altogether a very characteristic 'intermediate' state of decoration.

J. H. Wright

Plate 252. No. 2782 displays simplified livery with the post-1905 style, carrying the locomotive number on the tender side. There is no lining on the centres of the wheels and only the boiler band next to the smokebox is lined, together with the angle next to the cab front. The upper cabside lining has been simplified and there is no lining on the tender bogie springs or axlebox; however, the tender bogie frames are lined on the extreme edge, not inside the bolt heads as on No. 2788 (*Plate 249*). No. 2782 was renumbered 711 in 1907, superheated in 1922 and withdrawn in 1949, still carrying its LMS number.   *Collection Bernard Mathews*

Plate 253. This view shows '850' series 'Belpaire' No. 769 (formerly No. 859) now superheated and also equipped for oil burning. The livery is pure Deeley.   *Authors' Collection*

Plate 254. Superheated 'Belpaire' No. 720 (ex-No. 810) shows a typical early LMS condition (red livery in the Deeley 1907 style but with LMS markings); but it also shows the use of the former '990' type tenders with the odd example of the class 3 Belpaire 4—4—0s. This particular engine was superheated in 1925 — one of the last to be so treated — and was withdrawn in 1949, still carrying its LMS number.

Authors' Collection

Plate 255. Superheated 'Belpaire', LMS No. 726 (ex-No. 816) acquired a Johnson-style tender in LMS days and is depicted here in lined black LMS livery during the later 1930s. Note that by this time, the Ramsbottom safety valves had been replaced by the 'pop' type and the smokebox had acquired a considerable number of 'snap-head' rivets. No. 726 (as BR No. 40726) was scrapped in 1952.

Authors' Collection

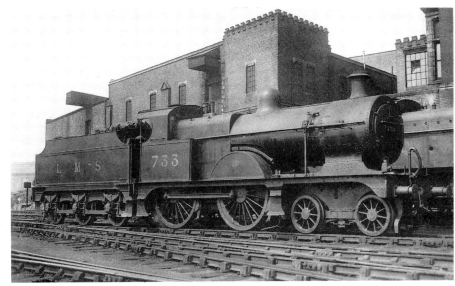

Plate 256. Superheated No. 733 (pre-1907 No. 823) shows a typical mid-1930s condition for the 'Belpaires'. The tender is now an LMS period replacement '990' class type (see text) but, interestingly, the Ramsbottom safety valves have not been replaced. The livery is lined black and No. 733 was withdrawn in 1936.
Authors' Collection

Plate 257. This view of No. 707 (pre-1907 No. 802) shows the engine at Elstree in 1938 bearing the short-lived 1936 style LMS insignia (sans serif characters) with lined black livery. It was withdrawn in 1947.
Authors' Collection

Plate 258. Some twenty-two 'Belpaires' reached BR in 1948, but by no means all were renumbered in the '407xx' series. One exception was No. 40741 (pre-1907 No. 831) depicted here c.1948-9. It was, of course, superheated and displayed a fair array of post-grouping rivets, especially around the smokebox. It also sported a 'Stanier' pattern chimney and trailed a tender carrying a standard Fowler 3,500 gallon tank. Even so, it still betrayed its early '820' series origins.
Photomatic

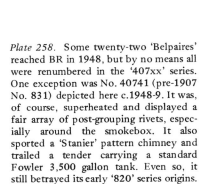

4-4-0 PASSENGER ENGINE

Fig. 41. Engine Diagram 55. This diagram was issued in 1910 and refers to the '2606' series, generally in original condition but showing the smokebox and safety valve changes which took place while the engines were saturated but before the tender rebuilding.

Authors' Collection

2606 SERIES

Summary

Built at Derby 1900-1.

Original MR numbers 2606-2610, 800-804.

1907 numbers 700-709.

When built they were equipped with GX boilers and the locomotive was coupled to a 4000 gallon tender.

All were rebuilt with G8 AS boilers from 1913 onwards. Most were withdrawn during the late 1920s/early 1930s but No. 707 survived until 1947.

The original style of construction, with a bogie tender, was allocated in 1910 to Engine Diagram 55 but, when superheated in their final form, they were allocated to Engine Diagram 70.

Plate 259. No. 2608 was built in 1900 and became No. 702 in 1907. Superheated in 1914, it lasted until the end of 1931 when it was withdrawn from service. The bogie wheels were 3 ft. 6½ in. on the first ten locomotives built, 3 ft. 3½ in. on the remainder of the class. There were no footsteps forward of the leading driving wheels and a different style of casing was provided around the safety valves when compared with the later construction. On superheating, this 'series' received new frames of identical wheelbase to the rest of the class, but the cabside panel remained smaller than the rest of the series. In this picture note also the original chimney and the pre-1903 lamp iron configuration.

Bernard Mathews Collection

Plates 260 & 261. These two views give a very clear impression of both sides of the superheated '2606' series, late in the Midland period. Nos. 705/6 began life as Nos. 800/1, they were superheated in 1914 and 1921 respectively and withdrawn in 1927 and 1932. The high-sided rebuilt ex-bogie tenders are of the more common variety with 'turned under' bottom corners between side panel and side frame. Note the new frame shape and the new valance/footstep arrangement, both features being unique to this particular series of rebuilds.

Authors' Collection

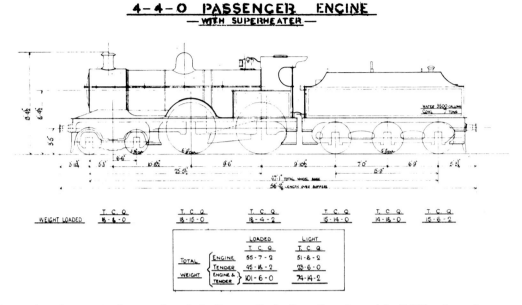

Fig. 42. Engine Diagram 70. When superheated, the 'front end' wheelbase dimensions of the '2606' series engines were altered, thus necessitating new frames. The new diagram issued to cover the modified engines was subsequently regarded as applicable to the whole class in superheated form, but it clearly shows a rebuilt '2606' type.   National Railway Museum

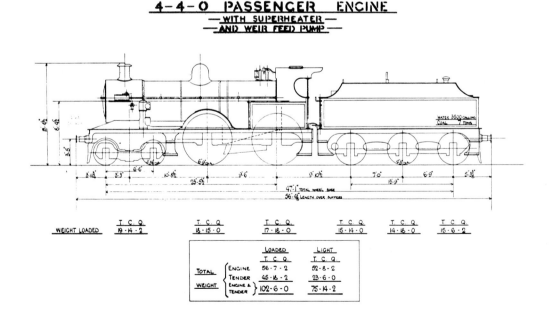

Fig. 43. Engine Diagram 70A. No. 700 was superheated in 1913 and later fitted with a Weir feed pump. Accordingly an amended diagram was raised to cover this modification (see also Plates 262 & 263).

Plates 262 & 263. These two views show '2606' series superheated Belpaire No. 700 in its final form when allocated to Engine Diagram 70A with feed pump. It is seen here in late Midland and early LMS livery respectively. No. 700 was withdrawn towards the end of 1927 and so never carried LMS black livery with red lining. *Authors' Collection*

2781/MODIFIED 2781 SERIES

Summary

Built at Derby 1902.

Original MR numbers 2781-2790, 810-819.

1907 numbers 710-729.

Original construction was equipped with G8 boilers and coupled to 4500 gallon tenders and in this condition they were allocated to Engine Diagram 56. This series established the wheelbase dimensions for all subsequent Belpaires. They were rebuilt with G8 AS boilers from 1916 onwards and as such they were allocated to ED 70 (*Fig. 42*).

This series was extinct in 1952 with withdrawals in general dating from the mid-1930s (No. 714 was withdrawn in 1928 following the Charfield accident in October of that year).

Plate 264. No. 2784 (later No. 713) was photographed in this condition in 1904, at which time none of the structural changes had taken place. The engine carries a fully decorated livery much in the fashion of No. 2788 (*Plate 249*).   *Collection Bernard Mathews*

4—4—0 PASSENGER ENGINE

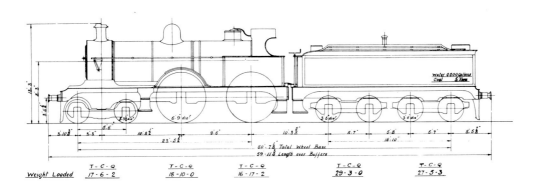

Fig. 44. *Engine Diagram 56 depicts the '2781' series in their original condition prior to superheating and exchanging their bogie tenders for the rebuilt straight-sided six-wheel version. The front end is, however, to the Deeley pattern. The diagram also shows the ascending steps, fitted originally only to Nos. 810-9.* Authors' Collection

Fig. 45. *This excellent drawing by Adrian Tester, specially prepared for this book, shows a '2781' series Belpaire in its original condition.*

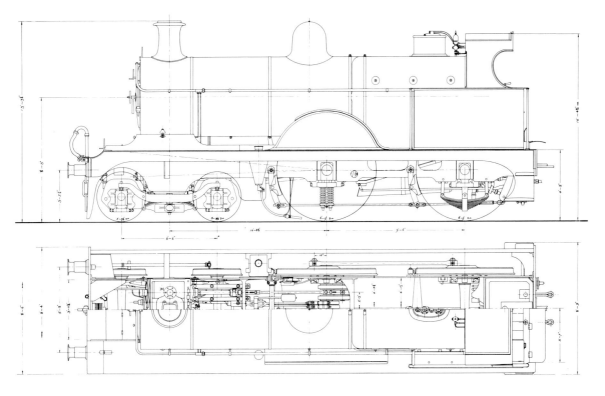

MR. JOHNSON'S 2781 CLASS 'BELPAIRE' LOCOMOTIVE - 1902

Plate 265. Saturated Belpaire No. 716 (formerly No. 2787) displayed many Deeley modifications — and a rebuilt tender — when photographed on express duty during World War I. There is a rudimentary tender cab fitted to cut down upward 'glare' from the firebox. The engine was superheated in 1923 and lasted until 1947.

Authors' Collection

JOHNSON/DEELEY CLASS 3 4—4—0s

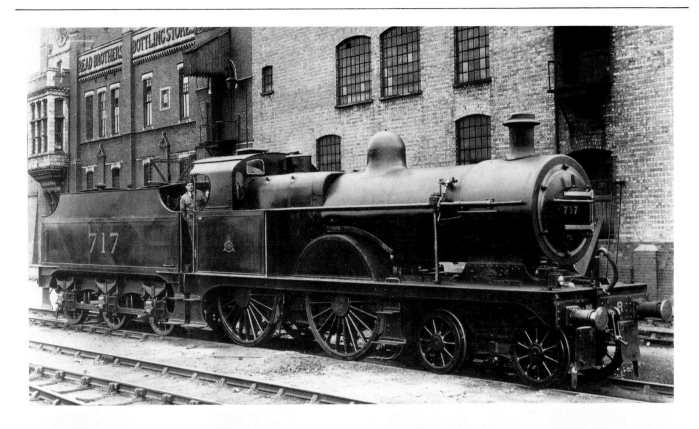

Plates 266 & 267. At about the end of the Midland period, bogie brakes became fashionable and many Belpaires were so equipped. These two views show superheated '2781' series 4—4—0s Nos. 717/726 (originally Nos. 2788/816) without and with bogie brakes. No. 726 was superheated in 1917, No. 717 in 1919 so it seems that the fitting of bogie brakes came very late in MR days. Later still, the LMS removed the fittings, generally during the 1930s. No. 726 was actually the last surviving Belpaire (1952) whereas No. 717 was scrapped in 1935. Note also that on these views the safety valves are still cased in, a by no means universal situation on the superheated engines. *Authors' Collection*

Plate 268. No. 743 shows a member of the '820' series (formerly No. 833), largely still 'as built' but carrying its new number with full Deeley livery. Note that the smokebox door has acquired fixing 'dogs' additional to the central fixing handle – a foretaste of things to come. There is, as yet, no visible indication of power class on the cabside. Superheated in 1921, No. 743 was one of the last survivors, as BR No. 40743, scrapped in mid-1952 carrying BR lined black livery.

Authors' Collection

Plate 269. No. 740 (formerly No. 830) as shown in this broadside view displays very little difference from No. 743 — the smokebox door may be Deeley — but the rebuilt tender imparts a totally different character to the combination. Note the variable blastpipe control mechanism on the smokebox side. No. 740 was another late survivor. Superheated in 1922, it lasted until late 1949, by then as BR No. 40740.

National Railway Museum

820 SERIES

Summary

Built at Derby 1903-1904.
Original numbers 820-839.
1907 numbers 730-749.
When constructed they were equipped with G8 boilers. The first five were coupled to 4500 gallon tenders and the remainder to 4100 gallon tenders and in this condition they were, in 1910, allocated to Engine Diagram 57.

Superheating commenced from 1917 but not all the series was rebuilt and three locomotives were withdrawn in 1925 in saturated condition. Withdrawal of the superheated locomotives commenced in 1929 but it was 1952 before the final locomotive was taken out of service.

When superheated they were allocated to ED 70 (*Fig. 42*).

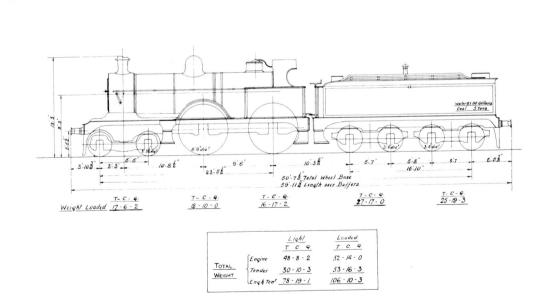

4—4—0 PASSENGER ENGINE

Fig. 46. In 1910 the Midland Railway issued a series of diagrams, and Engine Diagram 57 was the one allocated to the '820' series of locomotives when coupled to bogie tenders. We have been unable to trace a diagram for these locomotives when in saturated condition and coupled to six-wheel (rebuilt) straight-sided tenders.
Authors' Collection

Plate 270. Superheated '820' series No. 744 (ex-No. 834) was so converted in 1920 and this picture must have been taken soon afterwards. Note the bogie brakes and uncased safety valves. *Authors' Collection*

Plate 271. No. 740 again, still in pre-superheated condition but now with a full Deeley pattern 'front end', yet retaining original cab roof. *Collection Roger Carpenter*

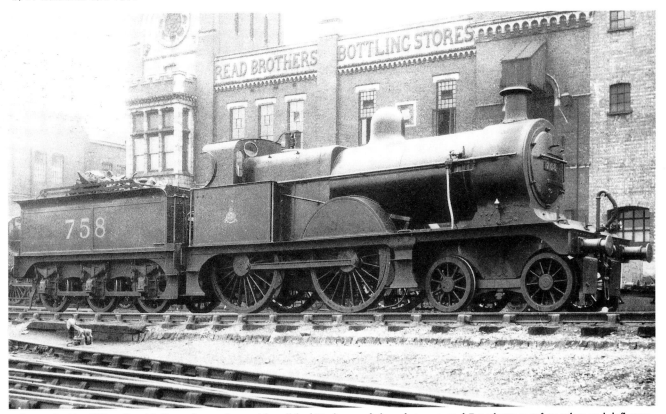

4—4—0 PASSENGER ENGINE

Fig. 47. Engine Diagram 53 was raised to cover the '840' series of Belpaires with the six-wheel Johnson style tender. The diagram shows original cab/safety valve housing but later pattern smokebox. This series started life with flower-pot chimneys and continuous handrail.

840 SERIES

Summary

Built at Derby 1904.
Original numbers 840-849.
1907 numbers 750-759.

When constructed, this series of ten locomotives was built with G8 boilers and they were coupled to six-wheel flared top tenders. With one exception, No. 751, they were all superheated from 1917, but withdrawals began in 1929 and this series was extinct in 1951.

Plate 272. No. 758 at Kentish Town is seen here with a dished Deeley smokebox door, uncased Ramsbottom safety valves and deflector plates attached to the front buffer beam. Built in 1904 as No. 848 and superheated in 1925, this locomotive was scrapped in 1951 as British Railways No. 40758.
Collection Bernard Mathews

Plate 273 (Plate 272). Like No. 758 (*Plate 272*). No. 756 (formerly No. 846) displays the '840' series 4—4—0 more or less in the condition shown by Engine Diagram 53. The livery is clearly the standard Deeley treatment and the engine is shown as converted for oil burning. Superheated in 1923, No. 756 was scrapped in 1949 before receiving its BR number.

National Railway Museum

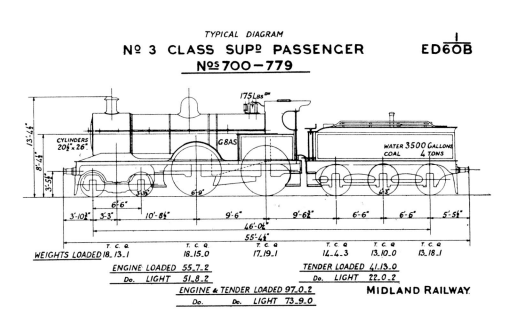

Fig. 48. ED 1/60B. This is a 1919 Midland Railway diagram intended to apply to all the superheated locomotives which were coupled to flared top 3,500 gallon tenders. However, the diagram is in error in showing a locomotive of the '2606' series in superheated condition coupled to a tender type, which in reality it never carried! This diagram underlines the importance of not placing too much reliance upon diagrams for accuracy of visible detail. The '2606' series ran in their superheated condition with straight-sided tenders, and ED70 (Fig. 42) is a more accurate version for this particular group.

Plate 274. Superheated '840' series No. 750 (ex-No. 840 itself) shows a mid-LMS period view in lined black with 'pop' safety valves. The engine was superheated in 1923 and withdrawn in 1939. This view shows it stored at Bedford in July 1935 and also reveals the more heavily riveted smokebox of those engines superheated in late MR/early LMS days.
A. G. Ellis

Plate 275. Now fitted with a Deeley dished smokebox door and Deeley chimney, No. 762 also represents a locomotive equipped for oil burning. Originally No. 852, it became No. 762 in 1907 and was superheated in 1923. This simplified livery picture taken c.1912 displays lining on the frames clearly visible by the bogie and running along the bottom edge of the valance. Note the step and the way in which the lining was treated, compared with other pictures where the valance lining continues around the foot step. *National Railway Museum*

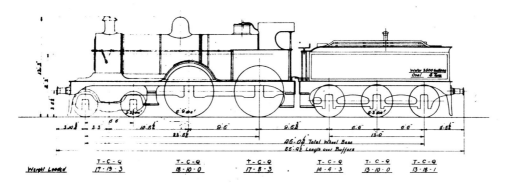

Fig. 49. Engine Diagram 61 was the 1910 Midland Railway diagram which referred to the '850' series of locomotives but shows a curious cab form which we have been unable to confirm photographically. When rebuilt and superheated, they were allocated to ED 1/60B.

850 SERIES

Summary

Built at Derby in 1904.
Original numbers 850-859. 1907 numbers 760-769.
When built, they were fitted with G8A modified boilers and six-wheel flared top tenders, and in this condition they were, in due course, allocated to Engine Diagram 61. All were rebuilt with G8AS boilers, starting in 1916, and withdrawals were spread over the period 1928-1951. This was the first series to be built with a straight platform from new.

Plate 276. This opposite side view of No. 764 (formerly No. 854) shows a coal-burning saturated '850' series Belpaire in much the same configuration as *Plate 275.* Both views also reveal the changed shape of the upper spectacle glass — compare, for example, *Plate 272.* This modification was introduced with this particular series of engines.
National Railway Museum

Plates 277 (opposite) & 278. When in superheated condition, '850' series No. 768 (ex-No. 858) was fitted with Weir feed pump and feed water heater. As such it was probably classified as Engine Diagram 70A (*Fig. 43*). These views show it on a train at King's Norton in 1921 and in more close-up detail from the opposite side. Note the 'oil burning' conversion and the 'cased in' safety valves. No. 768 was superheated in 1919 and scrapped in 1936. *W. L. Good & Authors' Collection*

Plate 279. This view shows another oil-burning superheated '850' series engine No. 766 (ex-No. 856) at Halesowen Junction in 1921. Note that this one has bogie brakes. No. 766 was superheated in 1917 and scrapped in 1928. *W. L. Good*

Plate 280. Saturated Belpaire No. 777 running as an oil-burner in standard Deeley livery. Originally No. 867, it was superheated in 1924 and withdrawn in 1939.

Collection Bernard Mathews

Plate 281. Photographed during the 1920s, this picture shows No. 774 in early LMS livery. The existence of the bogie brakes and Ramsbottom safety valves are not unusual for this date. Originally No. 864, this locomotive was superheated in 1923 and lasted until 1940 when it was withdrawn.

W. L. Good

860 SERIES

Summary

Built at Derby 1905.

Original numbers 860-869. 1907 numbers 770-779.

This series of ten locomotives was built with G8A modified boilers and coupled to 3500 gallon six-wheel tenders. In this condition they were allocated to Engine Diagram 62. Unlike the previous 70 locomotives, the final ten were fitted with a longer cab roof as shown in the diagram.

Three locomotives remained in saturated condition and were withdrawn during 1925/6; the other seven were superheated during 1919-1924 and as such remained in service until withdrawn between 1935-1947.

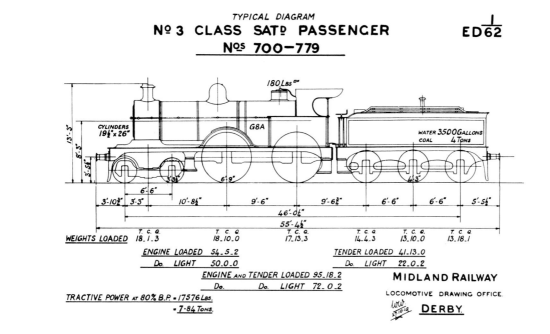

Fig. 50. ED 1/62 is the MR 1919 diagram supposedly covering all remaining saturated Belpaires still in service. It was, in fact, based upon the 1910 diagram for the '860' series.

Plate 282. This cab interior view of No. 758 was taken in November 1913 to illustrate the Geach lubricator fitted on the fireman's side of the cab. Intended to lubricate the coupled driving wheel axle boxes, it was not entirely satisfactory in service.

National Railway Museum

Plates 283 & 284. These two cab views of Nos. 720 and 754 were both photographed c.1912. Again they are worthy of careful study if only to illustrate that the footplate layouts of seemingly identical locomotives varied slightly. *National Railway Museum*

JOHNSON/DEELEY CLASS 3 4–4–0s

Plate 285. Saturated 'Belpaire' No. 748 at Trafford Park c.1914 while undergoing repairs. We have included this picture not just to illustrate this aspect of activity but more particularly to show the frame behind the driving wheels.

Collection Roger Carpenter

Plate 286. This rear view of Belpaire No. 741 (originally No. 831) gives a very clear view of the rear of a rebuilt bogie tender which we have classified type D2 at Table 16. The lack of 'footplate' on this type with 'turned under' bottom side panels is very clear. The picture was taken in 1921 at Derby during one of several 'oil-burning' experimental periods during the later part of the Midland period. *H. C. Casserley*

CONCLUSION

It cannot be denied that the Midland class 3 Belpaires were a visually complicated series, and we are conscious that there may well have been further variations of a small type which we have either not spotted or not recorded. At the same time, we are also aware that, from the Midland's point of view, these 80 engines were the mainstay for much of the heavier passenger working during the last twenty years or so of the company's independent existence. They well outnumbered the class 4 compounds and '990' class engines during the Midland period and were always in the 'thick' of things.

It is not, therefore, really surprising that they would be kept as up-to-date as possible, thus indirectly causing many of the visual changes we have identified. Of course, some of the changes were more cosmetic than anything else and many of the differences were more visually obvious than they were mechanically or operationally significant. In fact, on this last point, the fitting of larger 20½ cylinders to the superheated engines was clearly more important than anything which could actually be seen at the lineside.

That they were good engines has never seriously been questioned, even by non-Midland enthusiasts, and their long drawn out withdrawal, given their non-standard classification by the LMS, suggests that they had plenty of relevant work to the very end. Indeed, we have often wondered why the MR/LMS did not use the class 3 with G8AS boiler as the basis for its standard 'second line' 4—4—0, rather than the '483' class of engine. The G8AS boiler itself became an LMS standard, being used, *inter alia*, on the class 4 2—6—4Ts of the late 1920s, so the class 3 4—4—0 could have been adopted had things been different.

Like the more or less contemporary superheated 'George the Fifth' type of the LNWR, the superheated 'Belpaires' of the Midland were amongst Britain's best inside cylinder 4—4—0s, but the LMS did not seem to fancy either of them for further development and they both withered on the branch, the Belpaires lasting just a bit longer.

Plate 287. This shows No. 2632 in immaculate condition and should be compared with *Plate 291.* Note the raised running plate over the cylinders and the two separate reversing levers reflected off the boiler clothing. The different and deeper arrangement of the valance beneath the running plate should also be noted. Furthermore, the livery is not identical. It is post-1903 — note centre buffer beam bracket.

National Railway Museum

CHAPTER NINE

JOHNSON/DEELEY CLASS 4 4-4-0s

IT is an extraordinary fact, nonetheless so for having been remarked upon so often, that the Midland Railway (one of Britain's four largest private railway companies) came to the end of its independent existence with no more than 55 express passenger engines in what could be called the 'larger' size category. These, of course, were the forty-five Compound 4—4—0s and the ten simple expansion '990' class 4—4—0s, both rated power class 4 and the subject of this chapter. Even these were well outmatched by the offerings of several of its rivals.

How this came to be, has been commented upon and explained 'ad nauseam' by many writers including, let us be honest, ourselves; so we do not propose to dwell over-long on further cultivation of already 'well-tilled soil'. Nevertheless, some preliminary comment does seem appropriate by way of putting the whole story into perspective, and a useful starting clue is provided by a quotation from the well-researched RCTS monograph on the Midland Compounds by our friend David Tee who writes: 'It was during the period of construction of the Compounds that the Midland locomotive policy gradually changed from one of steady progress, often ahead of other companies, to one of almost total stagnation . . . '

We could not and would not doubt the truth of this statement, which also relates the change to the 'little and often' policy of small trains, upon which the MR had embarked at this time and to which, to its detriment, the LMS fell heir in 1923. The Midland, undoubtedly, felt no *need* to build larger or better engines — so it didn't! At the same time we have sometimes wondered if this was the only reason. There is no doubt that even in the class 4 category, the Midland did not exactly develop the concept with great rapidity after Deeley left. We have, therefore, sometimes felt that this may have been because Johnson and Deeley (by developing the class 3 Belpaire and, later by introducing class 4 engines, particularly the compounds) had moved the Midland such a 'quantum' step ahead of many rivals during the mid-Edwardian period that it created a sort of complacency around the headquarters at Derby. Something rather similar happened on the GWR after Churchward departed, so it would not be too surprising if this was so.

What is certain is that Deeley wished to proceed to a 4—6—0, in succession to the 4—4—0 (just as Johnson before him had wanted to build bigger engines — see page 133) and eventually left the company in somewhat unusual circumstances, thus leading to the appointment of Henry Fowler. Now Fowler was an admirable man in many ways — and did, after all, introduce superheating — but one feels that he was not the sort of man to 'rock the boat'. In consequence, he was more likely to go along with the newly developing Midland style of 'operational' management than, perhaps, Deeley would have been. At all events, nothing bigger than a class 4 ever emerged from Derby during Fowler's time until well into LMS days — and then only reluctantly!*

In part this slow movement was because the class 4 passenger engines were, on the whole, rather good for their time and this is where we feel there is an as yet less publicised aspect to the Midland locomotive story as far as its bigger engines are concerned and it is mostly to their credit. By way of introduction to the story, the engines concerned are compared at *Plates 288-290*.

The fact is, of course, that when discussing the Midland's class 4 passenger engines, the story really crystallizes around the compounds rather than the '990' class. The latter were built 'for comparative purposes' and, although always sound, they were never quite as efficient as the three-cylinder machines, and consequently not repeated. Had they proved to be serious rivals, then, given the contemporary thinking, it is quite likely that the MR/LMS management would have proceeded to a large build of these engines instead of the policy that was pursued. So it is that, without apology, we devote by far the bulk of this chapter to that most famous of types, the Midland Compound.

THE MIDLAND COMPOUNDS

We are prepared to 'stick our necks out' and assert, unequivocally, that the Midland Compound as developed during the pre-LMS period, was one of the truly outstanding British steam locomotive designs. Such a statement, of course, invites criticism and merits qualification; so why do we make this claim?

Firstly, let us quote a few facts of a quite unimpeachable nature:

1. The Midland Compound was the only truly successful British compound design built in quantity.
2. The Midland Compound was the largest single class of new 4—4—0s (simple *or* compound) *ever* built in Britain.
3. The Midland Compound was the largest series of three-cylinder compounds built by any country *in the world.*

It defies all logic to be able to make any of these statements unless the design itself was of intrinsically high merit. We do, of course, include the 195 LMS-built examples as justification for Facts 2 and 3 but we feel that neither the Midland nor the LMS would have built them at all if they had not been of exceptional merit. For one thing, it would have been cheaper to build two-cylinder simples had the difference in quality been only marginal. The Midland, and particularly the LMS, were very cost-conscious at the time so it is scarcely conceivable that the LMS after 1923 would have built so many had it not been convinced of their value.

---

* Excluding, of course, the Lickey 'banker' and the S & DJR 2—8—0s.

Plates 288-290. These three views show the 'as built' state of the Midland's class 4 passenger engines and allow visual comparisons to be made. No. 2632 is the second of the original pair of Johnson compounds, still very much in the Johnson idiom. No. 1000 represents the original Deeley compound of 1905, very different in shape and appearance; while No. 993 is an example of the 2-cylinder simple expansion '990' class in saturated condition and displaying pure latter-day Midland appearance. The three views together afford a graphic representation of the changes during the Edwardian period.   *Authors' Collection and Bernard Mathews' Collection*

Yet the Compounds were not always given a good press, either at the time of their building or subsequently. Why is this so? We cannot be certain but feel that the answer is probably nothing more significant than size. They were excellent machines but, in the context of LMS developments, never quite big enough in *absolute* terms. The LMS was much criticised for adding nearly 200 more Compounds after 1923 and in size terms this was probably a justifiable point. However, over the years, especially on the ex-LNWR lines, where memories of Webb's less than perfect compounds had gone into folk-myth, the criticisms 'homed in' on the 'compound' aspect rather than the size factor. These engines were suspect because they were compounds (and 'Midland' to boot!) whereas in fact they were simply not big enough for the tasks involved in many cases — and for this, LMS management must take the blame.

As *engines*, however, the Compounds had much 'going for them' as they say. They could out-perform almost any contemporary 4—6—0 (save, perhaps, the more sophisticated GWR types) and were more than a match for any contemporary 4—4—0. Their only serious British rivals in the latter wheel arrangement were the Gresley D49 (the 'Shires' and 'Hunts') and the superb Maunsell 'Schools' class which, if truth be told, was, for operational reasons, more of an eight-wheeled 4—6—0 than a true 4—4—0! Moreover, the Gresley and Maunsell designs were a generation or more *later* than the conception of the Midland Compound. We cannot honestly conceive a D49 running non-stop from London to Edinburgh, which achievement is 'on record' as far as the Midland design is concerned, albeit with a modified tender to carry the extra coal supply — but then, we are probably prejudiced!

The Midland Compound was successful *because* it was a compound, a fact not always accepted, or appreciated by British observers. We shall describe its 'gestation' in due course, but at this point we propose to indulge in a bit of 'lateral' explanation by way of trying to redress the balance — apologising again (as with our dissertation on 'single' driving wheel engines) to any engineers who may feel that we are merely stating the obvious in explaining the compound principle.

The compound steam locomotive developed, historically, out of a desire to make more use of the expansive properties of steam. Essentially, when a 'simple' locomotive exhausts its 'spent steam' from the cylinder(s), the steam is still at a very considerable pressure above that of the atmosphere — hence the 'puffing' sound, characteristic of the exhaust of a simple, as the steam forces its way to the external atmosphere via the blast pipe. Many engineers in the 19th century realised that this was wasteful. The steam clearly had 'work potential' when exhausted and the search was on to find a practical way of making use of this before exhausting to atmosphere. It almost seemed to offer 'something for nothing', as it were, once the steam had been generated in the boiler.

Thus the 'compound' locomotive makes more use of the expansive properties of steam. It is used first in the high

pressure cylinder(s) but then, instead of wastefully exhausting, it is allowed to expand further in lower pressure cylinder(s) before going to atmosphere. It does not need a profound knowledge of physics to appreciate that *theoretically* this has to be more efficient since once the actual creation of steam has been achieved, the more work which can be extracted before exhausting it to atmosphere, the better. Obviously, the working mechanism must be more complex to make this 'second use' of the steam and the final exhaust pressure will be lower. This in turn may cause problems because the reciprocating steam locomotive depends on the exhaust (via the blast pipe) to 'draw the fire' and create the necessary draught on the firebox to continue the 'steam creation' process.

It is all very much a question of calculation of the 'profit and loss' balance; but far better minds than ours have demonstrated that the increased complexity, compared with the 'simple' engine is more than offset by the gain in efficiency of the compound engine, all other things being equal. Unfortunately in the British context, all other things were *not* equal. For one thing, cylinder sizes have to be carefully calculated — and the restricted British loading gauge did not always help. Secondly, this country was blessed (or cursed, depending on one's viewpoint) with indigenous supplies of cheap, good coal which often meant that maintenance was more of a problem (costwise) than expenditure on fuel. The compound costs more to maintain (obviously) so — did it make an appreciable saving in fuel etc., sufficient to justify the extra complexity?

This aspect was further bedevilled by the various national approaches to crew training. Sadly, in Britain, footplate crews (as one of us can personally vouch) were seldom, if ever, encouraged to take an intelligent interest in what was actually happening 'up front' and if a locoman developed a real understanding of the whole business, he was often discouraged, ignored or even regarded with suspicion by his mates. 'Keep it simple' was the philosophy at all levels and this, unfortunately, endured to the very end of steam in Britain — and, as the other half of the partnership has personally experienced, it has not always changed in the era of preserved steam. To witness *Evening Star* being worked on the first valve and full forward gear with a 500 ton train on a 1:100 gradient as late as 1978 was pathetic, to say the least. However, we digress a little and *Evening Star* is not even a compound!

Thus it was that the compound never really had a fair chance in Britain for a variety of historical reasons. One has only to look overseas, particularly France, to see what might have happened. In France, fuel was not good and working efficiency was much more highly regarded. French enginemen were 'true' engineers, fully understanding their charges and the names of De-Glehn and Chapelon as their mentors, immediately spring to mind. Whether we in Britain like it or not, it was the French who really developed the steam locomotive to its ultimate state in the person of André Chapelon — and he built *compounds* to the very end! Moreover, such 'gurus' as Gresley and Stanier were only too willing to consult Chapelon in the 1930s. It is just a pity that they were, through force of circumstances, unable to make full use of what they discovered. To be fair, however, they both tried!

All the more credit, therefore, to this lone Midland attempt to 'break out from the mould' as early as 1902. Deeley tried and so too, as late as the 1920s, did the much maligned Fowler with his 4—6—2 proposals. There is even (at the NRM) a design study for a 4-cylinder *compound* Stanier 4—6—4 with full Chapelon treatment; but all to no avail. The British did not really want compounds and even the great Churchward, who bought a few French examples to play with, could not really see any advantage. However, mention of Churchward tempts us to speculate upon what the Midland Compound might have been like if it had also embodied Churchward's long lap, long travel valves. This never happened, more's the pity.

A further point must also be considered as far as the Midland Compounds are concerned — that of the Midland men themselves. Whether by force of circumstances or by inclination, many of the Midland locomen did not really appreciate just what a formidable machine they had in the class 4 Compound. Rarely, if ever, called upon to exert matters, most Midland crews, by the late pre-grouping period, tended to call for a pilot engine for any load even marginally above the stipulated limit, so they never really comprehended the sheer puissance of the Compounds, if properly handled. For this, management must accept some blame. Given different operational circumstances and attitudes, the Compounds could have created just as formidable a reputation as did the 'Georges' on the rival LNWR — but they never got the chance. Thus it was left to other enginemen, on other parts of the newly formed LMS after 1923, really to test the mettle of these excellent machines; it was only in the famed Settle-Carlisle trials of the 1920s that the 'home' team began to discover those thermodynamic truths which had been, theoretically, available for 10-20 years previously. It was all most curious and, in retrospect, more than a little regrettable, because by then it was too late — and, it must be said, many Midland men never really learned the lesson, even until the end of steam itself.

The net result was, as we were all to see, a perpetuation of the simple expansion philosophy against the typically British background of maintenance costs etc. It probably made a great deal of economic sense, as no less a person than the late R. A. Riddles has stated to one of us, but it also puts the Midland Compound into rather more favourable a position viewed retrospectively in more purely engineering terms. Too small — maybe; but not much good — never! Now if only Deeley *had* built his compound 4—6—0 and Midland men *had* learned some of the new ways . . .

From here on we shall not be tempted into too much further speculation, but merely record the Midland part of the story — the first 45 engines of this celebrated class.

To many, the Midland Compound, more than any other locomotive, personified the Midland Railway; yet the first five Compounds were very different from those locomotives which were developed later from the original design and which were continued in large numbers by the LMS, so much so that the LMS version survived in service with British Railways until 1961. Although it was this later form, of course, which most folk saw as typical, the real story started earlier.

The year 1900 saw the final series of Singles enter service, together with the last of the slim-boilered 4—4—0s. However, Johnson's long-expressed wish for bigger engines eventually bore fruit when the same year also saw the introduction of the Belpaires, a much more powerful class of locomotive designed to handle the heavier passenger trains coming into service. This increase in weight was due almost entirely to the use of many more corridor coaches on express passenger trains when compared with the 1890s, during which period, widespread use of non-corridor express stock in principal trains was normal.

By 1902 there was a need for even more powerful locomotives and this was answered in part by the arrival of 4—4—0 Compounds Nos. 2631/2. These new 3-cylinder Compounds worked on the Smith system which employed two outside low pressure cylinders with a single high pressure cylinder between the frames. Compounding had been tried on several British systems; but the spur to the Midland's use of compounding had been that introduced onto the North Eastern Railway when, in 1898, T. W. Worsdell's 2-cylinder 4—4—0 No. 1619 was rebuilt with three cylinders. At the time of this reconstruction, the chief draughtsman at Gateshead was a W. M. Smith who played a major part in the development and design of the compounding system employed subsequently by the MR from 1902 onwards.

Much has been written about how the Midland Railway at Derby, with no previous experience in compounding, came to use the Smith system. However, Smith was an ex-Derby man and knew Johnson well. Suffice to say that there must have been close co-operation between the two companies which enabled the Midland Railway to use Smith's design in their two new locomotives. The first two compounds were followed by three more basically similar machines; but these five Johnson Compounds were more different visually and structurally from the Deeley Compounds, which followed them in 1905, than they were from each other. Such variations as there were between the first two Johnson Compounds and the next three were small when compared with the differences between the Johnson and Deeley locomotives.

The 1905 Deeley batch had a new cab with a combined rear splasher, and a cab roof now extended well back over the footplate. This, combined with a running plate which was raised slightly over the coupled wheels in conjunction with the flat Deeley smokebox door and new straight-sided tender, produced a very different looking machine and saw

Plate 291. No. 2633, posed on a train somewhere south of Derby, clearly reveals the front end changes on the second series of Johnson compounds, especially above the cylinders. Note that like the engine in *Plate 287*, the cylinders appear to be unlined — somewhat surprisingly in view of the general elaboration of finish revealed elsewhere. No. 2633 was renumbered 1002 in 1907 and when rebuilt in 1919 it was the last of the Johnson compounds to assume the 'Deeley' form.
National Railway Museum

the introduction of what many regard as the classic Deeley stylistic features (perpetuated by Fowler) and evident, in a modified form, in the construction of Midland style locomotives of all kinds by the LMS until 1941, when the final series of class 4F 0—6—0s entered service. Thus, the compounds not only introduced new ideas in the loco-motive design sense, but, as developed, also became instrumental in helping to establish the visual 'face' of the late MR/early LMS period, and from this point onwards we shall pursue the story chronologically by batches, starting with a discussion of the two series in saturated form.

THE JOHNSON COMPOUNDS
(SATURATED STEAM PERIOD)

2631 CLASS

Built at Derby 1902/3.
Original MR numbers 2631-2635.
1907 numbers 1000-1004, all to LMS.
Superheated 1914-1919.
Withdrawn 1948-1952.
No. 1000 was restored as MR 1000 as part of the National Collection in 1959.
Allocated to engine diagram 58 (No. 1000-1001) and engine diagram 59 (Nos. 1002-1004) in 1910.

Early in 1902, less than eighteen months after Johnson had moved to the 'big engine' concept with his 'Belpaire' 4—4—0 (Chapter 7), and long before this latter design had been pursued to fulfilment, he startled the contemporary world again by building two even bigger engines — the pioneer Midland Compounds Nos. 2631-2. That they were considered something of an experimental notion cannot seriously be denied — the Midland rarely produced new designs in quantities of two only.

Visually, they owed much to the Belpaires and gave little clue to the ultimate stylistic character of the developed compound. They were very similar in concept to NER 4—4—0 No. 1619, employing a piston valve for the single high pressure cylinder and two slide valves for the (outside) low pressure cylinders. Two sets of independent reversing gear were provided and, all told, they must have seemed quite formidably complex in the context of 1902 and certainly demanded considerable extra sophistication on the part of the footplate crew.

They went first to Leeds (for the Settle-Carlisle line) and proved a great success, quickly demonstrating (in competent hands) a free-running, high speed capability quite unmatched by anything which had gone before. The separate reversing gear for the two steam circuits must, however, have met with some objections, for the next three to appear in 1903 had but one reverser, operating all three sets of valve gear. This was, theoretically, less efficient and already indicated the sort of compromises which prevented the compound being as acceptable as it may and perhaps *should* have been. Not to put too fine a point on it, the traditional mode of training British footplatemen on the 'sitting next to Nellie' principle without real attempt on the part of management to *explain* the business to their men, was already revealing its 'dead hand' characteristics!

None the less, all five compounds were a great success, both in haulage ability and economy, so the Midland must have been reasonably well pleased. The two series can be compared at *Plates 287 & 291*, from which the most obvious change was the 'straight through' running plate fitted to the second batch of three engines, Nos. 2633-5. 'Handsome is as handsome does', so they say, and starting from a first contemporary reaction of shock and horror at the quite alien visual characteristics of these new engines, we can, at this point in time, examine them more rationally.

They were not greeted with approval aesthetically, 'Great Ugly Brutes' being one recorded observation, but this was soon to change as they proved their worth. In point of fact, they were not too different from the Belpaires in stylistic treatment; but there were only ten of the latter by the time the Compounds first appeared, so maybe the criticism was levelled across the board at Johnson's new approach.

For our part, we find them not displeasing visually. That they were different cannot be gainsaid, but, viewed objectively, they still revealed the attention to detail which was characteristic of Johnson. The bogie tenders, for example, whilst necessary until the Midland instituted water troughs in 1903, had less of the ugly clumsiness of those first fitted to the '2601' class 4—2—2s or the first series of 'Belpaires', and there seems to have been a conscious attempt to 'clean up' the lines of the second series of three engines at the front end.

All five employed a new chimney shape, deploying a capuchon (or windguard) at the front upper rim. Chimney shape was always guaranteed to cause a furore in certain circles (it still does, for that matter) and we know of at least one eminent locomotive designer who deliberately put an 'absurd' chimney on some of his engines to divert attention from its more fundamental changes (!); but Johnson handled matters with his usual flair and, as far as we are concerned, it 'came off'. The finish, as always, was superb, as some of our pictures will reveal.

In due course, they were taken in hand, superheated and rebuilt (visually and anatomically) almost beyond recognition, to the standard Deeley style — but this was not until well after Deeley's departure. During his time, the only major change was the rebuilding of the bogie tenders to the high-sided six-wheel type. These rebuilt tenders were of the 'turn-under' side panel variety (see Chapter 8), having been derived from bogie tenders with individual wheel springs, and were not the most pleasing to behold after rebuilding. They tended to remain with the pioneer compounds well into LMS days and 'matched up' with the engines (whether original or rebuilt) rather better than with some classes (*Plate 292*).

The first five compounds were renumbered 1000-4 in 1907 which got rather bound up with the renumbering of the Deeley series (Nos. 1000-29 at first), but more of that in due course. During the whole of the saturated period they kept their Johnson lineaments, save for the inevitable 'front end' and livery changes of the Deeley period, and the pictures appended should serve to complete this first phase of the story.

Plate 292. This view shows Johnson compound No. 1003 (previously No. 2634) in a slightly intermediate state at Nottingham c.1908 before its full rebuilding to Deeley style in 1915. The most obvious change is the rebuilding of the tender to six-wheel pattern, but the smokebox has also been altered and the engine now carries the Deeley style of red livery. The upper cab spectacle glass has also been slightly changed (compare *Plate 291*). *Authors' Collection*

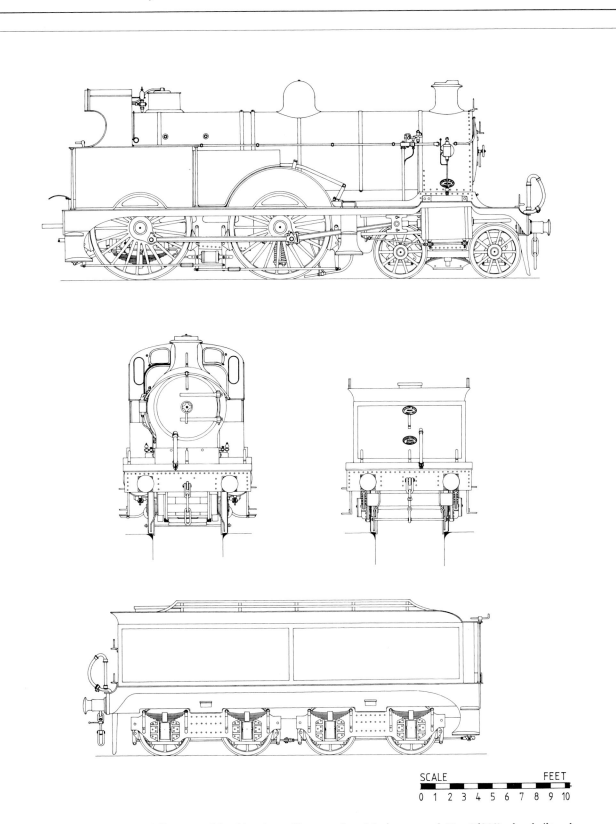

SCALE   FEET
0 1 2 3 4 5 6 7 8 9 10

Fig. 51. This drawing, specially prepared for this volume, illustrates the original compounds Nos. 2631/2 when built and coupled to a bogie tender.

B. D. Hunt

THE DEELEY COMPOUNDS (saturated phase)

Built at Derby 1905.
Original MR numbers 1000-1009. In 1910 allocated to Engine Diagram 67.
1907 numbers 1005-1014, all to LMS.
When superheated between 1919-1927 they were allocated to engine diagram 71.

Built at Derby 1906.
Original MR numbers 1010-1029.
1907 numbers 1015-1034, all to LMS.

Built at Derby 1908/9
Numbered 1035-1044 from new, all to LMS.
In this condition they were allocated to Engine Diagram 68 and following superheating they were allocated to Engine Diagram 71. Superheating began in 1913 (No. 1040) with the remainder superheated between 1919-1928.

Class extinct 1953.

In late 1905, by which time there were 50 Belpaires in service but still only the original five Compounds, Deeley built some more of the latter type and a series of ten engines emerged (Nos. 1000-9) of radically new appearance

(*Plate 289*). Not only were they different visually, but below the surface, as it were, more changes took place.

Essentially these mechanical changes were probably bound up, yet again, with the innate conservatism of the footplate men and Deeley may have felt that Johnson's compromises on Nos. 2633-5 did not provide the perfect solution for getting the best out of a compound, given contemporary attitudes. As well as a single reverser, Johnson's revised arrangement had also incorporated a reinforcing valve to allow high pressure steam to be admitted to the low-pressure circuit at the driver's discretion; but it seems possible that drivers had not fully utilised this added refinement. In its place, Deeley provided an ingenious new patented regulator which automatically provided live steam to all three cylinders on starting (always the most 'tricky' aspect of a compound) and then, when more fully opened, cut off the live steam to the outside cylinders while still supplying the inside (HP) cylinder with boiler steam. Thus, the engine would go 'fully compound' without too much thought on the part of the crew! It did, of course, demand that the regulator be opened more fully

Plate 293. No. 1000, after renumbering to No. 1005 in 1907, appears here prior to superheating. By now a dished Deeley smokebox door has been fitted and the continuous boiler handrail has been replaced. From a livery standpoint, readers should note that the fluting on both the coupling and connecting rods have been painted black. The deep front frames of this series show clearly on this view.

Collection Bernard Mathews

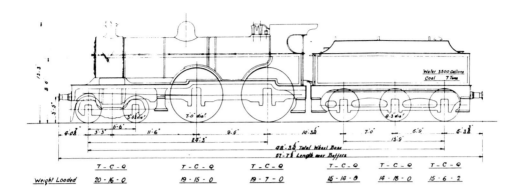

4—4—0 PASSENGER ENGINE

Fig. 52. *This Midland Railway 1910 diagram ED67, details the first ten Deeley compounds prior to superheating.*
National Railway Museum

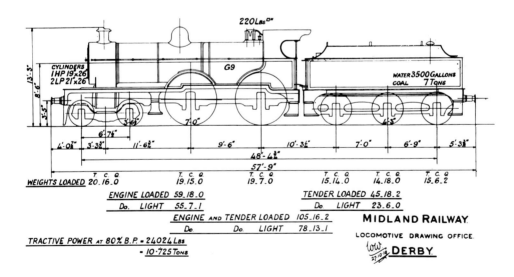

Nº 4 CLASS SATᴰ COMPOUND PASSENGER   ED68
Nᴼˢ 1005—1044

Fig. 53. *This 1919 Midland Railway diagram ED 1/68 was intended to cover all the saturated compounds at that date.*
However ED 1/68 is clearly based upon ED68, the 1910 diagram for the 'shallow frame' series, 1907 Nos. 1015-44.
National Railway Museum

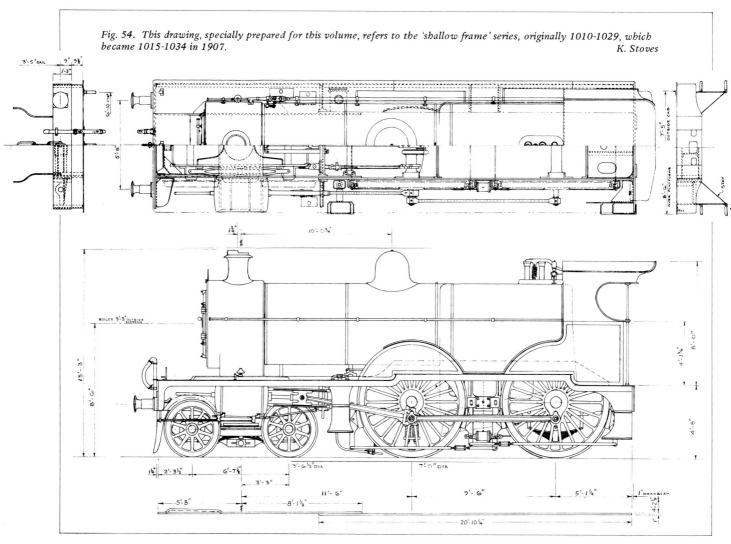

Fig. 54. This drawing, specially prepared for this volume, refers to the 'shallow frame' series, originally 1010-1029, which became 1015-1034 in 1907.

K. Stoves

to work compound and led to more than one instance where the 'first valve' devotees (quite prevalent on British lines) could sometimes find themselves working the engines as 3-cylinder simples and then complaining that the steam circuit was strangled! Neither did this make the compounds totally suited to the 'stop and start' nature of local passenger working with its consequential and frequent opening and closing of the regulator.

As already intimated, we cannot help but think that the French ordered things rather better, especially in relation to providing the sort of footplate training which allowed the compound to be given the more sophisticated controls which its very nature demanded — not the least being an ability to set the cut-off differently in the HP and LP circuits.

Tempting though it would be to go on in this vein, we are conscious that many accounts exist in print of the more technical aspects of compounding in general and the Midland Compounds in particular, and we would refer readers to these sources* for further exposition of this most fascinating business.

The new Deeley compounds established stylistic features which were to last for nearly forty years on many classes of locomotives, before the last, essentially Midland-looking engine was built in 1941 (the last of the class 4 0–6–0s). Raised running plate, new smokebox, much more spacious cab, new style tender, etc., were all incorporated to an extent which probably seemed even more radical than Johnson's earlier departures from the 19th century norm; but they were all to become Midland (and later LMS) hallmarks. One or two front end features did, however, hark back, if only peripherally to earlier days. The smokebox support, door, handrail and chimney had something of a hint of Johnson to them at first, but this was not to last (see *Plate 289*).

The next series of Deeley compounds (Nos. 1010-29) incorporated a few more changes, most obvious of which

* In particular: 'The Compound Locomotive' by J. T. Van Riemsdijk, BA — Transactions of the Newcomen Society Vols. XLIII-V, 1970-3.

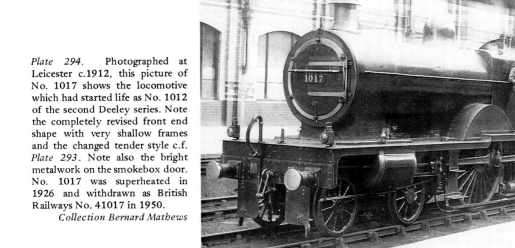

Plate 294. Photographed at Leicester c.1912, this picture of No. 1017 shows the locomotive which had started life as No. 1012 of the second Deeley series. Note the completely revised front end shape with very shallow frames and the changed tender style c.f. *Plate 293.* Note also the bright metalwork on the smokebox door. No. 1017 was superheated in 1926 and withdrawn as British Railways No. 41017 in 1950.

Collection Bernard Mathews

were the very shallow front frames, thus revealing a fully circular smokebox projecting forward of its support (*Plate 294*). This went with a slight redesign of smokebox door and handrail, a slight extension in length of the smokebox itself, and a subtle change in tender style.

The new flat-sided Deeley tenders, fitted to the first ten of his compounds, were of exceptionally neat design, well suited visually to the new engine shape. They had a clearly defined running plate level with the cab base and a

neat arrangement of footplate angle and footstep supports. With the next series, the running plate was 'cut back' between the front and rear footsteps to almost vestigal proportions and this became normal for the remaining Deeley compounds. The style was also used for the '990' class engines and is sometimes referred to as the '990' style tender. In fact most of them were built for the compounds. *Plates 293 & 294* reveal the differences between the two types of Deeley tender.

Plate 295. This view of the last of the Midland-built compounds, No. 1044, shows the engine almost exactly as per *Plate 294*, save for considerable additional riveting at the smokebox end and the now standard dished-shape door. The cylinders appear to be lined (see note on page 250) but the picture is not dated. No. 1044 was not superheated until 1926 and was scrapped as BR No. 41044 late in 1952.

Authors' Collection

It was this design of tender which formed the basis of the slightly later conversion of the former bogie tenders. These were given slightly deeper upper side panels and came in two varieties (already discussed in Chapter 8), including the five rebuilds for the Johnson compound series. They were, however, generally similar to the new tenders.

After Deeley had built his first 30 compounds, the 1907 renumbering caused some confusion. Deeley's engines were Nos. 1000-29 but the new system decreed that all the compounds should go into this series. Accordingly, Johnson's engines became the *second* Nos. 1000-4 and Deeley's were renumbered 1005-34. It can be very difficult at times in the 1005-29 series to know which is which as a result of this considerable overlap in numbers pre- and post-1907.

Finally, in 1908-9, a further ten Deeley compounds were built, exactly like his second batch and these were numbered in the new 1907 series as Nos. 1035-44 immediately following the renumbered earlier engines (*Plate 295*). This concluded the building of the Midland Compounds as such, and it was not until the onset of superheating (below) that further significant visual changes took place.

THE SUPERHEATED COMPOUNDS

The superheating of the Midland Compounds was, to some extent, related to the '990' class engines (see page 255). In 1910 one of this latter group was superheated, the first MR engine so treated, and this was followed by the gradual introduction of superheating on the Class 3 Belpaires and the introduction of the superheated '483' class rebuilds (see Chapters 6/8). The compounds came later, the first one to be converted being Deeley type No. 1040 in 1913.

The subsequent progress was somewhat sluggish, commencing in 1914 but not being completed until 1928, well into LMS days. Yet these engines were the Midland's 'prime' express types and the slow progress seems, in retrospect, somewhat strange. It can have had little or nothing to do with the relative newness of the engines. The '990' class were mostly newer still, but were all superheated by 1914, and the '483' class renewals frequently replaced engines which in their previous 'H' boiler state were only a few years old. We think the explanation may be more subtle and, conceivably, less flattering.

It seems probable that, once again, the Midland was taking a somewhat uninspired approach. Superheating greatly improved the performance of a two-cylinder simple, but the compounds, even in saturated form, were already more capable than a superheated Class 2 or Class 3 so 'why bother?' may well have been the prevailing approach at Derby for a few years. The fact that the

Plate 296. No. 1004 in superheated condition — note the misshapen coupling rod on the running plate at the base of the smokebox. Originally No. 2635, this locomotive became No. 1004 in 1907 and was superheated in 1914. It survived to be withdrawn as British Railways No. 41004 early in 1952.
Collection Bernard Mathews

Plate 297. The pioneer Deeley compound No. 1005 (originally No. 1000) was not superheated until the first few months of the LMS period and is shown here, soon thereafter, still in MR livery. The deep front frames were retained but the extended smokebox made quite a change in appearance (compare *Plate 293*). Ultimately, during LMS days, all the ex-MR compounds assumed this general front end configuration.

Authors' Collection

advantage of superheating was just as relevant, if not more so, on a compound, seems not to have been seriously pressed home by anyone. By its very nature, a compound is designed to take better advantage of the expansive properties of steam than a simple, and superheated steam, also by its very nature, has even greater expansive properties than 'wet' steam; so the benefit of *combining* these two advantages should have been a bit more immediately obvious than seems to have been the case. However, there does seem to have been some sort of contemporary belief that superheating could serve as a substitute for, or alternative to compounding.

Apart from No. 1040 (above), which may have been something of an experimental 'try out', the only compounds which came in for anything approaching early treatment were the pioneer Johnson quintet, now Nos. 1000-4. They, of course, were non-standard compared with the Deeley engines, so it probably seemed sensible to rebuild them to the Deeley configuration in any case (in the interests of harmonisation with the rest of the class) and this rebuilding took place during 1914-5 (Nos. 1000/1/3/4) and in 1919 for No. 1002. Taking the already superheated No. 1040 as the 'model', the Johnson engines were superheated and rebuilt beyond recognition, re-emerging as typical Deeley engines (*Plate 296*) and, of course, today exemplified by the preserved No. 1000 itself at the National Railway Museum.

It is, of course, possible that, as some writers have stated, Fowler was so busy with the '483' renewals and the

superheating of many of the Belpaires that the compounds came well down the list of priorities − and this may be true. If so, it was something of a short-sighted policy. Right to the very end of its existence, the Midland was double heading its heavier trains with virtually every conceivable combination of express power available. Although 45 super-heated compounds may not have been able totally to eliminate such practices, it is a stone cold certainty that the wastefulness of this policy could have been reduced to a noticeable extent if Derby had pursued a crash programme of upgrading the compounds, during, say, 1913-4 and then encouraged its drivers to use the engines properly! This, of course, never happened so the nonsense continued − and World War I then interposed further delays and difficulties.

Thus it was as late as 1919 that the somewhat leisurely programme of superheating the rest of the Deeley series began. By the time of the grouping, there were still 21 left in saturated state and it was not until 1928 that the LMS completed the business when No. 1022 was superheated. For the record, the engines superheated during MR days were as follows:

Nos. 1000-4: Original Johnson compounds	(5 total)
Nos. 1006-9/11-2/4: First Deeley series	(7 total)
Nos. 1015-6/20/3-4/31/5/7-40/2: Final Deeley series	(12 total)

When superheated, the Midland Compounds began to assume a somewhat more consistent appearance, tender styles excepted. The biggest visual change, of course, was found in the original Johnson series, but after this change

Plates 298 & 299. These two views, taken from virtually the same angle, show how relatively small was the visual change to the 'shallow frame' Deeley compounds when first superheated. No. 1030 (originally No. 1025) is in saturated condition and No. 1040 was the first of all the compounds to be superheated (in 1913). The extended smokebox was the main visual clue. No. 1030 was eventually superheated in 1925 and the engines were scrapped in 1951 (No. 1030) and 1952 (No. 1040), both carrying their BR numbers. *Authors' Collection*

took place, all 45 shared the characteristic extended smoke-box with standardised dished door, separate handrail and 'Deeley' chimney. The rest of the locomotive remained virtually the same as the original Deeley version and it was only really at the front end that a superheated compound differed significantly in appearance from the saturated Deeley types.

The principal front end variation, along with the extended smokebox, was the matter of frame shape. The first Deeley series had been given deep frames and these were retained

the study well into LMS days (which we have covered in another publication) and as far as the *Midland* period is concerned, the front frame configuration of the super-heated compounds was as follows:

	Nos. 1000-4	Deep frames after superheating
Between	Nos. 1005-14	Deep frames retained after superheating
Between	Nos. 1015-44	Shallow frames retained after superheating

The whole of the ex-MR-built series of superheated compounds survived intact until 1948 when the first with-

Plate 300. No. 1017 (originally No. 1012) was not superheated until 1926 yet still retained its shallow frames, as shown here on a down Tilbury line boat express c.1926-7.   *Authors' Collection*

after superheating, the extended smokebox being the main visual difference (see, for example, *Plates 293 & 297*). The Johnson engines, when superheated, were also given this arrangement (*Plate 296*). However, the remaining Deeley series (1907 Nos. 1015-44) had been built with shallow frames and slightly extended smokeboxes. When super-heated, all that really changed on this group was a further extension of the smokebox length, sometimes difficult to 'spot' but readily obvious if the angle of view was right — see, for instance, *Plates 298 & 299*.

This shallow front frame proved somewhat less than satisfactory, but it was not until LMS days that the front frames of the 1015-44 series were deepened to what became the standard form. As late as early 1926, superheat-ing was still being carried out retaining the original shallow frames (*Plate 300*), by which time only Nos. 1010/8/21-2/6-7/44 remained to be superheated. We have no record of whether these few were rebuilt from the outset with their original shallow or new style deep frames, but, by then, the front frames of some of the earlier engines of this series were being converted. However, this has now taken

drawals took place and the very last withdrawal from service was No. 1025 (as BR No. 41025) at the start of 1953. Although we cover the LMS period in detail else-where, we have thought it desirable to include a few pictures here (*Plates 301-306*) to round out the account of a long-lived class.

Finally in this survey of these famous engines and before giving additional details of livery and other visual variations during MR days, a note on the preserved No. 1000 will not be out of place.

MR No. 1000 was, of course, built as the pioneer John-son compound No. 2631 in 1902 (*Plate 307*). Withdrawn from service late in 1951 as BR No. 41000, it was selected for permanent preservation. Mercifully no attempt was made to put it back to 'as built' condition (it would have been almost a practical impossibility), but a superb restoration to its original 1914 superheated condition was achieved by BR in the late 1950s. However, it did not have a correct tender, having been one of the several ex-MR engines to receive that most curious LMS hybrid style, well shown at *Plate 308*. In its 1914 condition, and for much

Continued on page 246

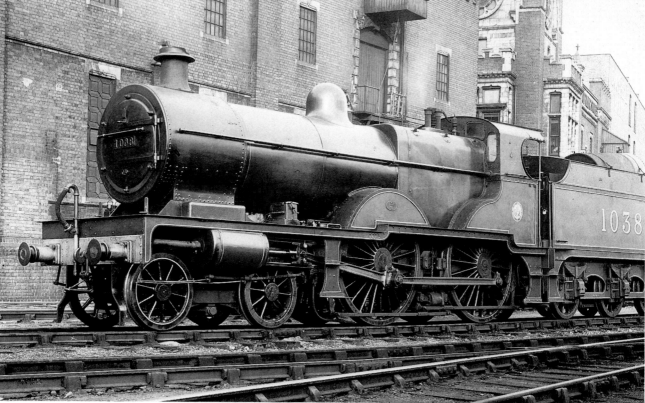

Plates 301 & 302. In due course the LMS fitted deep frames to all the erstwhile shallow frame compounds — but it was something of a drawn out process as these views reveal. No. 1038 had modified frames before 1928 as its early period LMS livery reveals (superheated as late as 1922) but No. 1023 (old No. 1018), also superheated in 1922, still had shallow frames as late as 1934 when photographed at Bristol in the post-1927 LMS colours. No. 1038 gives an excellent impression of the first LMS livery (essentially Deeley style) and both engines have lined cylinders (see page 250). No. 1023 was withdrawn in 1951 and No. 1038 in 1952, both carrying BR livery.

Collection Bernard Mathews and H. C. Casserley

JOHNSON/DEELEY CLASS 4 4−4−0s

Plate 303. Photographed at Saltley in 1935, No. 1014 displays the post-1928 LMS livery. Built in 1905 as No. 1009 and superheated in 1919, it was withdrawn in 1952 by British Railways as 41014. Note the extended and strengthened front frames (not an uncommon feature by this time) and the 'pop' valves, by then almost universal. The tender is still the original pattern. *W. L. Good*

Plate 304. No. 1004 started life as the last of the Johnson compounds, No. 2635 (see also *Plate 296*). By 1937 it had received the 1928 LMS livery with gold/black insignia, a new LMS pattern tender, tank and 'pop' safety valves — a fairly characteristic 'mix' of changes for these engines. This view was taken at Kentish Town on 22nd August 1937. *L. Hanson*

Plate 305. This view at Derby in August 1937 of No. 1029, originally built as No. 1024, shows a former 'shallow frame' compound now with deep frames. Like *Plate 304*, this engine, too, has 'pop' valves but has also acquired a replacement tall Stanier chimney. The tender is, however, the original version. *A. G. Ellis*

Plate 306. This picture of No. 41012 (originally No. 1007) taken at Derby in March 1949, shows the early BR lined black livery which was the final guise for this class. Note the short replacement Stanier chimney and squat dome when compared with the previous Midland version. Note also the tender. A replacement tank without beading has been fitted to the original frames, No. 41012 was to run until 1951 when it was withdrawn. *V. Forster*

Plates 307 & 308. Transformation of a compound. These pictures show the famous MR No. 1000 at the start and virtually the finish of its operational life as MR No. 2631 and BR No. M1000 respectively. The pictures tell their own story, but note particularly the curious tender on M1000. This was an LMS economy measure — a new standard tank fitted to serviceable existing frames. However, the standard tank was designed for a shorter-framed tender, hence the platform at the rear. *Bernard Mathews' Collection and Authors' Collection*

Plate 309. An immaculate ex-works view of No. 1000 in post-1927 LMS livery c.1930. The rebuilt ex-bogie tender was carried during most of the LMS period. *Authors' Collection*

of the LMS period, it ran with a rebuilt ex-bogie tender (*Plates 309/10*), but these too had gone so the only reasonable solution was to find the 'nearest to original' tender available. This turned out to be a Deeley tender first built for an ex-S & DJR 2–8–0 which was almost (but not quite) identical to the tenders given to Deeley series Nos. 1015-44. This was duly affixed and a not unreasonable 'pairing' was achieved (*Plate 311*).

During 1959-62, MR No. 1000 ran as a 'working' museum piece until it went to Clapham Museum in 1963 where it remained until that museum closed in 1973. Moved to the NRM in 1975, it was put back into working order against a series of unsubstantiated and quite idiotic rumours regarding its general state. There was even talk of it having replica 'wooden' motion parts! It remained on the working roster until 1984, when the mandatory boiler certificate finally expired and at the time of writing (1986-7) it is not known whether this very precious example of Britain's railway heritage will ever steam again. The issue is controversial. It is Britain's only potential working main line compound, but, by the same token, it is irreplaceable and in the museum business, long term conservation can often be in conflict with short term popularity of appeal. One of us has to live, daily, with this problem and only time will tell what might transpire. Emotionally, of course, there is not much doubt in the issue!

In the meantime, the engine still stands as a permanent physical reminder of this valiant attempt to move British locomotive practice forward. That it was only a partial success is hardly the fault of the engine as such, more the lack of vision of its various owners! It also happens to be possibly the most definitive extant example of the true Midland Lake colour and the Deeley style of lining, copied, of course, by the LMS — which brings us nicely to a brief analysis of some of the more noteworthy livery and detail variations of the whole compound family during their Midland days.

Plate 310. No. 1000 photographed at Derby and now in the post 1935 period carries a 22B Gloucester shed plate and is fitted with an exhaust steam injector — note the pipe running from the lower part of the smokebox to the running plate. It is, however, still paired with its original tender. *Collection Bernard Mathews*

Plate 311. MR 1000 as originally restored in 1959 with a Deeley tender of ex-S & DJR origin (see text). Compared with this view, the engine, as now displayed at York, has received a correct size shed plate, black painted 'fluting' to the connecting and side rods and lining on the cylinder covers. *Authors' Collection*

Plate 312. The locomotive and tender changing which became commonplace during the early years of the LMS (i.e. locomotives running with tenders belonging to other locomotives) was a practice not confined to the post-1923 era, as this picture of No. 2634 confirms, seen here coupled to the tender of Belpaire No. 821. The lining is reduced to the basic Deeley style. There are no lined splasher panels, lining on the smokebox or cylinder covers. Of the boiler bands, only those adjacent to the smokebox and the cab front are lined out but the outside motion has the fluting painted black. Finally note the cabside power classification '3', not to become '4' until c.1908. *Collection Bernard Mathews*

MIDLAND COMPOUNDS — DETAIL AND LIVERY VARIATIONS

Apart from the original Johnson series, the Midland Compounds were somewhat more consistent in appearance and finish than many Midland types — but there were some changes.

Starting first with anatomical details, the Johnson compounds were, of course, subject to most variation. They started life as 'pure' Johnson engines but, before rebuilding with superheaters, quite a number of peripheral detail changes had taken place. Most noteworthy was, of course, the rebuilding of the bogie tenders, but on the engines themselves several Deeley details had been instituted before the full superheated rebuilding took place and at *Plates 312-4* we give further examples of changes not covered earlier in the chapter. Most of these were concentrated at the front end.

The first Deeley series (Nos. 1000-9, later Nos. 1005-14) also came in for a few changes before final superheating. These were, again mostly confined to the front end where the original Deeley arrangement gradually gave way to the more familiar 'standard' Deeley pattern (*Plates 315-318*). However, before superheating, this particular group were always distinctive by virtue of their basic 'built up' smokebox support and their shorter smokeboxes compared with the final series. They also displayed originally two sorts of chimney. As built, Nos. 1000-4 (later 1005-9) had a slightly outward tapering chimney (*Plate 315*). It was surmounted by the new 'wind guard' (capuchon) and was not quite so recognisable as the approximately contemporary 'flowerpot' style of the Belpaires (e.g. *Plate 234*) but it was different from the final style of parallel-sided Deeley chimney which came into use on Nos. 1005-9, later 1010-4,

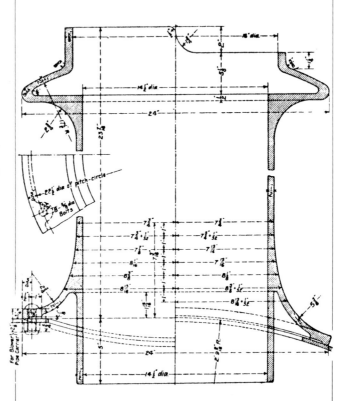

Fig. 55. The Deeley compound chimney, originally published in the 'Railway Engineer' in 1919.

Plates 313 & 314. By good fortune, Johnson compound No. 1004, formerly 2635, seems to have managed to get its picture taken at almost all stages of its existence and thus gives a potted history of all the changes (see, for example, *Plates 296 & 304*). In this pair of views, it is shown at Leicester in 1909, still with bogie tender and a few years later with rebuilt tender but still basically 'as built'. In both cases the engine carries Deeley livery but the 'front end' shows some changes. In particular, note the change from flat to dished Deeley type door between the two views, accompanied by a change in top lamp iron position and what looks like a change to a taller 'slimmer' chimney. Both these smokebox doors were, of course, successive replacements of the original version. Note, too, the change from seriffed to block style 'MR' on the front buffer plank.

Authors' Collection

Plates 315 & 316. These less than ideal views are amongst the few we have located which show the original ten Deeley compounds 'as built' with original chimneys and continuous front handrails. No. 1000 (later No. 1005) shows the slightly outward tapering chimney whereas No. 1013 (originally No. 1008) shows the later form. *Authors' Collection*

(*Plate 316*) and thereafter became standard for the whole class.

The final Deeley series (Nos. 1010-29, later Nos. 1015-34 plus Nos. 1035-44) hardly changed in style, except for the somewhat extended smokebox after superheating and a change from 'flat' to 'dished' smokebox doors in their saturated state.

The tender styles originally fitted, also reflected the 'as built' batches, viz.

Nos. 1000-4 (originally 2631-5)   Bogie style, later rebuilt to high sided 'turn-under' type.

Nos. 1005-14 (originally 1000-9)   First Deeley style 'continuous' running plate.

Nos. 1015-34 (originally 1010-29) plus Nos. 1035-44   Second Deeley style, 'discontinuous' running plate

Later tender changes, particularly in LMS days, tended to confuse the picture.

Turning now to livery, the only compounds to be given the full 'Johnson' treatment were the original five, and *Plates 287-8 & Plate 291* afford a good representation of the styles adopted.

The first Deeley compounds exhibited the new Deeley livery with large tender numerals, etc. This, of course, well preceded the 1907 renumbering, so Nos. 1000-29 (later 1005-34) *all* received their *original* numbers in the new livery. The cabside emblem was also of the old 'diamond' shaped style for Nos. 1000-9 (later 1004-13). The change to the new emblem took place during 1906 (old No. 1014 is also confirmed with this device) certainly by the time compound No. 1025 (later 1030) had appeared (*Plate 321*) in late 1906. This situation is further confirmed by a poor picture of No. 1016 (*Plate 320*) which could be either old No. 1016 or old No. 1011 (later 1016) also showing the old emblem. We are inclined to think this picture shows *old* No. 1016 since the 1907 renumbering almost always incorporated the *new* emblem. During 1906 the largest 'break' in construction sequence was between No. 1024 (later 1029) and No. 1025 (1030) and, in the absence of evidence to the contrary, we feel that old No. 1024 may have been the last compound to carry the old emblem. There must have been *some* reason why No. 1025 (*Plate 321*) was singled out for official photography and the new heraldic emblem may

Plate 317. No. 1011, originally No. 1006, is seen here following the replacement of the original smokebox door with one of the later dished style. No. 1011 was superheated at the end of 1922 and lasted to become British Railways No. 41011 with withdrawal from service taking place in 1951.

Collection Bernard Mathews

have been the justification. It probably does not matter in retrospect, but modellers may be interested, and if any of our readers can resolve the issue it would be welcome — especially when *Plate 322* is also put into the debate!

Be that as it may, the bulk of the compounds had settled down in new Deeley livery with new numbers and emblem c.1908-9 and the only remaining livery detail is in the matter of cylinder lining (*Plate 323*). Most contemporary MR period pictures of Midland Compounds in Deeley style seem to indicate that the cylinders were *unlined* during MR days and, indeed, MR No. 1000 was so restored by BR in 1959. However, when it went into Clapham, lining had been added to the cylinder covers and, in 1923 the LMS adopted lined cylinders as 'standard' procedure for all tender engines thus equipped. Now it was almost unheard of for the new LMS to *enhance* the old MR livery so the presumption must be that by late MR days, cylinder lining had been adopted — but we are not sure on this point and would welcome more information. What we are prepared to say is that in the post-Johnson period it seems most unlikely that yellow cylinder lining was carried by Midland Compounds until quite late in the Midland period but was always there in LMS days (*Plate 324*). There was, of course, always a black band between the polished cylinder end covers and the main red portion of the main cylinder cover and, in the pre-1905 period, some of the *Johnson* Compounds originally had had quite extensive cylinder lining (see Frontispiece). It is all most confusing and the NRM may be at fault in having retained the cylinder lining when correcting other minor errors of detail on No. 1000 after reception at York in 1975.

The compounds continued to receive somewhat 'different' painting treatment from most Midland engines in LMS days but this is beyond the scope of this particular survey and has been covered elsewhere.

Plate 318. This detailed 'head-on' view of No. 1006 gives a very good impression of the 'face' of the original ten Deeley compounds in their final saturated condition. The engine started life as No. 1001, was superheated in 1922 and scrapped as BR No. 41006 in 1951.

A. G. Ellis

Plate 319. Second series Deeley compound No. 1014 (later 1019) at Leeds (Wellington) clearly displaying Deeley livery with old emblem c.1906.   *J. H. Wright*

Plate 320. This poor view shows No. 1016 also carrying the old emblem with Deeley livery. The engine could be either old No. 1016 (later No. 1021) or new No. 1016 (previously No. 1011), both being from the shallow frame series. We think that old No. 1016 is the more likely candidate.

Authors' Collection

Plate 321. Works grey view of No. 1025 (later No. 1030) as built in 1906 and clearly displaying the new heraldic emblem.

Authors' Collection

Plate 322. Confusing matters even more, old No. 1010 (later No. 1015), the first of the shallow frame series, carried the new heraldic emblem before renumbering. This was probably a case of replacement insignia, late in 1906 just prior to renumbering.

Collection Bernard Mathews

Plate 323. This picture of No. 1024 in immaculate condition, photographed at Kentish Town in May 1922, displays a top link passenger locomotive in the correct Deeley livery of this period with yellow lines on the black wheels and black fluting to the coupling and connecting rods. The lining on the cab front angle is vertical and commences at the point where the rear splasher reaches the end of the firebox. The tender front is lined crimson lake and the cylinders seem to be lined (see text). Originally No. 1019, this locomotive became No. 1024 in 1907 and was superheated about two months before this picture was taken. Withdrawal was toward the end of 1948, still carrying its LMS number.

Collection Bernard Mathews

Plate 324. This typical LMS period view of No. 1027, even in fairly characteristically grubby 1930s condition, still reveals lining on the cylinder covers with the post-1927 LMS livery. It had received new front frames and was to last until 1948, being withdrawn without renumbering by BR. *Authors' Collection*

CONCLUSION

We are not unaware that we may have given the Midland Compounds more than their fair share of space in this book — and possibly diverted a little more than usual from the 'outward appearance' theme which is our main concern — but we are not disposed to apologise too much. They are not, if truth be told, our own personal 'favourites' but they were, by 1923, the Midland's 'flagship' engines, and their nature has been much misinterpreted in spite of the proliferation of published writing about them. We have merely tried to make our own contribution in order to redress the balance of debate on what we feel to be much misunderstood and underrated engines. For their time, they were a truly outstanding design, in British terms, and, as such, we think they merit a better press.

Finally it is interesting to note that when comparing the Midland and LMS general arrangement drawings of the compounds, there are surprisingly few differences once you ignore the front end frame shape, boiler and smokebox. Despite the reduced wheel size for the LMS-built machines, the splashers are the same. The apparent differences were in the position of the hornguides in the frame, shape of ashpan and inclination of the cylinders. Finally, it is worth noting that the LMS series reduced the frame length and returned to the original 6 ft 6 in wheelbase bogie.

4 – 4 – 0 PASSENGER ENGINE

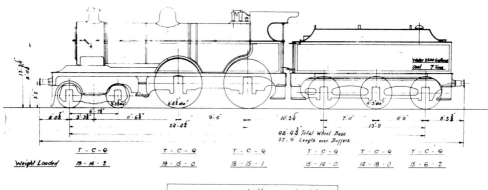

	T - C - Q	T - C - Q	T - C - Q	T - C - Q	T - C - Q	T - C - Q
Weight Loaded	19 - 14 - 2	19 - 15 - 0	18 - 15 - 1	15 - 14 - 0	14 - 18 - 0	15 - 6 - 2

		Light T. C. Q.	Loaded T. C. Q.
TOTAL WEIGHT	Engine	53 - 14 - 0	58 - 4 - 3
	Tender	23 - 6 - 0	45 - 18 - 2
	Eng & Tenr.	77 - 0 - 0	104 - 3 - 1

Nº 4 CLASS SIMPLE PASSENGER
Nºs 990 – 999
ED 1/74

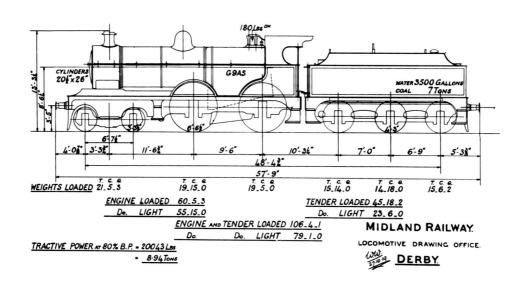

CYLINDERS 20¼″ x 26″
G 9 AS
180 Lbs ᴼᴺ
WATER 3500 GALLONS
COAL 7 TONS

WEIGHTS LOADED	T. C. Q. 21.5.3	T. C. Q. 19.15.0	T. C. Q. 19.5.0	T. C. Q. 15.14.0	T. C. Q. 14.18.0	T. C. Q. 15.6.2

ENGINE LOADED 60.5.3
Do. LIGHT 55.15.0

TENDER LOADED 45.18.2
Do. LIGHT 23.6.0

ENGINE AND TENDER LOADED 106.4.1
Do. Do. LIGHT 79.1.0

TRACTIVE POWER AT 80% B.P. = 20043 Lbs
= 8·94 TONS

MIDLAND RAILWAY.
LOCOMOTIVE DRAWING OFFICE.
DERBY.

Figs. 56 & 57. ED73 and ED 1/74 represent the saturated and superheated diagrams for the '990' class and are dated c.1910 and 1919 respectively. The quoted weights differ but the drawings appear almost identical and show the saturated configuration. When superheated, the smokebox extended well forward of the saddle, to a point almost directly above the centre line of the leading bogie wheel.

National Railway Museum

THE DEELEY '990' CLASS

Plate 325. The original '990' class engine, No. 999, in saturated 'as built' condition early in 1907. The neat lines are readily apparent. At this time the engine was carrying power class 3, soon changed to 4. No. 999 was superheated in 1911 and became LMS No. 809 in 1927.

Authors' Collection

Built at Derby 1907 (999) and 1909 (990-998), all to LMS. Original construction was saturated, they were superheated between 1910-1914.

All except 990/2/4 were renumbered in the 800-809 series in 1926/7.

Withdrawn between 1925-1928.

In saturated condition they were allocated to engine diagram 73 (*Fig. 56*) and in superheated condition they were allocated to ED 1/74 (*Fig. 57*).

These ten locomotives have, more than once, been dubbed the Midland's 'forgotten' engines and we are not disposed to argue with this overall assessment. They lived in the 'shadow' of the compounds and their lifespan was short — less than 20 years on average. By Midland standards this almost constitutes total failure, but this would be less than a fair assessment. They were, in fact, rather good engines and it was only the outstanding quality of the compounds which relegated them to a subsidiary place. They were unquestionably somewhat more effective than the class 3 Belpaires and their eventual concentration on and association with the Leeds-Carlisle line tends to prove this assertion.

The Settle-Carlisle section was not the easiest of the Midland's routes to operate, yet it is an undoubted fact that in spite of the greater number of both compounds and superheated Belpaires, the '990' class engines carved out for themselves a peculiar niche in the operational pattern of MR services on this most demanding of routes. This hardly denotes an inferior design and their short life was, we feel, more a consequence of their 'non-standard' nature than of any real deficiency in performance.

The '990' class originated in 1907 when a solitary, two-cylinder simple 4−4−0 with G9A boiler (a variation of the compound G9 boiler) was built for 'comparative purposes' with the Deeley compounds themselves. Numbered 999 in the 1907 Deeley series, this engine (*Plate 325*) remained the sole example for some two years and, in some sources, still gives its number to the class designation. No less an authority than D. F. Tee refers to the '999' class in his definitive RCTS monograph on the Midland Compounds, but we are assured by him that '990' class is in fact the more correct designation, based upon Derby drawing office records, and in 1909 a further nine engines were built to the same type. They were numbered 990-998, and since it was customary MR practice to classify engines on the basis of the *lowest* number, they became the '990' class thereafter.

They were typical Deeley-styled machines of exceptionally well-balanced outline and proportions. They had 6 ft

Plate 326. No. 991 was in saturated condition when photographed at Leeds Wellington in 1909. From this angle the class appeared somewhat similar to the '378' class rebuilds (see Chapter 5). Note the way in which the coal has been stacked well forward. This class was always in Deeley style crimson lake livery with either MR or LMS identity.

Collection Bernard Mathews

6½ in driving wheels, well suited to the gradients of the Leeds-Carlisle line and they all gravitated to this section of the MR in due course, after a few had been used elsewhere. Technically, their principal claim to fame was the valve gear, sometimes referred to as the 'scissors' type, which Deeley designed. It was, in principle, of Walschaerts type but eliminating eccentrics and it was the subject of some contemporary controversy as to whether Deeley was indeed the true instigator. The great G. J. Churchward (of the GWR) apparently had some views on the matter and the issue is still clouded in doubt. We will leave others to argue this point.

What can be said is that the engines were a great success, if never quite as good as the compounds. That the compound v. '990' issue was never fully resolved during the Deeley period is witnessed by the fact that although No. 999 was built after Nos. 1000-29 (later 1005-34) and before Nos. 1035-44, Nos. 990-8 did not appear until *after* Nos. 1035-44 had come into service, even though they were ordered 2 months earlier than 1035-44. It rather suggests that the superior merits of the compounds were as yet 'non-proven' in absolute terms when Nos. 990-8 came into service.

This aspect is further emphasised by the fact — already touched upon at page 238 — that it was the '990' class which was the first of the two Class 4 groups to be superheated. This started as early as 1910 with No. 998 and was completed in January 1914, by which time only one compound had been so treated. But, of course, compound superheating followed, as we have seen.

Like so many similar matters, the issue was not an exact 'like for like' comparison. The '990' class engines had smaller driving wheels than and different valve gear from the compounds, so there were other factors at play than compounding when accurately evaluated tests were made. These tests did, however, reveal that the superheated compound was superior to the comparable '990', so the latter design was never adopted as a 'standard' type either by the Midland or the LMS. We are inclined to the view that this was more a confirmation of the high quality of the compounds than any adverse reflection on the '990' class as such. However, given the then current late MR/early LMS thinking, it is not at all surprising that a small group of but ten engines in the Class 4 category were unlikely to survive the holocaust when 'standardisation' ruled the roost.

Neither did they. The engines were not even allowed to serve out their time until their superheated boilers had become life-expired. Several '990' boilers were later used on compounds. By this time, the LMS had renumbered most of them in the 800-9 series during 1926-7 (Nos. 990/2/4 being the exceptions) and the last survivors were engines Nos. 998/9 (now No. 808/9) in December 1928. They never suffered the indignity of being painted black, all being withdrawn in the first LMS style of painting, and they remained on basically 'front-line' duties to the very end.

Turning now to their visual appearance, these engines were amongst the least variable of all the MR tender designs ('483' class renewals excepted). When they were built, all the Deeley stylistic characteristics were well established and

JOHNSON/DEELEY CLASS 4 4—4—0s

Plate 327. This front view of No. 991 shows the front buffer plank lining arrangement with its wide black edge. Note the bright metalwork on the smokebox door. The water deflector plates attached to the front buffer plank were painted black. Superheated in 1913, this locomotive became LMS No. 801 and was withdrawn towards the end of 1927. *Collection A. G. Ellis*

Plate 328. No. 995 was superheated in 1912 and became LMS No. 805 in 1926. Withdrawal was in 1928. This picture has been included to illustrate a Midland railway locomotive fitted with an exhaust injector. Note the pipe emerging from the base of the smokebox.

Collection Bernard Mathews

Plate 329. No. 997 was withdrawn at the end of 1927. It had been superheated in 1913 and became LMS No. 807 in 1927. This picture is interesting in that it shows a pipe attached to the side of the firebox which was connected to the 'sight feed' lubricator inside the cab.

Collection Bernard Mathews

Plate 330. This opposite side view (c.f. *Plates 328 & 329*) shows superheated No. 999 in LMS pre-1928 crimson lake livery. The first of the class, No. 999, also had the distinction of being one of the final two survivors withdrawn in early December 1928 as LMS No. 809. The pronounced forward extension of the smokebox in superheated form is well displayed on this near-broadside view. *Authors' Collection*

the only significant change was the extended smokebox displayed by the superheated rebuilds. Livery was always 'standard Deeley' and the only change made by the LMS (1926 renumbering excepted) was to remove the 'MR' from the front buffer plank and substitute the LMS emblem for the MR version on the cabside. They also established, along with the compounds, the Deeley tender and Deeley 'look' to the MR tender fleet. *Plates 326-331* give a good representation of their lifetime.

END PIECE

. . . and so, we conclude our review of the Midland's passenger tender types as they existed in 1922. We would never claim that they were the 'best of the bunch' but neither were they the least interesting; and it was, of course, in the area of passenger tender engines that any railway was most 'on parade' to the public.

For all the latter day criticisms, it is an undoubted fact that the Midland Railway, as one of Britain's 'Big Four' before the grouping (the other three being the GWR, LNWR and NER), was a highly regarded and prosperous system. Well organised and superbly presented (in terms of its public 'face'), its somewhat conservative approach to locomotive matters, both in the late 19th century and again in the post-Deeley period, did not seem seriously to affect its overall prosperity. Its engines may not have been, in 1922, as much in the vanguard as they were in the late

Johnson and Deeley periods, but they seemed to do the job required of them as far as the MR directors were concerned and the public seemed content. That the engines were not quite as appropriate to the newly formed LMS in 1923 as the Midland men may have liked is another story . . .

Plate 331. This low angle view of No. 808 (formerly No. 998) in LMS colours c.1927/8 emphasises the smokebox end of the superheated '990' class. Note again, c.f. *Plate 327* the very broad black margin around the front buffer plank — very much a characteristic of this particular type. No. 808 was withdrawn in December 1928, having been the first Midland engine of any class to be superheated (in 1910).   *Authors' Collection*

TABLE 17: 4—4—0 COMPOUNDS JOHNSON & DEELEY

1903 Diagram Page No.	Order No. or Class	Built by	Qty. built	Date of building	Pre 1907 numbers	1907 renumbering	Cylinders	BOILER Centre Line	Diameter	Length	Tubes	Diameter	Working Pressure	FIREBOX Length	Grate Area in sq. ft.	Total Heating Surface in sq. ft.	WHEELS Leading	Driving	Tyres	ENGINE WEIGHT Empty	Loaded	REMARKS
6	2109	Derby	5	1902/3	2631-5	1000-1004	HP (1) 19" × 26" LP (2) 21" × 26"	8' 6"	4' 8"	11' 7"	261	1¾"	195 PSI	8' 6"	26.0	1598	3' 6½	7' 0"	3"	53.15.1	58.9.0	These details apply to 2631, 2633/4. No. 2631 and 2635 were fitted with 120 Serve corrugated tubes 2¾" dia which gave a total heating surface of 1719.8 sq ft. Nos 2633-5 only had one set of reversing gear—see text. Serve tubes replaced in 1904. ⊕ see below.
N/A	2889	Derby	10	1905	1000-9	1005-1014	HP (1) 19" × 26" LP (2) 21" × 26"	8' 6"	4' 7¼"	11' 11"			220 PSI	9' 0"	28.4	1458.3	3' 6½	7' 0"	3"		59.16.0	
N/A	2998	Derby	20	1906	1010-29	1015-1034	HP (1) 19" × 26" LP (2) 21" × 26"	8' 6"	4' 7¼"	11' 11"			220 PSI	9' 0"	28.4	1458.3	3' 6½	7' 0"	3"			Longer bogie see below.
	3410	Derby	10	1908/9	N/A	1035-1044																
	As Superheated various o/nos	Derby	45	1913/28	N/A	1000-1044	HP (1) 19" × 26" LP (2) 21" × 26"	8' 6"	4' 7¼"	11' 11"	148 21	1¾" 5¼"	‡	9' 0"	28.4	1681	3' 6½	7' 0"	3"		61.14	

4—4—0 '990' CLASS

N/A	3139	Derby	1	1907	N/A	999	19" × 26"		4' 7¼"	11' 11"	249	1¾"	220 PSI 200 PSI	9' 0"	28.4	1557.4	3' 3½	6' 6½"	3"		58.10.2	Altered to 200 psi in April 1907.
	3371	Derby	9	1909		990-998																998 was first MR loco to be superheated in 1910. Cyls enlarged to 20½". No 995 fitted with steam reversing gear between 1912-1922. ⊕ The 1910 Engine Diagrams gave different weights 2631/2 55.1.1 empty 59.10.1 loaded 2633-5 54.7.0 empty 58.16.0 loaded

Wheelbase when built   O/N 2109   6' 6" + 8' 3" + 9' 6" = 24' 3"
                       O/N 2889   6' 6" + 8' 3" + 9' 6" = 24' 3"
                       O/N 2998/3410 6' 7½" + 8' 3" + 9' 6" = 24' 4½"
‡ Various boiler pressures were used at various times 190-220 PSI although 200 PSI was the most common.

SOURCE—1903 Midland Railway Diagram Book
'The Midland Compounds' by D. F. Tee, 1961.
'Derby Works and Locomotives' by J. B. Radford, 1971.

AN INDEX TO ILLUSTRATIONS OF
MIDLAND RAILWAY PASSENGER TENDER ENGINES
IN VOLUMES 1 & 2

'Old' refers to a pre-1907 number.